Angels in My Valley

Angels in My Valley

Adeline Kulig Puccini

To Annette
Adeline "Jo" Puccini

Copyright © 2001 by Adeline Kulig Puccini.
Library of Congress Number: 2001117996

ISBN #:	Hardcover	1-4010-2361-4
	Softcover	1-4010-2360-6

All rights reserved. No part of this book may be reproduced or transmitted in any form or by any means, electronic or mechanical, including photocopying, recording, or by any information storage and retrieval system, without permission in writing from the copyright owner. .

This book was printed in the United States of America.

To order additional copies of this book, contact:
Xlibris Corporation
1-888-7-XLIBRIS
www.Xlibris.com
Orders@Xlibris.com

Contents

ENDORSEMENTS 7
INTRODUCTION 9

CHAPTER 1
    THE TRAGEDY 13
CHAPTER 2
    LIFE AT UNCLE BERT'S 25
CHAPTER 3
    BACK TO BROTHERS AND SISTERS 37
CHAPTER 4
    THE COUNTRY SCHOOL EXPERIENCE 48
CHAPTER 5
    PIETY AND PAROCHIALISM 59
CHAPTER 6
    LIFE ON THE FARM IN THE THIRTIES 75
CHAPTER 7
    THE STORM THAT SAVED ME 99
CHAPTER 8
    HIGH SCHOOL AND WORLD WAR II 118
CHAPTER 9
    CHICAGO: A WHOLE NEW WORLD 137
CHAPTER 10
    BETTY AND LYMAN: MY MENTORS 157
CHAPTER 11
    COLLEGE 169
CHAPTER 12
    CAREER AND GRADUATE SCHOOL 184

CHAPTER 13
    MARRIAGE, FAMILY, AND CAREER 206
CHAPTER 14
    PIETY REVISITED 268
CHAPTER 15
    REFLECTIONS 284
CHAPTER 16
    RESOLVE 300

BIBLIOGRAPHY 317
APPENDIX A 321
APPENDIX B 341
APPENDIX C 351

ENDORSEMENTS

"This is a compelling narrative and should be read by every person, young or old, who subscribes to the *Mind Your Own Business* school of thought."

Suzanne W. S. Shoemaker

"It is always amazing how some people overcome the obstacles in their lives. Adeline 'Jo' Puccini is a survivor of child abuse and neglect. Her book tells of a child's inner strength to overcome the abuse and of the support she found along the way. It was the support of caring individuals who made the difference in Jo's s life, enabling her to overcome her fears and excel in life. An inspiring story of caring people making a difference in a child's life."

Maggie Thorpe
CASA Program Director

Holger R. Kjeldsen, M.A.
Executive Director

"I have known the author as a student, as a professional, and as a friend for almost fifty years, and until she wrote this powerful story, I knew nothing about her tragic childhood. Her achievement as a scholar and her long and successful career in speech and language pathology are a tribute to all who are determined to rise above misfortune."

Mary S. Farquhar, Ed. D.

Speech and Language Pathology

"From a childhood of abuse, Jo (Adeline) recounts the events in her life that contributed to her success as an adult. Her early development of independence and academic proficiency were key factors that shaped her ability to cope with the vicissitudes of later life and maintain a positive and cheerful outlook toward the future. Her challenges of being a Navy wife—separation from her Navy-flyer husband for long periods, frequent moves to different regions in the country, child rearing through changing schools and friends, all built on her strong independence and self-confidence developed as a youth. Her life's story is an inspiration to anyone who has suffered abuse as a child and has faced the tough decisions needed to overcome the adversity of abuse and mature into a fulfilling and rewarding life."

Rear Admiral and Mrs. R.C. Avrit, USN (Retired)

INTRODUCTION

W HAT started as an unembellished documentary intended for professionals and volunteers working with abused children has become a memoir of a life of survival. My intention in writing this narrative is to give hope and encouragement to all children living in fear, to those physically and psychologically abused youngsters who believe they have no one to talk to or nowhere to go, to those voices silenced by fear and shame.

I also hope that this story will, in some small way, acknowledge the work of those dedicated people who hear these "cries in the dark" and are moved to do something about it. Although a lost childhood can never be replaced, the interest and concern of those working with the abused and neglected will help immeasurably in repairing a fractured young life. The ravaging effects of a protracted stormy childhood can be long lasting. The importance of salvaging these young lives, of restoring the self-confidence necessary to become useful and contributing members of society, can never be overemphasized. Unfortunately, this book cannot directly acknowledge the work of those who contributed to my rise above what seemed like a hopeless future. They, I feel certain, have passed on to enjoy their rewards for the good deeds they considered to be a normal part of their lives.

At a time when major changes were taking place during my teenage years, my name changed from *Adeline* to *Jo*. To my family and the friends I left in Wisconsin, I am always remembered as *Adeline*. To my colleagues, professional associates and friends, I emerged as *Jo* and am remembered by this name to this day. This story takes *Jo* back through a life where she is able to rediscover *Adeline* as a survivor.

Above all, I wrote this book to honor my siblings, who through the years, provided psychological support, and, with the writing of this book, shared the pain of reopening old wounds that had been festering for years, in hopes that proper healing could take place. The cohesiveness of my siblings has undoubtedly sustained us all in times of real stress. From them I drew the courage to finally tell this story, and I thank them for their corroborative contributions. And for the young surrogates, Verna at age eleven and Ben at age ten, who felt the responsibility for caring for and protecting their six younger siblings, I have the greatest admiration.

I am thankful for the support I have received from friends and from total strangers as I worked to make this book a reality. I am especially grateful to Florence Gordon whose artistic talents help to lighten the heavy subject matter of this book. It tells us what we already know—that humor is a necessary ingredient for survival. I am thankful for the suggestions that my editor, Linda Wolfe Keister, provided; they were most helpful in bringing this book into proper focus. She made me keenly aware of the need to understand the reader's perspective. To my computer support engineers, Lyle Bowman and Gary Bucy, I offer my sincere thanks. And my sincere appreciation goes to Megan Fenton, who repeatedly rescued me from the wizardry of the computer. Without her help this story may have been irretrievably lost in that scientific wonder.

CHAPTER 1

THE TRAGEDY

My trips back to the valley of my birth continue to evoke special feelings of excitement mixed with traces of melancholia that are difficult to explain. One thing is understandable. Visiting our brothers and sisters reinforces ties to our roots and makes us reflect on the different courses our lives have taken.

It has become customary, almost ritualistic, during these visits that Ed, my youngest surviving brother, and I take our cameras and drive around the scenic areas of the Trempealeau Valley in the western part of Wisconsin. We travel the smaller valleys that originate as deep gulches formed by melting snow and widen to become coulees that branch off the main valley.

As we drive we recall how these hills, valleys, and coulees of Trempealeau County welcome each season as a special time for renewing and redecorating. In spring, snow-covered hills and valleys become fresh green pastures and fields of carefully tilled crops. Hay and grain appear as alternate strips in attractive designs that follow the contours of the hills. Before long, neat and orderly rows of corn begin sprouting as if a race is on to reach knee-high by the Fourth of July. A visitor must drive the winding roads up to the high ridges to look down and capture and appreciate the scenic beauty of the area.

The summers are pleasant and if rainfall is adequate, teaming fields of grain and tall corn may swallow the narrow country roads. The harvest in late summer and autumn invites another time for redecorating. The hills become vibrant with color, the wild geese fly south, and the season fades into a time for this land to rest and rejuvenate.

During our drive we stop at a scenic overlook at the top of one of the many ridges. We photograph the vibrant fall colors of the trees capping the hills and the strip-cropping that makes the area unique in its beauty. As I try to frame each scene, Ed asks if I remember Phil Newman, our high school teacher who taught strip-cropping to his young farm students. Ed goes on to describe how this technique, introduced about 1940, enabled farmers to safely till the hillsides without fear of erosion. I wonder if this teacher, and many others like him, was ever appropriately rewarded for his contribution to the scenic beauty of the area.

Our drive culminates in a delicious lunch of local beef at a log-style restaurant on the crest of an especially scenic ridge. While we wait for our food, I decide to walk out onto the huge deck with its large stone fireplace and grill for cookouts and outdoor eating. I need to take another look at the surrounding beauty. It is magnificent. Yet I cannot deny the trace of sadness I feel, because somewhere amidst all this beauty is a lost childhood never to be recovered.

It was in this beautiful country setting that I was born into a happy household—the eighth of ten children. My sister Verna, nine years older than I, recalled those happy days when my father played the harmonica for the family, when my mother sang as she worked, and when the family gathered around the Victrola as it played the popular songs of those times.

We lived on a farm in the Trempealeau Valley not far from the Mississippi River. My paternal grandfather, Jacob Kulig, purchased the rich, black loam of this unglaciated land in the 1870s. He improved the land with attractive buildings. A large frame farmhouse, a large red dairy barn, two large granaries, an oversize machine shed for farm equipment—along with a sleigh, cutter, and buggy—a corn crib for storing unshelled corn, a large chicken coop, a woodshed, and hog sheds were carefully constructed and conveniently located on a flat area that served as the hub of his farm operation. A creek flowed around these buildings through the low-lying areas of the pastures where cows and horses grazed together.

He later acquired farms for his sons in the same valley or nearby. Although the area was named *Maule Coulee* after the property owners at the entrance to the coulee, Kuligs owned most of the farms located there. Actually, the area would be more accurately described as a valley with rolling hills and meadows. As my grandfather acquired more of the valley, Kulig homes were built every half-mile along Maule Coulee Road, and the Maule Coulee red brick country school was established for our early education.

When my father came of age, he inherited my grandfather's property. And when he married my mother, his farming program was well established. Large families were common to the area. As our family grew, so did that of other Kuligs. For every sibling in our family there was a cousin about the same age or grade on Maule Coulee Road and at Maule Coulee School. Verna recalled the various housekeepers, or "hired girls" that were necessary to help Mother with her active brood. Likewise, a "hired man" to help my father with the farm work was added to this family constellation. The dining room table had expandable oak leaves to accommodate our growing family. After we said grace in unison, my mother served food "family style" with older siblings and hired help assisting younger siblings with portions served. Before I was old enough to remember, a large Studebaker with pull-up seats in the floor between the front and back seats provided transportation for the expanding family and hired help. Later, a second, and probably faster, car was added—the car I remember, with elegant leather seats and pull-down window shades. A fruit orchard, a large garden, chickens, ducks, geese, hogs, cows, and horses all added up to a farm teeming with resources for a thriving, wholesome, and busy life.

Electrical power for the house and barn was provided by a unique, private system, which we called the Delco Plant. I remember the Delco Plant, located in the cellar of the house, that provided electrical power for the entire farm, including the water well and pump, the barn with an early model milking machine, the separator in the milk house, and the chicken house. In the 1920s, this was considered to be an efficient, state-of-the-art system. To provide adequate power, the Delco had to go through a noisy process of charging up on a carefully planned regimen. I recall one not-so-carefully-planned occasion when the lights began to go dim one evening, a clear signal that power would not last through the night. To my father's chagrin, it was necessary to start the Delco and re-energize the system late in the evening, with its noisy engine keeping everyone awake until the wee hours. The noisy putt-putt-putt was even noisier outdoors where the engine's noise came out through the exhaust pipe and could be heard in the quiet of night by neighbors in the surrounding one-half mile area. When rural electrification through the Rural Electrification Administration (REA) was made available during the Roosevelt era, the Delco Plant was retired, and the nostalgic era with the sound of putt-putt-putt was over.

Sharing space in the cellar with the Delco was the water pump. Because water could be reached within 15 or 20 feet below the soil's surface in much of the area, pumps, wells, and hydrants could be located almost anywhere. Replacing the old rusty pump in the front yard was a simple matter. Driving a sand pipe several feet into the cellar floor and adding a pump powered by the Delco provided excellent-tasting water. Also in the cellar, large bins were filled with potatoes, carrots, and other root vegetables. Another section held large crocks of fried pork, dill pickles, and sauerkraut. When this supply of fresh food ran out, a canned supply of fruits, vegetables, and pickles, lined up neatly on wooden shelves, would carry the family through the long winters. Putting up a supply of food for family and animals required an organized effort that included the entire family. A strong work ethic was encouraged and valued.

A tragic turn of events in January 1930 would change our lives forever. Mother became seriously ill after the birth of my youngest brother and four weeks later lost her battle with puerperal septicemia. I was barely two-and-a-half years old and had two younger brothers. Because these were my precognitive years, my memory of the events immediately following her death remains blank. A phone call to my oldest sister Verna on February 11, 1996, the sixty-sixth anniversary of our mother's death, recalled the sad event that led to the drastic changes in our lives.

Although Verna was only eleven years old at the time of our mother's passing, she vividly recalled the evening my father came home from the hospital with an old alarm clock and told her that our mother had died at 5:40 p.m. Why she remembered the alarm clock, she didn't say. But surely time was about to have a different meaning from then on. At eleven years of age and wanting to take care of her siblings—in descending order, Ben, Adolph, Eleanore, Clifford, Clarence, Anton, Adeline, Edward, and the new baby, William, Jr.—she had the weight of the world on her young shoulders. She recalled relatives discussing separating us for placement in different orphanages, and the idea brought nothing short of terror to her young mind. When this plan was rejected, she was relieved; nevertheless, her anxiety over the welfare of this large family must have been overwhelming. As the oldest, she naturally had much of the responsibility for caring for the younger siblings, even when our mother was still alive. My brothers remembered how they were amused by her concern for us. Verna, on the other hand, recalled how she took her responsibilities seriously. After family outings she felt it was her responsibility to make sure that all siblings were back in the Studebaker before the drive home. If anyone moved from his assigned position in the car, she became annoyed at her need for a recount.

On the sixty-sixth anniversary of our mother's death, Verna recalled the burial on February 14, 1930. The day for exchanging valentines at school took on a somber note. Maule Coulee School was closed so that the teacher and all her pupils, most of them brothers, sisters, and cousins, could attend the funeral. The scene at the cemetery, with my father, brothers, and sisters surrounding the coffin as it was lowered into the frozen earth, must have been indelibly etched on the minds of everyone present. Wisconsin in February can be bitterly cold. I'm sure that day was no exception. Yet in spite of the cold my four- and five-year-old brothers, along with their older brothers, reverently removed their hats during the graveside ceremony as they watched Mother's casket being lowered until it disappeared from view.

Verna's conversation wandered back to happier times. She described how Mother would drive her horse "Kate" to town to do the marketing. Mother did not like to drive the large Studebaker. Depending on the time of year, my father would hitch Kate to the buggy or cutter and bring her to the front yard. As Mother climbed aboard, she smiled and waved to the children watching in the window before proudly turning Kate toward the road. Naturally, the children ran to the opposite window where they could see Mother disappear down Maule Coulee Road for the two-and-a-half-mile drive to town. Mother's younger sister was left in charge of baby-sitting my brothers and sisters, probably numbering about four at the time. At any rate, Verna remembered the four boxes of Cracker Jacks Mother brought back from one of her trips, and the children's excitement over the surprises inside.

I recall the self-rocking cradle that faithfully rocked ten of us to sleep. It was a bit of a marvel for those times. The solid oak bed hung from supports that allowed free-swinging movements. After cranking a spring mechanism until it was tightly coiled, the swinging movements of the cradle were activated by releasing a clutch. The ratchet-like gear kept the cradle rocking rhythmically until the spring unwound, long enough for an infant to fall asleep. The inventor of this marvel must have known how long it took for a baby to fall asleep before the spring mechanism uncoiled and stopped.

The cradle was retired to an upstairs storage area where it collected various mementos of our infancy—baby booties, baby dresses and bibs, and pieces of baby clothes. Sometimes I would go upstairs and clear the storage space around the cradle, crank the spring to tighten it, and listen to the click-click-click of the ratchet gear as it rocked the baby contents in the bed. My brother Clifford enjoyed telling about an incident involving the cradle. He remembered a warm August day in 1927 when my older brothers and sisters were invited to visit their cousins in the Joe Kulig family. He was three years old and couldn't understand why they would be visiting on a weekday. Visiting cousins was always a Sunday event, unless there was a special occasion like a birthday or wedding. After an enjoyable afternoon they returned home, tossed their straw hats in the cradle in the kitchen, and were stunned by the noise coming out from under their hats. While they were gone, Dr. MacCornac had come to the house and delivered a baby girl—Adeline Kulig—who made her presence known from under a pile of straw hats!

My arrival, as the eighth family member to use the cradle, may have confirmed the need for a second family car—a safer model—that mother learned to drive. This new car—a Chandler—was a classy kind of sedan with a lot of chrome, elegant leather seats, and window shades. No infant seats of course. Verna had to hold me in her lap while Mother drove. The elegant car had neither side-view nor rear-view mirrors; so, as Mother drove, Verna checked on traffic. Along with being copilot, she had to be infant seat and rear-view and side-view mirrors, all in one—

a real challenge when the back seat was full of active children.

Yet, it was the old Studebaker that evoked exciting memories for my older brothers and sisters. Verna described how the convertible top of this long tour-mobile could be recessed and secured. The result was a convertible that exposed the car so completely it became a hazard to youngsters in the back seat. The doors were small and low, and on one occasion when my father made the quick turn into our long driveway, Verna stood up and fell out. After Verna sustained a broken ankle, children in the back seat treated future trips in the old Studebaker with caution. They learned to anticipate Father's turns on winding roads and automatically slid down to the floor for safety. I never had the opportunity to be part of the horse and buggy or the old Studebaker experience because the classy Chandler and I arrived at the farm the same year.

Before she died, Mother told Dad to be sure to take care of the three youngest—the baby, William, Jr.; Edward; and me. But her death came at the time when the Great Depression years were adding misery to the entire country. Dad's attempts to find homes for the three youngest were met with some reluctance by the large families with too many mouths to feed, too many bodies to clothe, and too many feet to be shod. Many years later, my brother Ed reflected on this scenario. He compared our father to someone desperately trying to give away three puppies in a basket. Eventually, he found homes for the three of us—homes that were close enough for us to be able to visit our older siblings. Family friends, whose children were already grown took William, Jr., my four-week-old brother. Edward, one-and-a-half years, was taken by my Uncle Louie, my father's oldest brother. And, at two-and-a-half years, I was taken by my father's youngest brother, Uncle Bert. Seventy years later, Clifford recalled the day when Ed and I were taken away. Clifford was five years old and watched curiously as the Chandler was loaded with our belongings. He was told to go back into the house, where he watched us through the kitchen window as the Chandler pulled out of the yard. He said, "I waved good-bye, but they must not have seen me because nobody waved back."

William, Jr., Edward, and I were now separated from the rest of the family. During the winter months, Verna and Ben often stayed with grandparents while they attended parochial school, leaving their younger siblings without their help and support. That left Adolph, Eleanore, Cliff, Clarence, and Anton at home with the housekeeper, which must have been too hectic for my father and the housekeeper to manage. Turnovers with housekeepers were not surprising. Keeping track of school ages and grades was probably left up to brothers and sisters. Consequently, in the fall after Mother died, Clarence at age five, joined his six-year-old brother, Clifford, as they enrolled in the first grade together at Maule Coulee School. They followed Adolph and Eleanore as they walked the mile up the dirt road to school. With no real supervision at home they walked barefoot, carrying dinner pails with bread and lard sandwiches. It wasn't until one frosty morning, when the teacher called them in to ask why they were still walking barefoot, that shoes were added to their school wardrobes. With the Depression getting worse, things were not likely to get better for the father of ten motherless children.

CHAPTER 2

LIFE AT UNCLE BERT'S

I have often wished that I could recall experiences from the first two-and-a-half years of my life. I'm sure they would have been happy ones. The late Twenties were a time of peace and plenty in Maule Coulee. For me, those were the years when I was in that nebulous state of precognitive development; that time when impressions are made, yet cannot be recalled later.

I have no doubt that my language environment was extremely stimulating. As an infant, the cacophony of seven older siblings speaking in two languages must have overwhelmed my immature language system. Nevertheless, this competitive language environment must not have had a negative effect on my language development, because I always remember understanding and speaking two languages—Polish and English. To prepare me for public school, however, I was encouraged to speak English.

What amazes me to this date is how I suddenly went from my precognitive period, that time of my life I am unable to recall, to a state of complete awareness. It was as if I went very suddenly from a total absence of being to a rational individual with feelings of anxiety, loneliness, and fear. I recall that instant very vividly. I was two-and-a-half years old and standing alone on the front seat of the Chandler. The passenger door was left wide open and I wondered why the adult in charge was not concerned about my safety. I expect my sisters were in school and wouldn't have been present for this scenario anyway. As I stood in the middle of the front seat, I clung to the leather with both hands, afraid to turn around for fear of falling down, and out through the open door. I remember my curiosity about the contents of the back seat, which I fleetingly noted as I was placed in the car. As my curiosity overcame fear, I turned around, looked at the back seat and saw all my clothes and possessions stacked in a heap. On top of the heap was a beautiful red wool coat and matching bonnet. I kept on thinking about the pretty red coat and bonnet, and I don't remember my father's driving away from the farm. We were on our way to Uncle Bert's, my new home. And for some strange reason, I never saw that pretty red coat and bonnet again.

Uncle Bert and his wife, Clara, whom we called "Mrs. Bert," lived less than two miles from our farm.

They had two sons, Marcel, about eight years old and Peter, about three years old. The Berts had lost a daughter in infancy several years earlier. Perhaps I was to be a replacement for her. Uncle Bert was very kind and had a warm smile. I felt he was very pleased to have me join his family. Mrs. Bert was very business-like and probably very efficient; however, I was too afraid and too shy to respond to any conversation either of them directed to me. At two-and-a-half, and just discovering my very being, how communicative can a child be? At supper that first evening, I recall being placed in a high chair with a plate of food set before me in the tray. I remember being coaxed to eat by Mrs. Bert, but each bite seemed to get stuck in my throat. The fear, loneliness, and confusion about the sudden change in my whereabouts caused an ache deep inside that seemed to be moving up to my throat, and I just couldn't swallow. I wanted to cry but was afraid to. Uncle Bert smiled kindly and understandably, but it was Mrs. Bert who made the decisions. She moved me to a rocking chair and went about serving her two boys. I was afraid to cry, so I sat in the rocker without rocking, while Mrs. Bert efficiently cleaned up the kitchen. I must have fallen asleep sitting in the rocking chair because I don't remember being put to bed. I woke up the next morning in a room off the kitchen, hearing the two boys speaking to each other. As they ignored me, I wondered why I was in these strange surroundings. No one explained why I was separated from my siblings, or that I used to have a mother and that she was gone forever.

I soon adjusted to my new surroundings on a nice farm with a comfortable home, a scaled-down version of our farm in Maule Coulee. Located on a bend of the Trempealeau River, it was appropriately named "River Bend Farm." I don't remember Uncle Bert's having a car, perhaps because I don't remember "Mrs. Bert" driving. Therefore, trips to town were limited and may have been with horse and wagon or buggy. I recall one trip to Whitehall, a pretty town on the Trempealeau River about two miles east of Uncle Bert's farm. Mrs. Bert dressed me and the two boys in our best clothes, loaded us in the one-horse buggy, and drove us up the paved road to Whitehall. The purpose of the trip was a photographic session at the professional studio there. The photographer coaxed us to smile while Mrs. Bert warned us not to move. The results fell far short of what one might consider to be a happy scenario, but the photographs do give a pretty good likeness of my appearance at age three. On the ride home, the weather turned cold and rainy, which brought out the best in Mrs. Bert's driving skills. While she clung to the reins, the horse responded to her ever-increasing demands for speed, as if he understood the gravity of the situation. While we made the most of our inadequate clothing and cover, the horse moved boldly on against the driving wind and rain. We arrived home safely to find a very concerned Uncle Bert busily adding wood to a well-established fire in the kitchen. The warmth of the fire was a welcome relief from the wet and windy ride; but alas, it was too late—we all got sick and Mrs. Bert had to contend with menthol rubs and hot water bottles for the next week. Since the trip provided me with the only photograph of me as a child, I feel it was worth it.

Uncle Bert usually made the trips to town—to

the feed mill and the grocery store. Mrs. Bert simply sent him with a grocery list and he just handed it to the store clerk. I remember this as the way husbands did the marketing for their wives. Mrs. Bert occasionally wrote special instructions on her shopping lists, but they were usually unnecessary because choices were limited, or the clerk already knew what Mrs. Bert wanted. I doubt if the need for exchanges ever came up. If choices were available, the store clerk made them. It was as simple as that. Special trips for a shortage of any kind, a spool of thread, some sugar, or condiments for baking, were considered frivolous. It became standard procedure to borrow such shortages from neighbors. Before I was four years old, I usually accompanied Uncle Bert's older son, Marcel, to the nearest neighbor about a half mile away, for "borrowings." I would walk with him on the side of the paved road to the home of Mrs. Leo Marsolek, a widow we affectionately called "Lewonka." But before long, Marcel was needed for other chores around the farm and I was expected to make these "frivolous" trips alone. The walk around the sharp curve in the road, with the steep hill on one side and the view of the Trempealeau River bend on the other, was scenic but spooky. At four years of age my imagination had no bounds. Were there wild animals or loose farm animals around the curve? Or would the next car coming around the curve stay on its half of the road? The road had no center line, and cars coming around the curve would usually cut the corner short. Everyone gambled on curves. Although I was prepared for these gamblers, the sight of a car coming toward me was always unnerving.

Whether it was my awareness of time, or the

absence of the bustling environment of life with my brothers and sisters, I recall the days at Uncle Bert's as very long. I tried to help with little chores around the house. Obedience was not taught to me; I knew instinctively what was expected of me. I wonder if during my precognitive years I was told to be a good child so that my new family would keep me and not give me back. But who would tell me that? Surely my older brothers and sisters wouldn't have mentioned anything as outrageous as that. Perhaps the housekeeper thought there would be less responsibility for her with my being gone. That would leave only one preschooler at home, my older brother Anton. It was difficult for me to feel that I belonged at Uncle Bert's. That feeling was exacerbated when I was suddenly moved from the little bedroom downstairs to a large bedroom upstairs. I will never forget my first night alone in the dark in the big room up there. It never occurred to me to object to this move. As I lay alone in the dark, in the big bed, in the big room, I felt totally rejected.

The feeling of isolation I felt made me try very hard to please Mrs. Bert. Uncle Bert didn't seem to need pleasing. He had the sweet and kind temperament I would later note in my father. Neither of them ever lost control of their feelings. Mrs. Bert, on the other hand, was very firm and decisive in her approach to life—decisive and efficient. Although I don't recall her losing her temper, I knew that displeasing her would be a big mistake. I don't know why I knew, but I did. Yet, I remember feeling safe and secure around her. I suppose her orderliness and efficiency somehow translated into a kind of guarded security for which I am truly grateful and still appreciate. Her parenting skills like many in her day were not appreciated as much as they should have been.

In spite of the isolation I felt, the environment was not altogether sterile. Mrs. Bert was very religious and soon taught me to pray. This seemed to help. She made me realize that I could communicate with those supreme beings represented in various reproductions of oil paintings around the house. I was deeply impressed with the Bert family's reference to them as holy pictures. Not only did Mrs. Bert teach me to pray, she taught me to sing many religious songs—in Polish. When she took me visiting to relatives and friends, I was always asked to sing. I remember standing on a wooden chair and how all conversation stopped while I sang:

> *Serdeczna Matko, opiekunko ludzi.*
> *Niech Cię płacz sierót do litości wzbudzi.*
> *Wygnańcy E~wy do Ciebie wołamy.*
> *Zmiłuj się smiłuj niech się nie tułamy.*
>
> *Do kogóż mamy, wzdychać nędzne dziatki.*
> *Tylko do Ciebie ukochanej Matki.*
> *U której Serce otwarte każdemu.*
> *A osobliwie nędzą strapionemu.*

The English translation of these lyrics follows:

> *Beloved Mother, guardian of our nation.*
> *O hearken to our supplication.*
> *Your loyal children kneeling we beseech you.*
> *Grant us the graces to be loyal to you.*
>
> *Where shall we seek our solace in distress?*
> *Where shall we turn, whom guilt and sin oppress?*

Thine open heart, our refuge e'er shall be.
When trials assail us on life's stormy sea.

I also remember the serious expressions on the faces of uncles and aunts as they listened attentively, how other children in the room were hushed, and how everyone smiled after I finished; but I didn't know if it was because of the sanctity of the songs or my mastery of those challenging Polish lyrics.

Mrs. Bert's religious fervor was especially great during the Holy Week before Easter. When I was about three-and-a-half years of age, she told me about the stations of the cross and the crucifixion. I became so depressed, I don't remember learning about the joyous resurrection, and if the Easter bunny came to leave Easter eggs for everyone, or for good children only. Regardless, by the time I learned the complete story of Easter, I was singing in three languages—Polish, English, and Latin.

I can recall four frightening experiences while I lived at Uncle Bert's. In the first one, I had somehow contracted a scalp infection that required shaving my head and treating the infected areas. It was serious enough that my father was called to join the Berts for our visit to Dr. Peterson, the local doctor. I remember Mrs. Bert being very much in control as Dr. Peterson tried to complete treatment without anesthesia. My father, Uncle and Mrs. Bert, and the doctor soon realized that omitting the anesthesia wasn't going to work. I remember fighting the nose mask, being held down by someone, and later being held by the doctor who showed me the pool of blood on the pillow. I was too groggy to be aware of my head being totally bandaged. On the first Sunday afternoon after I returned home from the doctor's office, my brothers and sisters walked over the hill from Maule Coulee to see me with my head bandaged, which seemed to have left a lasting impression on Verna. She talked about it for years afterward. Uncle Bert's two boys had different reactions. Peter seemed frightened by my headgear and avoided me, thank goodness. Marcel, his older brother, was impressed and seemed to treat me as some kind of hero. Both, I think, were envious of the attention I received. I recovered with no problems.

The second episode came and went so quickly it hardly deserves mention, except that it shows how Mrs. Bert could hardly be outdone in her decisiveness and remarkable efficiency. She was in the middle of her special technique for preserving the large quantity of mushrooms she had picked. As I watched her work, I decided to taste one of these strange looking things. As soon as it was in my mouth I realized I had made a mistake. For some strange reason it took the wrong course and became lodged in my throat. When Mrs. Bert saw that I was choking, she immediately grabbed me by my ankles, turned me upside down, and shook me violently. The mushroom came dislodged on the first shake, but she continued to shake me until I felt I was going to suffocate. The skirt of my dress covering my face and nose made breathing so difficult, I thought I was going to die. This weird orientation in space may have been terrifying, but this Heimlich-a-la-Mrs. Bert was extremely effective.

The third episode occurred in the spring when I was approximately four years old. Mrs. Bert ran out of sewing thread, so she sent me to Lewonka's house, less than a half mile away. Lewonka lent me the thread, and I started back down the side of the paved highway as I had done many times before. I remember feeling weak and unsteady, but I managed to get back with the thread. Then I remember sitting down in the rocking chair by the stove and feeling chilly. Mrs. Bert soon realized that I was ill, very ill. I lost consciousness, and the next thing I knew, I awoke in the master bedroom bed, with my father, Uncle Bert, Dr. Peterson, and Mrs. Bert all rejoicing at my recovering consciousness. Since it was early spring, the unpaved road in Maule Coulee was thawing out from its frozen winter state and was virtually too muddy for the Chandler. The late night telephone call must have been startling for my father. He walked over a mile and a half in the dark, over the hill and through the woods, from Maule Coulee to Uncle Bert's. I realized I must have been terribly ill to have my father and the doctor there, especially since I rarely saw my father other than on Sundays when we stopped at my grandfather's house before going to church. But I will never forget my embarrassment when the doctor insisted that I use the potty before he left, with everyone watching.

The fourth episode was more complex. Actually, it was a series of circumstances that eventually led to my return home to my father, brothers, and sisters. When I was about four-and-a-half, Mrs. Bert thought I was old enough to help Marcel and Peter tend the cows and keep them out of the cornfields. The grazing fields were less than a mile from the farm, and we were to drive the cows up the winding road through the woods, to the pasture to graze. I soon learned that when cows are determined to graze in forbidden areas—corn or grain fields—it would take a very determined four-year-old to stop them. Marcel thought I should run and turn back the animals when they headed for the cornfields, knowing full well the cows would ignore and terrify me. I dreaded these days in the hot sun, and spent most of the day crying. Furthermore, when it was time to chase the cows back down the hill toward the barn, Marcel would send me on ahead to open the gate and then chase the cows to overtake me as I screamed in terror. He did this every day, even when I asked him not to chase the cows before I got to the gate. Then one day, I remember a neighbor quietly cultivating his corn in the field next to where we were tending cows. I remember thinking and hoping that he might hear my cries for help. But it wasn't until the day we were tending the cows in a field adjoining my father's back forty acres that my oldest sister, Verna, masterminded a rescue.

My father's back forty was teeming with vegetables that year. Verna and four other siblings were picking cucumbers one Friday when they heard me crying and calling for Peter to help me chase the cows away from the cornfield. He didn't come to help me. Verna and Eleanore became upset and decided to take action. Two days later on Sunday after church, my sisters approached Mrs. Bert to say they were coming over that afternoon and planned to take me home "for a visit." Mrs. Bert packed a change of clothes and a few items for the "short visit." I never did return to Uncle Bert's. And I expect they never did know why. At age thirteen, Verna realized I was being mistreated and she wasted no time in coming to my rescue. I always felt that the man on the cultivator was pleased with Verna's decision.

CHAPTER 3

BACK TO BROTHERS AND SISTERS

I had been living with Uncle Bert's family for more than two years when the Sunday afternoon visit to my brothers and sisters was arranged. This was going to be my first visit with my brothers and sisters at our home in Maule Coulee, and I remember feeling very excited as Mrs. Bert packed a few of my belongings in a paper bag. To this date, I'm not sure how the Berts felt about this visit. Was Marcel sorry about scaring me with the cows? Actually, there were times when he made me laugh with his clowning. And was Peter sorry about not helping me chase the cows away from the cornfields? Would Uncle and Mrs. Bert miss me when I was gone? I hoped the answer to all three would be yes, because they were the only family life I knew. I had no memory about anything other than life at Uncle Bert's.

Because of the circumstances leading up to the planned visit, I doubt that anyone other than my sisters knew that this was going to be more than just a visit. At any rate, the wait for Verna and Eleanore, ages 13 and 10, seemed like an eternity. They finally appeared at the opening of the winding road through the woods, that same road along which I helped chase cows to and from the fields where they grazed. Although I was at once relieved and excited, I noticed a change in Mrs. Bert's demeanor as she made some reference to my father's "hired girl." I was too excited to understand what that might have to do with my visit. After all, I was going to see my "real" brothers and sisters and nothing else mattered.

After the usual polite greetings, we wasted no time in starting our hike back over the hill. With Eleanore carrying the paper bag containing a change of clothes, and Verna holding my hand, we started our trek. We followed the road through the woods to the clearing at the top of the hill, continued along the side of the cornfield to the line fence from where we were able to pick up the grassy road down the hill to our farm. We chatted excitedly the entire time. In fact, it seemed like I talked more on that hike than I had in the past two years. But soon our noisy chatter took on a guarded kind of hushed speech as we crossed the creek in the pasture to the gate at the eastern entrance to our yard. It was as if we were trying not to disturb the chickens in the hen house a few feet ahead on the left.

Suddenly, our happy hike over the hill turned into a kind of nightmare. Down the path from the house toward the gate we had just closed, came this big, very tall woman, ranting and raving in a language I had never heard before. My sisters froze as she came, half running, in our direction. I was terrified. She shook her arms and fists at us, screaming what I later learned were obscenities. As we kept a safe distance, she reversed course and continued screaming all the way back to the house. Verna left Eleanore and me hiding behind the hen house, while she went looking for my father and older brothers. It seemed like she was gone an eternity. My father and brothers were doing the evening chores and we would have to wait until they were finished before we dare go into the house. Finally, Verna came back with an all-clear signal and we cautiously approached and entered the house. Inside, Julia, the hired girl, was waiting.

Although the food on the stove seemed to be ready, the table remained to be set. My sisters quickly set the table for ten people as my father and brothers greeted and welcomed me. One after the other, they either remarked about my dark suntan, the result of too much time in the sun while tending the cows. This must have made a strong impression on them because they continue to mention it to this day. I felt safer, yet I did not remember being in that house before. I could recall nothing from my precognitive years spent in that house and I felt a bit disappointed about that. I didn't even know that it was over two years since I came alive with awareness standing on that front seat of the Chandler, with the doors wide open, parked in that very front yard.

After my father and brothers each had their turns washing up before supper, they took their regular places at the table. I sat between my sisters at the far end of the long table, as far as possible from the hired girl Mrs. Bert had alluded to earlier that afternoon. After my father led us in our Polish grace before meals, food was passed around family-style and the happy chatter of brothers filled the room. My sisters said very little and were probably concerned about how Julia would behave when she learned I was staying permanently. My father maintained a quiet, pensive mood. I learned later that that was his nature, pleasant and quiet, very much like Uncle Bert. Julia, on the other hand, complained about the table being too crowded as she leered in my direction. She towered over everyone at the table, including my father, and it was hard to ignore her. Yet the youngest three brothers ignored her completely. My two oldest brothers seemed to feel the same uneasiness my sisters and I felt.

That evening I tried to remain inconspicuous by staying close to my sisters and helping them with cleaning up the supper table. Verna hand-washed the dishes, Eleanore dried them, and I helped put them away. The boys went outdoors and played sponge-ball until dark. My father read the paper, and I don't know what Julia did or where she went during that interim. After my brothers came indoors, they waited for the usual signal from my father to let them know it was time for bed. Without further discussion, they all knelt down on the large kitchen floor, recited their prayers in unison, and were off to bed. I waited for my cue from my sisters, and soon we followed my brothers upstairs to bed. My father retired to his downstairs bedroom, and Julia went to her room upstairs.

From the raving welcome I received from Julia, I felt that I had jumped from the frying pan into the fire. The long hike over the hill followed by the nightmarish meeting with Julia, however, left me physically tired. It was wonderful being with real brothers and sisters. I must have felt safety in numbers because I was off to sleep before my sisters finished chatting.

The next morning at breakfast my father assigned jobs to my brothers, including a horse team assignment for Ben. Certain horses worked best when they were teamed up together. My father and Ben were aware of which combinations to avoid. After helping my sisters do the dishes and clean up the dining area, I went out on the front porch to watch the horses, hitched to their cultivators, obediently take off for the fields with my father and Ben at the reins. With the cows turned out in the pasture, Adolph, Clifford, and Clarence had already begun cleaning the barn. Anton joined his older brothers for whatever assignment they meted out as appropriate for a six-year-old.

Monday was laundry day, and water had to be heated on the wood stove in a large boiler. Julia barked orders at my sisters as they helped load the Maytag. I had seen Mrs. Bert go through a similar process, but I had never seen so much laundry in separate heaps all over the kitchen floor. Ten people can make a difference. The Maytag seemed up to the task as it washed load after load after load. The difficult part was fishing items out of the hot water with a round wooden stick and getting them through the wringer without breaking or tearing off buttons.

The old wringers with their two rubber rollers could be controlled more easily because they were hand-cranked. Of course these old wringers probably required three hands. The updated wringer on the new Maytag was powered by the electric motor under the machine. Although this newer version of the old hand-cranked wringer was more efficient, it could be difficult and dangerous for a novice operator. Julia, however, was good at it. She would watch intently as the clothes were swallowed on one side of the wringer and forced out the other side into a huge basket. When the basket was full, my sisters each grabbed a handle and carried the load out to the clothesline in the back yard. It was not unusual to take up eight or ten lines when hanging family laundry. And it made me feel a part of this large family to see my underwear flapping in the breeze next to that of my sisters.

Although Julia ranted about my visit, she soon calmed down and ignored me. It was my sisters who taught me how to help them. Since they were my protectors, they became my caretakers, and they naturally showed me how to become a part of their work ethic. Verna, at thirteen, became the mother figure and took her responsibilities seriously. She told Eleanore what to do, and soon Eleanore was pawning off little jobs on me. We became very close, and soon I forgot all about my returning to Uncle Bert's. If I thought Eleanore was pawning off jobs I didn't want to do, I would tell her I was going back to Uncle Bert's. Of course she didn't believe me, and before long Mrs. Bert returned what few clothes I had left there, or they somehow ended up in our car parked at church on Sunday. My contacts with the Berts after that remained cordial. We had our usual gatherings with my paternal grandparents, and I enjoyed seeing Marcel and Peter. I remember one occasion when I felt that Peter expressed his feelings about my leaving his family. Marcel and Peter had a new baby brother and our family, along with other Kuligs, was invited to the baby's christening party. Someone in the large gathering made a teasing remark by telling Peter they were going to take his new baby brother home. Peter became very upset and lashed out, "They took Adeline away and she never came back. No one is going to take our baby."

Julia's temperament did not improve with time. Verbal abuse came naturally to her. Before long she followed up verbal abuse with slaps across the head and face, which soon developed into what we referred to as the "poundings." On one occasion she ordered Verna to get her a drink of water. Verna saw no reason why Julia couldn't get up and get her own drink and before she had a chance to answer, Julia hit her across the mouth with such force that Verna thought Julia had loosened a front tooth. When my father was away or working in the fields, she didn't hesitate to hit or kick my younger brothers. She was big, and they were little. It broke my heart to see how she slapped them around. I still wonder how she could kick them, send them flying across the room, and not break any bones. And, of course, Verna and Eleanore were always targets for her verbal and physical abuse. When one of us got upset about seeing another sibling punished, she would simply say, "If you tell, you're next." So we didn't tell. Somehow she made us feel as if it was our fault that she acted this way.

Then, to our good fortune, Julia suddenly left and was replaced by her sister, Clara. By then I was five years old, and since Maule Coulee School had no kindergarten, I stayed home with Clara while my older brothers and sisters were in school. My two younger brothers, Edward and William, Jr., remained with the families that took them after Mother died. Clara, Julia's younger sister, was a kind and responsible housekeeper. After she cleaned the house and cooked the meals, she would crank up the Victrola and play records. I enjoyed that. It made the days seem shorter. I whiled away the time by copying the newspaper in the margins where there was no print. Before my brothers and sisters got to the paper, the bare and unprinted spaces were covered with my early attempts at printing and writing. Then I would make up card games that I could play by myself. The highlight of my day came when I saw my older brothers and sisters coming down the road from Maule Coulee School. I would watch the clock and then pull a chair up to the window at the expected time. I remember the long waits kneeling on the chair in front of that kitchen window. In the freezing winter time, condensation from boiling water on the stove would freeze on the inside of the window pane. Because there were no storm windows, ice would collect as much as a half-inch in thickness and I was unable to see through the pane. I would suck my little fingers to warm them enough to be able to melt little peepholes in the ice so I could see my brothers and sisters coming home. It made my fingers hurt from the cold, but it was worth it.

I think we all enjoyed Julia's absence. A respite

from Julia's temperamental outbursts was most welcome. I watched my brothers play horseshoes and ball outdoors, and cards indoors. The house and yard resounded with the happy excitement of brotherly competition. Unfortunately, this pleasant time was not to last. I learned from my older sisters that Julia left to have a baby and would be coming back. After the birth, she left her infant son with her parents and was back on the scene. Her return must have been her idea, because my father reportedly told my aunt Sophie that he did not want her back. Julia came back more brazen than ever and refused to leave. I was the only preschooler at home and witnessed several arguments between Julia and her mother, who often visited while my brothers and sisters were in school. On one occasion, I left them arguing in the house and went out to play near the milk-house where my father was working. Before long, Julia's mother came rushing out to talk to my father. At five-and-a-half, I was bilingual and understood most of the conversation. What transpired after that surprised and saddened my brothers, sisters, and me.

Suddenly, a lot of activity took over our house, much of it involving Julia's mother, brother, and sister. While my brothers and sisters were at school, Julia's family was busily making plans at our house. What kind of plans? Wedding plans. My father was going to marry Julia, and the date was set for June 12, 1933. Ben was suddenly ordered to leave the front passenger seat of the Chandler and join us in the back seat, so that Julia could sit next to my father. After the wedding bans were announced in church, friends and cousins asked my older brothers and sisters how they felt about it. Ben and Adolph expressed their disapproval, while my sisters, along with Clifford, Clarence, and Anton withheld comments. They were already conditioned to being cautious in their opinions of Julia who made sure of that. I probably would have reacted the same way, except nobody asked for my opinion on the subject. In fact, it probably didn't occur to my father to discuss the matter with his family. If he had, things might have turned out quite differently. I doubt that he was aware of Julia's behavior and her violent outbursts, because we were afraid to tell him. Furthermore, if he had discussed his plans with his brothers and their wives, they would not have been able to advise him wisely because they had no idea how risky this union would be for us. In the end, it was our fault for not speaking up. It all happened too quickly for any leaks about her violence. Perhaps her family wanted it to be that way.

We all dressed up for the wedding and hoped for the best. I don't remember much about the ceremony in the big church. I remember Julia's wearing a long white dress with a rather attractive hat, but I don't remember my father being with her until the reception at Julia's parents' farm, about ten miles out in the country. We were treated nicely by her family and given preferential seating at the dinner. That would be the last time we were given that consideration. After the festivities, Julia moved out of her quarters upstairs, into my father's bedroom downstairs. I was five years and ten months old and somehow knew that things were not going to improve in our home in Maule Coulee. It wasn't long before my doubts were confirmed.

Soon after the wedding Julia announced that, by some mysterious decree, we were required to call her "Ma." Ma! We were accustomed to calling her Julia, so this change was going to present a big problem. She went on further to say that if we forgot, she was required to slap us across the face or mouth. I decided that she was a stupid woman, trying to validate her right to abuse us, until her mother visited and told us we had to do this or God would punish us. Well, God didn't seem to help me remember, because I was sustaining more slaps and hits than I could count. My older brothers and sisters were subjected to the same treatment, which only escalated with time. Ben seemed to be spared. Privately, the "Ma" issue was resolved by referring to her as "she," and we all knew who "she" was. Since I would be starting my first grade at Maule Coulee School in the fall, I tried to focus on school activities and time away from Julia. I was really looking forward to the experience. Julia had a whole lot to do with how I felt about that.

CHAPTER 4

THE COUNTRY SCHOOL EXPERIENCE

WITH Julia as self-proclaimed dictator of our domain, my father seemed to have withdrawn from his parenting role. It was only natural for the younger members of our family to look up to my older sisters for motherly advice and to see my oldest brother, Ben, as the father figure. Although we respected our father as head of the family, we found ourselves looking up to Verna and Ben for parenting. Verna and Ben had completed their two years of parochial training and were back at Maule Coulee School to complete their elementary school years. With both of them now available, we went to them with questions arising from our responsibilities in managing the farm during the Depression. As a result, it seemed normal for Verna to arrange for my first country school experience. I looked forward to the opportunity to get away from Julia and her unpredictable tirades.

Kindergarten was not available at Maule Coulee School; therefore, Verna arranged to have me visit the school one spring day before my fall enrollment. Although Adolph and Eleanore were enrolled in the middle grades at the parochial school, I had five older siblings enrolled at Maule Coulee country school, one mile north of our home. With my enrollment, the one-room school, with its eight grades, accommodated six members of our family, along with cousins who lived on Maule Coulee Road and friends from the valley over the hill. In many ways, it was a pleasant adjustment to school routine, with no trauma over leaving home for the first time, because older siblings more or less took care of their younger brothers and sisters. School was a disciplined, extended family under the guidance and tutelage of the teacher.

I don't remember walking the mile to school that spring day for the visit, but I distinctly remember meeting the teacher, Doris Anderson. Along with teaching eight grades, she must have played a surrogate mother role to my brothers and sisters. I remember her as a beautiful young lady with a warm smile and a peaches-and-cream complexion. Her farm family of eight girls included the nurse who took care of my mother in the hospital before she died. Miss Anderson welcomed me warmly with an air of professionalism I had never been exposed to before. She had several sheets of workbook exercises—coloring circles and squares—to keep me busy while she called each grade up to the reading corner of the one-room school. I found myself so fascinated with the activities of the upper grades, especially those of my older brothers and sister, that I found it difficult to concentrate on my own paperwork. When Miss Anderson came to check on my progress, she gave me additional pages to do. I remember feeling that I was failing preschool, because I had not completed the first page. She assured me that it was okay, and that I could continue coloring after recess. My older cousin in the second grade took me outdoors for recess, where after we took our turns in the outdoor girls' toilet, I was included in simple games.

After recess, I returned to my desk and seriously began working on the coloring assignment and picture-pasting project. I was intent on showing Miss Anderson I was capable of coloring, cutting, and pasting. By the time the lunch bell rang, I was well into my project. I especially liked the taste of the paste. The first through fourth grades were dismissed for lunch and I joined the girls on the hillside of the schoolyard to eat my sandwich and cookies. Later, when the upper grades were dismissed, Verna asked me to join her and her friends. Verna seemed proud of me and told them I would be in first grade that fall. They all seemed happy to see me, probably because a preschool visitor was a rare change in their routine at school.

Afternoon recess was a bit more exciting. Everyone ran down the hill to the large merry-go-round and jumped on. I was afraid of it and chose to stand by and watch. The merry-go-round not only went round and round, it could also be maneuvered by the stronger children, usually boys, trying to scare the little girl riders, to sway horizontally in an inverted arc. I followed the swirls, swings, and sways with fascination and amazement as the children screamed with delight. As I watched the rotation of the merry-go-round, I soon realized that the strawberry jelly sandwich I had for lunch was about to reverse course. At that moment my sister came running down the hill to get me. As my stomach churned, she grabbed my hand and we ran up the hill together. Miss Anderson wanted to talk to me about starting school in the fall. I was so thankful she wasn't going to give me another paper of circles and squares, because I'm sure another circle would have been colored with the strawberry jelly sandwich I had for lunch. It was late in my first year at Maule Coulee School—the spring after a hard winter—before I had the nerve to get on that merry-go-round. Actually, my merry-go-round experience was delayed for other reasons as well. During the winter months the merry-go-round was all but abandoned as snow drifted around it, making it difficult to push fast enough to be enjoyed. Furthermore, the steel pipes, which we grabbed for support, were so cold that even the warmest mittens could not protect our fingers adequately. So we took to the hills with our skis, sleds, and toboggans instead.

Wisconsin winters were always a challenge and it continues to amaze me to this day how Miss Anderson started her teaching day by building the fire in the huge furnace in the school basement before writing class assignments for eight grades on the blackboards. Each grade had its own section of blackboard, with blackboards covering two walls of the classroom. As a first grader walking a mile to school, I faced other challenges. We packed our lunches in metal dinner pails, and because our mittens did not protect our fingers from the cold metal handles, they would become numb and painful. Our lunches literally froze on the way to school. Snowsuits for girls were unheard of. Instead, we wore knit woolen leggings, which were of little comfort in deep snow, because they simply did not stay in place. When we headed for the hills with our sleds and toboggans at recess and lunch hour, we often came back with wet legs from snow that had worked its way into our leggings. If we ventured over the hill, we were unable to hear the bell in the school tower clanging the end of recess or lunch hour, and Miss Anderson would be very displeased. But when the leggings failed to keep us dry during our trudging in the deep snow, displeasure gave way to compassion as we sat on the large heating vent, drying out while we had our reading session.

We mastered winter sports under the most challenging of conditions. On school days, our sleds, toboggans, and skis would be lined up along the south brick wall of the school, ready for recess. On weekends, we had no shortage of hills for long sledding or ski runs. My brothers would make jumps for sleds and skis, which iced over to become a bit treacherous. I would rush through my indoor chores to get outdoors as much as possible; but it was tolerance for cold weather that determined how long anyone stayed out doors. In zero temperatures, time spent outdoors could be shorter than time spent getting dressed to go out.

"Snow days," as we know them today, were not

an option in the 1930s. I remember many walks to and from school in which the snowbanks made by the snowplow in some sections of the road were four to six feet high. One day in the second grade, as I was walking the last half-mile home alone, I became curious about the big snowdrift on the drainage culvert. I walked to the edge and was looking into the big drainage ditch when the edge of the snowbank gave way and like an avalanche, practically buried me in the hole. I tried to climb out, but the snowbank kept breaking off, burying me deeper in the big hole. I wasn't worried because I knew my older brothers would be coming soon and could rescue me. I sat down on the caved-in snow and thought about the stories Miss Anderson read to us about Eskimos living in igloos. I was sheltered from the wind and felt rather comfortable down there. My concern for Eskimos being uncomfortable was somehow left down in that hole as I decided to try again to scramble out, out into the brisk wind, which was beginning to form picturesque snow drifts along the road. This time I got out of the ditch and back onto the road. As I walked on, I wondered if Eskimos sat around the fire in their igloos and told stories about white man's way of dealing with snow, or white children wearing leggings falling into ditches.

We somehow always managed to get to school, regardless of the temperature or snowfall. Julia wanted us out of the house, and we were glad to be away from her. Staying home because of weather never occurred to us or to any of the other pupils at Maule Coulee School. On very bad days, Miss Anderson let us play in the basement of the school, and we ate our lunches on little benches around the big furnace. One winter day after thawing out our lunches, the fourth grade pupils found a way to improve our meals by opening the big furnace door and toasting our sandwiches, using coat hangers as skewers. Remember that big heating vent that we sat on while drying our leggings during our reading session? Well, apparently the aroma of toasted sandwiches found its way through that vent and up to the classroom because soon we heard the quick steps of Miss Anderson's high heels heading for the stairs. Before she made it down the basement steps, however, the fourth graders had secured the furnace door and we were back on our benches, swinging our legs and eating our toasted sandwiches. She looked relieved to know we hadn't set the building on fire. When we returned to our desks upstairs, we could still smell toast. The upper grade students never asked about it, and we didn't tell. Self-sufficiency and imaginative resourcefulness were always appreciated and encouraged in our homes, and school was no place to discourage such initiatives.

Several events highlighted our days at the country school. Miss Anderson arranged for appropriate and beautiful music for every holiday. I loved to sing, and so did many of the boys and girls at our country school. I was so impressed and happy to be singing, I hated to stop to go back to reading and arithmetic. I will always remember Miss Anderson's playing the pump organ while we all sang patriotic songs from *The Golden Song Book*, and how "The Battle Hymn of the Republic" brought goose bumps to my little arms. "Twilight Has Gone from the Gray Autumnal Sky," sung in three-part melody, brought a hint of sadness as we wondered about the severe weather of the coming winter. It must have been around Halloween because I have always associated that song with pictures of pumpkins and witches hanging around the classroom. Later, we went on to "Over the River and through the Woods" for Thanksgiving. Although this song was supposed to make everyone happy about the coming Thanksgiving holiday, I don't remember any special joy associated with vacations from school.

The big event of the winter season at Maule Coulee School was the Christmas program. There was standing room only, as all the parents turned out to see and hear their children perform. Electricity at the school was limited to a single light fixture hanging from the ceiling in the center of the large room. Flickering candles lit the Christmas tree, and tinsel stirred with each cold draft from the opening door. Any movement within the room seemed to excite the tree, and all eyes would turn toward the flickering lights. Anticipation about presents under the tree was overshadowed by anxiety over recitations and songs we had rehearsed the previous weeks and were about to take turns presenting. Although as a first-grader I was very nervous about singing my little solos, I did remember the lyrics for *Silent Night* and a jolly number about Santa and reindeer *up on the housetop*. After Santa presented the gifts, Miss Anderson announced the carols to be sung by all present. The voices of all the students, older brothers and sisters, relatives, parents, and grandparents in the candle-lit, one-room school brought the spirit of Christmas into every heart. This scene on a lovely hillside in Trempealeau County, on a cold crisp December night, remains forever special in my heart.

After that Christmas performance in my first grade in the country school, one might think anything else would seem anticlimactic. Not at all. We continued to brave the cold winter with sleds, toboggans, and skis as accessories for recess and lunch breaks. In February, we had our Valentine's Day activities, although at the height of the Depression, our large family had limited cash flow for other than bare necessities, and valentine cards were not considered necessities. Although some classmates considered making valentines to be less than first class, in our family, this was often necessary. My brother Clarence admitted his embarrassment about making our own valentines. I didn't mind because I knew my mother was buried on Valentine's Day, four years previously, and my cousins and friends could take heart by knowing their mothers would be waiting for them when they returned home from school that day. In other words, who needs valentines if you have a mother?

To make Valentine's Day memorable, Miss Anderson decided to have a taffy pull, an event for which we were all ill suited. The older boys felt it was sissy-like to be kneading and pulling taffy, and they ultimately made a sticky mess on the waxed paper covering their desks. The girls seriously tried, and I was confused about having to eat something I messed up with my fingers, but gave it a whirl. After licking our fingers and washing our hands, we exchanged valentines. Then, we all got to walk home together—a rare occurrence since the upper classes always had a longer school day. I don't remember what happened to the taffy.

Clarence described another notable event that occurred at our country school before I was enrolled in the first grade in September 1933. It was recorded for posterity, but unfortunately never repeated in following years when I was a pupil. The results of that carefully planned occasion probably warranted removing it from the school agenda. It was the day a professional photographer came to take the school picture. Students sat obediently at their desks, while the photographer set up his bulky camera in front of the schoolroom. The photographer came prepared with his own flash equipment, and from my brother's description, the younger pupils were totally unprepared for the events that followed. The photographer disappeared under the black canopy attached to camera, and when the sulfur flash-fired they naturally assumed the cameraman was blown off the planet. The photo, which I saw many years later, shows the upper class students looking happy, probably impressed with the reappearance of the cameraman through the smoke wafting across the school room. Not so for the young pupils. Their worried looks were captured in various poses. Some of them appeared to be poised to bolt, while others looked ready to dive under their desks.

My final event at Maule Coulee School was the school picnic at the end of my second grade. Since I didn't know that I wouldn't be back for the third grade, I never got to tell Miss Anderson good-bye. I always felt a bit sad about this. The picnic included all the farm families along Maule Coulee Road and those from the valley over the hill. I played games with girls my age and enjoyed the delicious homemade food brought by all the families. Someone decided on an avant-garde approach to the traditional farm-style picnic and brought green olives. It was my first introduction to olives and I wasn't at all sure about trying one. I remembered trying the mushroom at Uncle Bert's four years earlier and was taking no chances. This time my curiosity was suddenly appeased by the distraction of upper class girls giggling as upper class boys threw olives at them. Olives were not a Wisconsin farm staple, and I doubt that they were ever a part of any school picnic after that. During the summer my father decided that I should attend the parochial school two-and-a-half miles from the farm, and my country school experience was sadly over.

Many years later while I was away at college, my brother Ben bought the farm that included the land on which the school was built. The school was sold and dismantled, and he bought a good portion of the building material. He built a lovely home, using the oak floor from the classroom. It was very nostalgic to visit him and marvel at the beautiful oak floor that held the desks bolted to two-by-fours in straight rows; the floor on which I marched to the tune of "Amaryllis" in the first grade; the floor that held the stage from which I sang my Christmas carols; and, most of all, the floor that reverberated with the sound of Miss Anderson's high-heel shoes. Out in his front yard Ben placed the school bell that stands in memory of our early education years.

CHAPTER 5

PIETY AND PAROCHIALISM

LONG before I was enrolled in the parochial school near the village of Independence, about two-and-a-half miles from our farm, piety was instilled in my siblings and me as part of our daily lives. Regular church services, the Sacraments, grace before meals, morning and evening prayers, and respect for parents, teachers, nuns, relatives, and all adults were part of our upbringing. That we should honor our parents was never questioned. Although accepting Julia as dictator was difficult, we never questioned her role as mistress of the household. We had learned not to cross her, and we made every effort to please her. We were well into our third year of poundings before I was enrolled in the third grade at the parochial school. By then, slappings and other manual maneuvers no longer satisfied her. She progressed to weapons such as wood sticks and the long iron poker hanging near the stove. On occasion, if the poker were hot, she would use it to burn my brothers. We were her slaves, and she beat us for our efforts—my sisters' cooking and housekeeping and my brothers' hard work with the farm and dairy.

My two younger brothers, Edward and William, Jr., were fortunate to be spared this brutality. Both were living in happy, wholesome environments where sensibility prevailed. Edward became an integral part of the Louie Kulig family and enjoyed the role of baby brother. Our close relationship with that family made him well aware of his double set of brothers. He knew he was fortunate to be a part of that family.

William, Jr., whom we always called Junior, was especially privileged. When he was two weeks of age, an aunt took him temporarily. Mother's younger sister remembered her words as she entrusted Junior in her care: "Take good care of him because I'm coming back to get him." Junior was soon given a permanent home with the Peter Mlynek family, where he became the living toy for the older brothers and their parents. Then, tragedy struck again. Around Christmas time, just before his sixth birthday, Junior developed painful, abdominal symptoms, which grew progressively worse. The doctor thought he was suffering from scarlet fever, which was prevalent in the area at the time. The Mlynek family transferred him to the Whitehall Hospital, where he was diagnosed with complications from a ruptured appendix. I remember joining my brothers and sisters in the hospital to see him. He was all but lifeless in the hospital bed, with the only treatment available at the time, an ice pack on his head. On December 27, 1935, my father came home from the hospital to tell us Junior had died. Years later, my aunt told me, "Your mother made good on her dying promise."

I remember the devastation felt by the Mlynek family. Before closing Junior's casket, the two older brothers clung to each other and sobbed uncontrollably. My brothers and sisters and I stood back in silence, holding back tears, as the Mlynek family followed the casket to the funeral hearse. After the funeral Mass, we followed the casket to the short graveside ceremony. The freezing January weather may have reminded my older siblings of a similar service six years earlier. Now I, too, had one to remember. We left the cemetery to go home and finish our Christmas vacation in mourning. When I returned to my third grade class after vacation, I did not want to discuss how I spent my Christmas vacation; the nun and all my classmates seemed to understand. Yet, I could not forget the images of the Mlyneks' grief during the funeral. When Peter Mlynek came to our home in Maule Coulee almost a year later to discuss the tombstone for Junior's grave, he broke down and cried. As my father maintained his stoicism, Peter remarked about Dr. Peterson's misdiagnosis: "He's no doctor!" he said, "He's just plain Charlie!" And when my brother visited Mr. Mlynek in a nursing home many years later, he still talked about Junior and "Plain Charlie." At the time, Mr. Mlynek was 101 years old.

The Mlyneks' grief made a lasting impression on me. I couldn't understand why our family didn't express their grief. I often thought about how the grown Mlynek brothers cried. I wished I could have cried, but I couldn't. I only cried when Julia was unfairly punishing me. Back in school, my third grade nun knew nothing about that. All she knew was what she saw in church each Sunday—the pious charade Julia played as she sat in the pew a couple of rows behind the nuns. Although the nuns did not know about Julia's behavior, my father gradually learned of her abuse the painful way—before he could lift his eyes off the newspaper at the sound of our screams, it was too late. Julia had already struck someone with one of her weapons.

I had special difficulty reconciling Julia's behavior on Sundays in church with what usually transpired after the service. I remember how, before the service, she made me piously follow her up the long side aisle of the church to the fourth pew from the front. Behind me, my father followed as we took our places in full view of our parish priest. My older brothers and sisters met with cousins or friends and sat with them further back in the large church. After the service, we all met at the car for the drive home. No sooner had the car doors been closed than Julia's long arm reached into the back seat to begin pounding some member of the family. What triggered her explosive outbursts with pounding and swearing was anybody's guess. The ravings would sometimes continue all the way home, while my father drove in silence. The pious charade in church had everyone fooled. Yet we never exposed her.

My sisters took turns preparing the Sunday dinners while the rest of the family were in church. If Julia's family were invited to join us, she would take part in serving them the food my sisters had prepared. Since the long dining room table could not accommodate all of them and my brothers and sisters also, my young brothers sat on the floor along the wainscoted wall and ate whatever her family had left. I usually joined my sisters in the large pantry and ate what was left in the roasters on the stove. The wedding was definitely over. No special consideration for children of the bridegroom.

On one of these Sundays, after a pious performance during Mass, Julia became especially enraged during the drive home from church. As usual, her outbursts were unpredictable, and we learned to keep our distance until her rage ran its course. But this particular Sunday was different. She continued screaming as we entered the house and prepared to eat our noon meal. She went to the oven, looked inside, and with the fury of a madwoman grabbed a plate off the table. With the plate in a vertical position, she crashed it down on Eleanore's head. As Eleanore went crumpling to the floor, blood streaming from her head, Julia reopened the oven, pulled out the large roaster of the Spanish rice hot dish and dumped it on the floor. Then, in full view of my father, five older brothers, and myself, she raised her skirt, pulled down her underwear, and gave all of us the "full moonie," all the while screaming, "Kiss my a—, Kiss my a—." Why did she do it? Probably because she was not going to see her illegitimate son that afternoon, as she usually demanded. Or, perhaps she had planned to give the meat Eleanore used in the hot dish to her mother. A lot of our prepared meats and other items were channeled in that direction, probably as payment for taking care of the illegitimate son.

The next day, we went to school as usual, too ashamed of life at home to mention this episode to anyone. I tried to lose myself in the parochial school routine. It was quite different from Maule Coulee School. When the time came for story reading, I would always request "Cinderella." The nun teaching the class would smile amusingly and jokingly refer to me as Cinderella. Little did she know about the stepmother at home. Nor did she know how we were expected to accommodate the wishes of the half sister and half brother who had joined the family constellation as favored members.

Along with the regular school curriculum, the nuns taught us catechism daily. On certain days of the week, Father Kufel came into each classroom to verbally test us on our mastery of this subject. I remember the "Ten Commandments" as an important guide to our early training. Father Kufel didn't need to impress me with the importance of the fourth commandment, "Honor thy father and thy mother"; Julia had already done that. Of the rest of the Ten Commandments, I'm not so sure. The nuns worked diligently to teach us, and I expect it was Father Kufel's way of checking on how good the nuns' teaching was.

By the time I reached the end of my third grade, I was preparing for my first confession, the Sacrament of Penance. After the nun provided pious instructions in catechism, including special emphasis on the Ten Commandments, we were prepared to make our first confession. My third grade nun felt it would be easier for us to remember "our sins" if we wrote them on a sheet of paper. I remember the day she walked up and down the aisles of our classroom as we all contemplated and wrote. Shy and embarrassed, I partially covered my paper as she walked by. I viewed this as a private matter, and she was sweet and understanding. When the day for my first confession arrived, I was terrified of going into the big dark confessional, afraid I would forget that long list of sins I had memorized. Julia had made me feel so unworthy and guilty at home, I naturally felt I had violated all Ten Commandments, except "Honor thy father and thy mother," of course. But what could Father Kufel have thought as I confessed to having "committed adultery" and "coveting thy neighbor's wife"—in the third grade. Well, how does a dedicated nun explain coveting a neighbor's wife or committing adultery to a third grader? I knew all about living with physical and mental abuse. But that was not part of the Ten Commandments.

One of my experiences with piety left me totally bewildered. I always took pride in my appearance, especially in how I dressed. Dresses had to be clean and pressed. Accessories had to match, and hats were required in church. On one particular Sunday in the third grade, I realized the new petticoat I was going to wear beneath my dress was a bit too long. Without much ado, I quickly resolved the problem with two safety pins—one for tucking up each shoulder strap. I saw no need to remove them as the petticoat went through the laundry. After the laundering, drying, and ironing process, this garment shrank to a size that fit my dresses perfectly. I didn't pay much attention to the rust markings made by the safety pins as I removed them, but Julia noticed them. She told me that I had rusty crosses on the shoulder straps of my new petticoat, and that was God's way of telling me I was bad. I went upstairs to check it, and indeed, the rust markings were in the shape of little crosses following the woven pattern of the cotton fabric. I didn't feel I was disobeying my parents and wondered if somehow I needed to be a better person. Julia said the crosses would not go away until I improved. Well rust markings never go away, and neither did the little crosses. I never spoke of them to anyone; I just tried going over and over those Ten Commandments. I was confused and filled with anxiety.

I don't remember much about the fourth grade, except that the dear elderly nun was well organized and experienced. We had one thing in common. Her mother was also dead; therefore, while all the fourth graders got to color their Mother's Day carnations red or pink, mine had to remain white. To offset this disappointment, she let me outline hers and my mother's carnation with blue crayon. I was honored with this privilege. The fourth grade was also the age that Julia expected me to care for her two young children—a girl and a boy. Caring for them meant keeping them happy. Julia couldn't stand to have them cry, and if they did, it was my fault. Their crying carried a penalty of a surprise blow to anyone within striking distance, usually me. To avoid this punishment, I learned to seat them in the rocking chair side-by-side next to me and sing to them. For some reason, this singing and rocking always worked, and I remember my father saying that I should sing in the junior church choir. I really wanted to, but

Julia decided I could not stay after school for choir practice. I was needed at home to baby-sit and do other chores.

It was about this time that Julia found various excuses to keep us home from school. I was expected to baby-sit her children, while my older sisters were often kept home to do housecleaning and cooking. What made this difficult and nerve-racking was the fact that she refused to write a note to the nuns, giving them the reason for our absence. The nuns naturally thought we balked at coming to school and let us know their displeasure. We were caught in the middle. Many tears were shed over this dilemma and the unfair treatment at each end. Julia apparently was not well educated and saw no real need for good school attendance. To add to our misery, she would tear up our homework or burn it in the kitchen stove during her rages. In a letter, Clarence tells about Julia's tearing up his homework, and his running to school to get there early enough to redo the assignment. And he never told a soul.

In spite of Julia's interference with our school attendance, by the fifth grade I was beginning to rise above the beaten-down effect she had on my psyche. That year I was fortunate to be enrolled in Sister Leonitia's class. She was an excellent teacher and way ahead of her time. It was under her wise tutelage that I stopped "committing adultery" and "coveting my neighbor's wife." I also hoped that Father Kufel would never figure out who I was. Nevertheless, I started preparing in earnest for my First Holy Communion. I was very excited and treasured the mementos of this event for a long time. Along with the usual prayer books and scapulars we all purchased, Sister Leonitia gave me a beautiful medal commemorating the event. I didn't know why I was the only recipient of this special medal until she took me aside and complimented me on my schoolwork. She encouraged me to continue working hard. This experience not only helped me rise above the problems at home, but it also was my first exposure to an important principle of behavior modification—rewarding behavior to see it repeated. Yes, Sister Leonitia knew that rewarding good behavior for good academic performance would promote better learning. Today it is called positive reinforcement, as opposed to negative reinforcement (or punishment) in learning theories.

Of course, the two-and-a-half mile walk to the parochial school had to be reckoned with. When our mother was alive, and my oldest sister and brother, Verna and Ben, were ready for the middle grades at the parochial school, my mother and father thought that a little cart and pony would be good transportation for them. With my retired grandparents living near the school, the pony and cart were sheltered at their place while Verna and Ben attended classes all day. After school they hitched up for the return trip home. This may sound like a marvelous idea, but the plan was never repeated for Adolph and Eleanore, the next two to enroll. Perhaps it was because only Ben could handle the "pony problems" that made storytelling interesting later on. It turned out that boarding with the grandparents during the severely cold weather, and walking two-and-a-half miles during warmer weather, was simpler than pony run-a-ways.

And so it was. By the time my pious father decided it was my turn for parochial school, walking was the only option. After boarding with an uncle and aunt for one year, I joined my older brothers and sister for the long two-and-a-half mile walk. Those enrolled in high school either caught up with or passed us. It was a nice social time with peers. As classmates reached their homes, however, only my brothers and sister were left for the final stretch and conversation immediately changed to a discussion of home chores awaiting each of us and how best to complete the work at home along with the homework from school.

The long walks home were rarely boring. Quite often some kind neighbor or my father would be driving home from town and would give us a ride, which meant getting home earlier, with more time to get our work done. If we didn't get a ride, part of the way or all the way, we kept our ears peeled for the sound of gypsy cars. We were "tuned in" to the sound of our family cars. I'll always remember the unique sound of the Chandler as it came down the highway. It was easy to recognize the clattering sound of gypsy vehicles with their camping gear, including pots and pans, hung on the outside. Fortunately, I was with a group of walkers when we witnessed a vehicle of this type. Whether true or not, we had heard stories about gypsies who kidnapped children walking alone, so we stuck together as much as possible.

When it became very cold and the Chandler refused to start, Ben would prepare the sleigh with warm blankets, hitch a team of horses, and drive us to school. We were the envy of all the walkers who came from other routes. The center of the road would be covered with packed ice and lined with ridges made by tire chains. Horses usually trotted along the sides, where traction was safer. Their steamy breaths made long frosty beards, sometimes covering their eyelashes and the hair of their necks. Their winter coats of long hair served them well as they trotted along. On one of these sleigh rides, I sat under heavy blankets with one leg tucked beneath me. Shortly before reaching the school, I decided to shift my position and get ready for stepping off the sleigh. I was unaware that my tucked-under leg had gone completely numb; and, as I put my weight on it to shift position, I must have misjudged my strength and flipped backward over the sideboard landing in the icy street. I remember the worried look on Ben's face as he stopped the horses to pick up his fallen cargo. My sister jumped out to rescue me. She told me that was a stupid thing for me to do and never to do that again. I knew I wasn't injured, but I felt embarrassed about scaring everyone with the crash of my lunch bucket and schoolbooks hitting the road. Ben returned with the sleigh and horses at three-thirty that afternoon to take us back home.

I can recall some mornings when my father, coming in after checking the animals, told us it was 40 degrees below zero on the outdoor thermometer. This message was his way of telling us to dress warmly, whether or not it was a school day. He always announced the outdoor temperatures as he came in for breakfast. He would have driven us to school, but of course, the Chandler wouldn't start. In any event, when Ben didn't hitch up the horses to the sleigh and take us, we dressed warmly and walked the two-and-a-half miles. I can remember the air being so cold I didn't want to breathe. My fingers and toes would ache from the cold. On the first Friday of each month, we would leave for school in the dark, to get there in time for the 8:00 a.m. Mass and Holy Communion. One advantage to leaving that early was that the wind seemed not to have yet awakened, and we could hear our boots crunch on the frozen snow as we walked.

During my fifth-grade year, a blizzard had come up while we were at school. I was somehow separated from my older siblings at parochial school, so I started home on my own. I was fortunate to be taken part way by a family who lived on the highway. The highway was open, so they probably assumed I could manage the rest of the way on my own. As I left their yard, I found the snow on the road getting deeper and the wind getting stronger. I looked back for cars, hoping for a ride the rest of the way. No luck, so I trudged on in the deep snow. As the snow got deeper, and the wind grew stronger, I found myself becoming very tired. By the time I reached the entrance to Maule Coulee Road, I could hardly breathe. To add to this frightening experience, Maule Coulee Road was not even plowed out, and I still had a half-mile to go. Now I was really in trouble. Out of breath, I would take a few steps and stop to rest, standing in knee-deep snow. It was during one of these stops that through the noise of the wind, with snow blowing horizontally, I could hear the sound of a car. The snowfall was so heavy, I couldn't see if it would continue down the highway or turn into the entrance of Maule Coulee Road. In fact, I couldn't even see that the car *did* turn in my direction. I could only hear the car engine as it downshifted into the lowest gear to make it up the incline of the unplowed road. I knew it wasn't my father, because the Chandler had its own unique sound, especially when it shifted gears. I waited as the car came in my direction. I felt relieved when the driver, our neighbor, Mr. Sandelbach, stopped to pick me up. As the car churned through the deep snow in its lowest gear, Mr. Sandelbach asked where my brothers and sisters were. I didn't know. I was only grateful for being safe. I didn't want to die in the snow on Maule Coulee Road. I had remembered hearing about animals dying in the snow and not being found until it melted in the spring. Not long after I was safely home and placed my snow-covered snowsuit, parka, mittens and boots behind the stove to dry, the Chandler pushed its way into the yard. The split doors of the garage could hardly be opened because of the deep snow, and the Chandler pulled into its shelter for a well-deserved rest. Ben was probably relieved that he didn't have to hitch up a team of horses to rescue the Chandler stuck in the snow somewhere along the way home. My father, sister, and older brothers came into the house and were very surprised to find me home. They looked for me at school and along the highway, and just assumed I rode home with cousins, as we often did. We didn't discuss my scary experience; I just sat down at the table to do the homework assigned by Sister Leonitia. The books stowed in the school bag had managed to stay dry through the long trek in the deep snow. My lunch bucket didn't fare as well; it was half-full of melted snow. Although Julia was not disposed to being concerned about my welfare, she allowed me to do my homework in peace that day. She ignored me and ordered my sisters to start preparing supper.

After the inspiring fifth-grade year with Sister Leonitia, I found it easier to dissociate myself from problems at home and really take an interest in schoolwork. Eleanore and Verna were taking abuse for their work around the house, and I was physically pushed around and slapped for anything that displeased Julia's children—now numbering three. It seemed that Julia's day was not complete unless she had beaten some member of the family. If Verna or Eleanore sat down to read the paper, she would come up from behind and hit them on the head. My brothers were yelled at constantly, for no reason other than for being in the house. My father withdrew into silence, which must have taken on a form of depression, because he hardly spoke to any of us, a marked change from his earlier years. So, as my sixth-grade year got under way, it was a matter of trying to avoid school absences. It was also my confirmation year at the church. I chose Mrs. Bert, who I saw regularly at church and family socials, as my "sponsor," and she was very pleased. Being very religious, she took the occasion more seriously than I did. I was happy to give her the opportunity to follow up on that very early preschool religious training she gave me. Unfortunately, those religious songs she taught me as a three-year-old were all but forgotten. Singing to Julia's children to keep them quiet defeated my purpose for singing in the first place. Furthermore, I was deeply disappointed in not being able to sing in the junior choir. It was as if singing had become a painful experience, so I avoided it.

I enjoyed school. The seventh and eighth grades were successful years in spite of Julia's demands that I stay home from school often to help with her children. I was proud of the report cards I presented to my father to sign. I actually had other classmates asking for my help with their assignments, and I was happy to oblige. By the time my eighth grade graduation day arrived, my efforts at school were acknowledged with a special scholarship award—the medal presented by the Knights of Columbus each year. My father was quiet and reserved at my graduation, but I felt that deep down inside, he was very proud of me.

CHAPTER 6

LIFE ON THE FARM IN THE THIRTIES

THE difficulties of life during the Depression years were keenly felt in Maule Coulee. Although our farmland was rich and productive, cash flow was a real problem. Farm produce did not bring in much cash, and "trading" became common practice. A case of twelve dozen eggs taken to Lyga's or Garthus' store could be traded for groceries, shoes, boots, and clothing. Christmas and birthday gifts were sacrificed to the times. In addition to the economic problems affecting the entire country, Wisconsin was experiencing several years of severe droughts, adding another hardship for farmers. And for a farming father of ten children, the difficulties were compounded. A good dairy and feed business was no cause for celebration when butter brought 8 cents a pound and milk prices per gallon even less. Farm produce could be traded for groceries and very basic food items, but doctor and dental bills presented major concerns for the large families everywhere. I doubt that we were the only family who traded a cord of wood or other farm produce for medical and dental services.

Although cash flow was a problem, we were fortunate to own very productive land. In addition to our garden—almost an acre of sweet corn, peas, carrots, beans, lettuce, tomatoes, cabbage, and any other vegetable known to our community—we had cultivated several acres of potatoes and cucumbers grown for sale. Later, in the late 30s and early 40s, strawberries and green beans were grown for sale, all of which meant long hours of hoeing in the hot sun. I can recall those days, wearing a bonnet and long sleeves for protection from the sun, as I joined a hoeing party with my brothers and sisters. There was never an idle hoe on the farm during that season, and after being hoed, those long rows of potatoes and sweet corn looked beautiful.

In the summer we picked and scrubbed cucumbers before preserving with homegrown dill and a briny solution in heavy, five-gallon crocks. Similarly, we made cabbage into sauerkraut. I remember the long thirty-inch wooden cabbage shredder placed over a large metal tub. A square frame held the cabbage in place as it was pushed back and forth over three or four sharp blades. We had tub after tub of shredded cabbage because we all vied for turns with the shredder. Fortunately, cabbage "settled" into the crocks as it was preserved.

If it hadn't, we might have had a house full of sauerkraut.

I thought making grit baloney was every bit as exciting as pickling cucumbers and cabbage. I particularly liked placing the prepared meat formula into the iron gadget that filled the casings. During the pressing process the operator of this gadget had to restrain any enthusiasm. If he or she pressed too hard, putting too much force on the holding tank, the meat would spew out too quickly and force the casing off the pipe at the other end. Catching and tying the slippery sausage—a skill I never mastered—required quick, skillful, and strong fingers to make sure the string did not come off as each ring of sausage was immersed in boiling water for the final process.

As a dairy business, we made our own butter, although I thought it was not as much fun as making sauerkraut or grit baloney. In fact, it was downright tedious. The special cream that had been set aside for making butter was poured into a large churn—a large wooden barrel built around a shaft with a crank at one end. The barrel, with a large cover over an opening at the opposite end, was placed horizontally on strong supports attached to a firm base. The shaft supported the barrel and its contents as the crank rotated it. The status of the cream contents could be checked at any time by looking at a small glass viewer at the center of the barrel. The tedious part for me came during the cranking of the filled barrel. I don't recall how long it took to churn a batch of butter, but it seemed endless. My sisters and I would take turns with the crank, and I still remember what a relief it was to see the film clear off the viewer, as butter finally appeared. The butter would then be stored in small, half-gallon crocks. As the Depression lifted, our family once again used butter freely for cooking and sandwiches. Because we were not interested in either the buttermilk from the churn or the skim milk from the separator, we probably had the fattest, most pampered, hogs in the county.

During the Depression, necessity became a great motivator. My father became proficient as a barber, cobbler, farm mechanic, and auto mechanic. He maintained all the farm engines that powered various machines and the Delco Plant. I remember how I was warned to stand far back as my father cranked the engines with the large, heavy flywheels—just in case the flywheel would actually fly. With my oldest brother Ben as their role model, the younger brothers became self-sufficient journeymen. They all thought Ben could do anything—and he could. So the farm program continued in spite of the Depression.

The same initiatives applied to cooking and housekeeping. When Julia and my father began having children, Julia more or less—mostly more—excused herself from the responsibility of cooking and cleaning for my brothers, so my sisters became primary caretakers for our family. Only the limited resources under which they were forced to work hampered their enterprising programs. Julia found ways to control the cash flow from the farm, but Verna and Eleanore were never at a loss for ideas about home decorating, sewing their own clothes, or styling their hair. Besides cooking mouth-watering meals and sewing the fanciest of dresses, they styled our hair just as beauticians would. When Julia disallowed any allowance for hair-setting lotion, Verna would beat egg whites to a consistency that served just as well—perhaps better. I remember how Eleanore spread the beaten egg whites on my head and "finger-waved" my hair quickly before this setting concoction dried or became stiff. It wasn't long before our cousins on Maule Coulee Road noticed our beautiful finger waves in church on Sunday, when they too asked to be finger-waved each Saturday. They, of course, brought their own hair-setting lotion, thinking it unfair to use our supply. I doubt that they ever learned why we had such firm "sets" that lasted so much longer than theirs.

In addition to helping my sisters with household jobs, I had the primary responsibility of taking care of Julia's children, which was a seven-day-a-week job. I had no freedom from this responsibility, except when I went to school or church, and even those times could be denied. If the children cried, Julia screamed at everyone, but it was my fault if they were unhappy and I usually paid the price. We stood by as she spent our hard-earned money on toys, treats, and clothing for them. She gave them toys we were not allowed to have. Why not? She controlled the purse.

One particular occasion, related in a letter from my brother Clarence, was especially cruel. When Clarence was in the fourth grade, he became seriously ill with acute appendicitis. While he was hospitalized for his appendectomy, our aunt, Mrs. Joe Kulig, visited him and gave him a clever "Popeye" toy—a wind-up Popeye pushing a wheelbarrow. Clarence loved it. In fact, later we all enjoyed watching the grinning Popeye, pipe in mouth, scooting around the kitchen floor. After his recovery and return to school, Clarence came home one day and searched and searched for his Popeye. But Popeye was nowhere to be found. He learned later that Julia had given the beloved toy to her illegitimate son.

There was never a question of what happened to items that disappeared—from our pantry, or from our wardrobes. Julia had several younger sisters. One day I found my sister Eleanore in tears standing under the large elm trees behind the house. She had come home from school to find that Julia had taken a number of her freshly washed and ironed dresses, blouses, and skirts, and given them to her mother. We never complained. It was safer to avoid Julia's violence. Not long after that, for no apparent reason, Julia stormed out of her bedroom, into the kitchen, and delivered a blow to Eleanore's head that not only gave her a severe headache, but also left her with ringing and a permanent loss of hearing in one ear.

Verna didn't fare much better. Unlike Eleanore, who never spoke up in response to Julia's abuse, Verna would try to hold her ground. Although she sustained similar abuse, on one issue she stood firm. When Verna and Eleanore were old enough to date, they usually joined cousins and friends at the local dances and parties. Julia decided that her younger brother would be socially accepted if Verna dated him. Verna refused, for reasons quite obvious to all of us, and instead went to a dance with her cousins. When Verna and Eleanore came home, they quietly went upstairs to their bedrooms. Julia was waiting for them. Julia began screaming and breaking down

Verna's bedroom door and awakened my brothers and me. Clarence got out of bed and went to Verna's rescue. I believe Verna won, but poor Clarence took the brunt of Julia's rage. I hid under the covers and pretended to be asleep, because I knew I was no match for her. The next day Julia went upstairs with a hammer and nails and tried to repair the door she had kicked in. Verna never did date Julia's brother. I think he got the message. But Julia was determined to get her revenge. When Verna developed an infection in one of her ankles, Dr. Peterson recommended soaking it in warm water. As Verna sat near the stove soaking her foot, Julia went to the stove, took a kettle of boiling water, and poured it on the infected area. Verna screamed in agony as Julia walked away; but Verna had a few choice words for Julia—some right out of Julia's vocabulary. Not long after that, Verna accepted a job as a telephone operator in Elk Creek, a small unincorporated village nearby, from where she plugged in connections to other telephone operators in Trempealeau County. She was thrilled to be salaried. Julia lost one of her slaves, and Eleanore and I would have to make up for that.

Eleanore and I did our best to manage the housekeeping and take care of Julia's children. In addition to cooking, cleaning, and doing laundry for five brothers working the farm, we worked the large garden. Julia did help with the canning, but my brothers, sister, and I did most of the vegetable picking, especially the large quantities of cucumbers, strawberries, and beans that were sold. But we never saw any money from the sales. We never questioned my father in these matters. It was Julia who decided what should be done with that income. She always provided well for her offspring. She also decided when we could afford new clothes. My father would have given my hardworking older brothers "spending money," except that he never seemed to have any. When it was time to pay for our books and supplies at parochial school, we had to make several requests before he found the money. It wasn't until the mother of a seventh-grader who sold me her sixth-grade books called Julia to ask for payment, that I realized why my father never had any money. Julia, embarrassed by the phone call on our party line, immediately came rushing out of the bedroom with full payment for the books.

It would seem that a hard day's work in the fields, garden, and dairy, would be rewarded with a well-deserved good meal in a quiet environment. Hardly. It was almost impossible to get through a meal without Julia shouting or throwing things. If the food or the conversation displeased her, missiles began to fly, sometimes immediately after the "Amen" following grace. On one occasion she threw a table knife at Clarence. He ducked and it hit the wall. Another time she threw a fork at him with such force that it took a chunk of wood, four inches long, out of the wainscoting behind him. Fortunately, he dodged that also. In a letter, Clarence writes about his fifteenth birthday, the day Julia took a china coffee cup and smashed it on his head, causing a two-inch gash. When questioned about his head wound at high school the next day, he told of "making up a story." And that's what we all did. Many years later my brother Anton jokingly told us how our life with Julia prepared him for boot camp in the Marines.

I remember how discrete Julia could be during her time as our housekeeper and later, during the first few months of her marriage to my father. She avoided being violent and abusive when my father was present. But the first time he saw her hit me I was horrified and deeply hurt. I realized immediately that we were vulnerable and unprotected and that her abuse would very likely escalate. And it did—slaps and blows were replaced with wood sticks, butcher knives, and hot poker burns. I remember one occasion when she burned Adolph's back with the hot poker. Why? Because his work jacket slipped off an overcrowded coat hook and fell to the floor. Clifford got the same treatment when he tried to play the radio.

What my father was thinking as he witnessed this brutality remains a puzzling secret. We know he was extremely pious and naturally took his marriage vows seriously. For him, the precept of "permanency" in the marriage vow precluded any consideration of divorce. We all felt trapped and hoped our faith in supreme beings would sustain us. In fact, it was our faith that did just that. Our faith, our cohesiveness as a family, and our early upbringing gave us the strength to stick together and rise above Julia's boorish behavior.

Our opportunities for restoring body and soul came, ironically, through one of Julia's idiosyncrasies, although sometimes at a price. Julia insisted that my father take her to town on Wednesday and Saturday evenings where he would park the car so she could sit and watch the people coming and going. He had to leave the farm early to get the parking spot of her choice. These were the times when we happily shared our experiences, made fudge, popped popcorn, and cracked hickory nuts. Unfortunately, on one of what was supposed to be an evening for brothers and sisters to enjoy each other, or join their friends in town, Julia executed another of her cruel acts. It was haying time, and the boys worked very hard all day on a neighboring farm. They rushed to get the last load into the barn before coming home and doing the milking and chores. This caused a delay with supper and Julia's "people-watching" plans. She became so angry that she took the food left for my brothers, dumped it in the yard, and ordered my father to take her to town. My exhausted, hungry brothers came in from the barn to watch Julia's ducks and geese eating their supper on the front lawn.

Word of Julia's behavior was beginning to leak to some of our cousins, especially the Maule boys at the entrance to Maule Coulee. On the Sunday when Clarence had his skull injury, one of the Maule boys was tending cows in a field near our road. Clarence walked over to talk to him. The obvious head wound, on Clarence's birthday no less, made Ben Maule so angry that when he saw Julia near the mailbox he walked over and gave her a verbal thrashing she was bound to remember. She responded with her usual tirade and tried to hit him with the bucket she was carrying. Mrs. Maule was my grandmother's youngest sister and was appalled at what her sons were telling her about Julia. Furthermore, she was not a part of Julia's clan and their gossiping ways; she was an independent thinker and was not fooled by Julia's charade in church on Sundays. And we were especially fortunate that the Fourth Commandment did not apply to the Maule boys when it came to "advising" Julia.

In spite of Julia's behavior, my brothers, sisters, and I had some good times together. Julia's need to spend long days in town, or to shop in the nearby cities, gave us opportunities to exercise our skills as entrepreneurs. As soon as word got out of her plans to be away, we secretly organized our work force and meted out responsibilities, and before the Doppler effect of the Chandler faded down Maule Coulee Road, we were well into executing our plans. Homemade ice cream was often the choice. Eleanore and Verna would make the custard, someone would dig up a block of ice from the sawdust in the ice house, another would gather some eggs from the chicken coop, another would get the cream from the milk house and another the salt. By the time the ice was chipped, we were ready to start the process of freezing. We all took turns at cranking the ice cream freezer until the ice cream got too thick. Then only my older brothers were strong enough to turn the crank. The results were delicious. What a shame that we couldn't share it with my father. He would have enjoyed it and been very proud of us.

Clarence and I remember only one time when our ice cream program was almost thwarted. Julia and my father left for town with a case of eggs—*all* the eggs from the hen house. After a short argument over who allowed such a catastrophic situation to interfere with our plans, we quickly decided to distribute our forces around the farm to search for a maverick chicken—one whose unorthodox ideas and attitude caused her to leave her colleagues in the hen house and move to some secret place on the farm to lay her eggs. Clarence was the first to find her and came running with the eggs. The next hurdle increased our anxiety even further. How long had this hen been protecting these eggs? We were used to fresh eggs, and surely none of us could conceive of a partially hatched chick getting beaten into our ice cream recipe. We were fortunate that Eleanore was an expert on eggs and she lost no time in making the custard for the ice cream. And we were all experts at cleaning up after our "party." By the time our Dad returned with Julia, there was no trace of events that had taken place during their absence, and everyone was back doing the chores assigned each of us.

In contrast to the poundings, bloody noses, hot poker burns, and woodstick beatings, there was a "company" side of Julia that gave us respite from her usual behavior. When we had company, usually her family or visiting cousins, Julia wisely postponed her rages. Although we enjoyed these breaks, we knew she would be back to her usual behavior after the company left. These were as predictable as the outbursts at the dinner table after "Amen." I often wished she would skip the "company" behavior and show everyone her true colors. She didn't, and I felt betrayed.

One of the most exciting times for me as a child on the farm was grain-harvesting or "threshing" time. This amazing joint effort by the Kulig brothers—my uncles—was always a summer highlight for me. My uncles shared the massive equipment required for this cooperative effort. Uncle Joe provided the threshing machine; Uncle Sam, the tractor with the pulley that powered it; and my father, the grain elevator and special motor that powered it. The equipment was set up on each Kulig farm along Maule Coulee Road during threshing season. The older sons in each family drove teams of horses that pulled hayracks loaded with bundles of grain from the "shocks" in the fields. In an orderly and carefully timed plan, each load was pulled along the side of the thresher where bundles of grain were tossed into an opening with huge rotating teeth. Timing was important because keeping the thresher operating steadily not only kept the process moving efficiently, but also avoided the possibility of added delays caused by bad weather.

 Before any equipment was set up on each farm, the "cooks" or the wives of the farm owners gathered at each farm home to prepare the meals for the threshing crew. The social atmosphere accompanying this event brought ladies from town who wanted to help, but more likely who wanted to be a part of the action. This event inevitably brought out the company side of Julia's behavior—a most welcome relief. While waiting for the threshing crew, the cooking crew happily baked apple pies, grated lemons for lemon pies, beat egg whites for the meringue, peeled potatoes, and prepared the vegetables and meat. They extended the large oak table to its limits, with every available leaf inserted, and covered it with a special, oversize tablecloth that they brought out of storage. These women were so adept at big-event meal preparation, they could tell jokes and maintain a lively discussion without a break in their animated conversations—and without a peek in any cookbook. I can still visualize the scene and recall the aroma of freshly baked pies. My excitement could hardly be contained as I saw the first team of horses coming down the road to begin loading in our fields, then a second team, and the next several teams systematically heading for our fields. These teams were followed by the long grain elevator with its power source, and the large tractor pulling the huge threshing machine. This parade down Maule Coulee Road was one of the most exciting events of my childhood. It heralded a special feeling of security for me because I could expect at least a couple days of company behavior on Julia's part.

Because we didn't tell anyone about Julia's usual cruel behavior, this clan of cooks socially accepted her. Those who knew about her tantrums either were not invited or declined the "invitation" to help. Some of her friends looked at us as fortunate to have her as our "mother." We didn't tell them that we were actually taking care of her—and her children. And, of course, they would have no way of knowing about her embezzling of our family income. The charade at home was working just as well as the one at church. This dilemma often sent me to the large woodshed, where I could quietly ponder my very being as I smelled the freshly split wood. Why was I born? What will happen to me when my brothers and sisters are gone? Will anyone ever know the truth about our life at home?

My worries about my future would abate whenever I thought about my brothers and sisters, how I was an integral part of this family, and how they would always be there for me. We worked harmoniously together because we knew and did what was expected of us. If our resources were limited, we made up for it by becoming a family of young entrepreneurs. Even before Julia became the albatross on our scene, young entrepreneurs in the family were busily making games out of nails, boards, and discarded rubber fruit-jar rings. Using a sponge ball, we would play outdoor ball games until dark. When we were fortunate enough to be able to attend a county fair, we would observe many of the games or competitive activities and then copy them and play them at home. Five brothers could devise any number of games, with complex rules to be followed. As the rules became more complex, they made adjustments to accommodate arguments.

When weather was not conducive to outdoor play, we often gravitated to the retired Studebaker in the lean-to next to the old granary. It was a wonderful, gigantic toy, with a convertible top and extra seats that pulled up from the floor between the front and back seats—a very appropriate kind of limo for a family of ten children. This spot was where we went to "play car," where we took turns behind the huge steering wheel. Although the old Studebaker had been resting for many years, it was later to be revived in a most clever way as my brothers grew up and became interested in driving.

During our early years on the farm, before the advent of the tractor, horses accounted for the force behind the successful farming and harvesting experience. I was always fascinated with these huge, willing creatures—their strength, their temperaments, and their different personalities.

Counterpoised with their willing nature was the occasional, frightening breaking-in procedure of the novice horse. It was critical that a mature horse be patient in tolerating the antics of the novice as the latter was hitched up to a wagon for the first time. I don't know which required more patience—my father or the mature lead-horse harnessed next to young trainee.

Recent phone conversations with my brother Clarence refreshed my memory of these marvelous creatures. Nance and Florie were two brood mares that provided the young foals that later became the work force for the farms. I don't remember much about Nance, except that she had three foals—Dewey, Pearle, and Babe. Florie was a dapple-gray mare that had a series of beautiful offspring—Bob, Dick, Colonel, Prince, Robin, and Silver. Two other horses, King and Clyde, were the "experienced" members of the stable. King, the oldest, was the old-faithful worker and "training assistant" for the young novices. Clyde, purchased from our neighbor, came with an "attitude" to the work force. Clarence said he and Florie were known for a trait that proved to be very frustrating for the driver. When they considered the load to be too heavy, they absolutely refused to move. On one trip for a load of wood from the back forty, Ben returned with a "load" of six small logs. Florie or Clyde's idea, of course.

As is typical with all horses, our farm horses had distinct personalities. Although one might expect some similarities among these siblings, personalities and talents varied widely among this group. Bob was Ben's favorite for riding. But it was Robin I remember best. He was foaled on a beautiful spring day, a day when the first robin also appeared on the farm. Robin was a delight from the first day I saw him. His dark chestnut coat was highlighted by his white blaze and white, spotted rump. But most of all, his quiet temperament made him a favorite as an all-around performer. Although I was not allowed to ride (riding was considered not to be a "girl thing"), my brothers enjoyed riding and driving him. I wish I had some photos of the time Clarence and Clifford hitched him to the cutter and drove him in deep snow almost two-and-a-half miles toward town. Although Robin was a bit apprehensive about the passing cars fitted with noisy chains, he safely brought a couple of young high school boys back home.

All the horses were trained to work with farm equipment, but an amazing feat was getting them to stand quietly near the noisy threshing machine and grain elevator during the harvest. The threshing machine, with its long moving belt to the tractor that powered it, must have been frightening to the novice horse, to say nothing of the big, long pipe that spewed the threshed straw into a huge haystack. Yet these horses were trained to stand quietly as each driver tossed the bundles of grain into a gaping mouth with revolving teeth at the front end of the thresher to be blown out the other end through the big pipe into the haystack.

While the grain was being separated from the straw during the threshing process, another team of horses would take wagonloads of grain to the elevator set up near the granary. The elevator was a long trough-like ladder that could be raised at an angle so that its upper end fit into an opening in the roof of the granary. Metal steps attached to moving chains within a metal trough channeled the grain up to the roof from where it could be directed to different bins inside. Added to the noise of moving metal against metal, was the noisy gasoline engine that powered this huge apparatus. Remarkably, the horses stood quietly while the grain was shoveled from a double or triple box into the noisy elevator. In fact, I have actually seen them sleep as they stood.

Unfortunately, not all was pleasant or tranquil with this workforce. During one of our phone conversations, Clarence and I talked about several conditions that may trigger the "fight or flight" instinct in a horse. One of them is the smell of hogs. He recalled two incidents where hogs played a major role in causing a team of horses to run away. On one occasion, my father had a wagonload of hogs to be driven to town with a team of horses. It took over half an hour to get the horses near the wagonload. After finally getting hitched to the wagon, the horses, with my father at the reins, took off in a full gallop on the two-and-a-half mile drive. The return trip wasn't any safer. The smell of hogs from the empty wagon pursued the horses in full gallop back to the farm.

Clarence also remembered a time when it was his and Clifford's responsibility to pick up the fallout—grain that spilled under the thresher—and transport it to the hog pens on the south side of the farm. With a team and wagon loaded with fallout, they checked to see that the hogs were asleep in the hog sheds and proceeded through the gate to the feed pens. Unfortunately, the hogs heard the activity near their feeding pens and came running en masse to the area where Clifford and Clarence were unloading. Bob and Clyde took one look at the approaching invasion, combined hog smell with instinct, and took flight through the open gate. They galloped all the way back to the buggy shed where they waited to be unhitched. Remarkably, they made it around the curve at the open gate without damage to horse, hitch, wagon, or gate. Good judgment on their part. And good judgment on my father's part to shelter the hogs on the south side of the farm, far away from the horses.

On another occasion, my oldest brother, Ben, was returning to the barn with a team of horses and a cultivator. Propped up in the metal seat, about as protected as a statue on a post, he held my five-year-old brother, Edward, for a quiet ride home. Suddenly, the pole attached to the neck-yoke came unhooked, hit the horses, and both of them were off. Unable to jump with my young brother in his arms, he held firmly as the horses broke loose and ran for the barn. One can easily imagine the jarring effect of having the pole driven into the ground at that speed and force. An experience like this might have intimidated the average driver, but as we learned later, Ben would never meet life's challenges in an average kind of way.

These frightening incidents were more than offset by the pleasurable experiences my brothers had with horses. When they used the "walking cultivator" in our large garden, potato patches, or cornfields, one brother could ride the horse pulling the cultivator while the driver walked behind. I remember wishing I could ride also; but then, riding was not considered to be a girl thing.

The excitement of a run-a-way occasionally followed a day of cultivation. Like young novice horses, young novice drivers were not always prepared for "spooking" conditions. Horses often take a dim view of any changes in their familiar environments. On one occasion, while one team was working in the fields, another was moving some sheds and farm machinery to another location on the farm. In this instance, they were moving a hay tether and some sheds used to shelter the ducks and geese from one location to another. As Clarence was walking King and Clyde back to the farm, this team took one look at the relocated hay tether and sheds and ran off. They ran so fast they failed to negotiate the sharp turn into the driveway and ended up straddling a tall power line pole. This stopped the horses, of course. Clarence was left far behind trying to catch up with his run-a-way team, now entwined around the power pole.

One of the most fearful of farm creatures was the bull guarding his herd in the pasture. He was a sure-fire reason no one took a short cut through the pastures—ours, or anyone else's. I recall vividly how uncomfortable I was, walking home alone from school, especially the last half mile past the bull guarding his herd. I remember thinking that if I didn't look at him he wouldn't feel challenged by me, a timid first-grader, walking alone. Yet I couldn't resist the impulse to look around to determine his whereabouts. It was always a relief to see him grazing on and ignoring me. I never told my older brothers and sisters that I would have gladly stayed on for a longer school day, just to be able to walk home with them.

While I was struggling with my fear of the dangerous bull in the pasture beside the road, my father and other farmers in the area had greater concerns. A serious epidemic of equine encephalitis—at that time called "sleeping sickness"—was affecting many horses in the 1930s. The cause was yet unknown, and a cure was not available. My father thought it would be safer to have the horses in the barn at night and asked three of my brothers to go out in the dark pasture, where the horses grazed with the dairy cows, and bring the horses in. Clarence took a flashlight to see the horses, but unwittingly he flashed the bull, which came charging full speed in his direction. In the dark and hilly pasture, Adolph, Clifford, and Clarence ran to the large culvert that drained the opposite field across the road. Fortunately, the culvert was large enough to allow them access and small enough to stop the angry charging bull—and the horses did not get brought in that night. Fortunately, none were lost to the disease.

A truly frightening episode with a raging bull took place around 1940 when I was in the seventh grade. My father had purchased a young bull from a farmer living in an isolated part of another county. As Clarence explained, it came from isolation to a busy, well-inhabited farm. The poor creature was not accustomed to people, and as he matured, he became a real challenge around the farm. My brothers managed to move this animal between our farm and the neighboring Bringsosen farm we were renting by guiding it down the country road. Returning it by the same method and on the same route, however, turned out to be a disaster. First he got away as he neared our home farm, ran across the fields through barbed-wire fences on a neighbor's property, and charged down the paved highway toward town. Fortunately, after frightening several onlookers, he veered right, ran across the fields, and disappeared into the woods. By that time it was dark, and my brothers were unable to find him.

Early the next morning, Clarence took off a day from high school and joined three older brothers to look for this angry, frightened animal. Ben picked up a piece of a branch as they looked for signs of the animal. They saw him resting in a field near the woods on property about five miles from our farm. As the four of them surrounded the animal he arose and quickly charged in Ben's direction. With the wooden branch, Ben stood poised in batting position. As the bull charged, Ben swung at the angry animal. This, of course, did nothing to improve the bull's temperament and he reversed direction for a wilder charge. Ben swung at him from the opposite direction, and back again. With each swing of the branch, a section of wood broke off, until Ben was left to fight the bull bare handed. He tried to catch the animal by the ring in his nose, but at that instant the bull miraculously turned and ran for the woods. As three brothers watched nineteen-year-old Ben fight a bull barehanded in an open field, the bull decided to run in the opposite direction into the woods.

From my classroom at parochial school I could

see the open fields where my brothers were in pursuit, but I didn't see the actual bullfight. I had difficulty focusing on my classwork, however, as concern for my brothers' safety overshadowed any reading, rhetoric, or even recess. When I got home from school, I was relieved to learn that my brothers were safe, and the events of that day were a closed chapter in farm events. Someone had arranged to shoot the animal and he was prepared for beef, although no one in the family enjoyed the meat. It tasted "wild" to me.

Four years later, in July 1943, the story of Ben's encounter with a German tank in Sicily was documented at length in the August 9, 1943, issue of *Life Magazine*. After World War II, the movie *Patton* showed the jubilant residents of Palermo, Sicily, welcoming the U.S. Second Armored Division that liberated them. Unfortunately, the movie failed to show the German 88 tank that held up the American soldiers who were fighting fiercely to take the city. And it also failed to show the half-track from which Ben fired one shot to "take out" the German tank, and the following shot with which he blew up the German ammunition dump fortifying the city. Without Ben's skill in executing this feat, General Montgomery, who had the same objectives for Palermo as Patton did, would have thwarted General Patton's triumphant march into Palermo. The mismatch between the German tank and the American half-track in Sicily in 1943, and the young man and the angry bull in Wisconsin four years earlier, did have one thing in common. They both took place in the most dangerous of places—an open field.

Clarence recalled another truly remarkable incident with a bull on the farm. As youngsters, Clarence and Cliff often liked to play horses, by pulling a little wagon, side by side like a team of horses. In this case, the little wagon had long since lost its wheels and resembled a rusty toboggan. Out in the pasture was the large bull with a long heavy chain around its neck, long enough to be dragged behind its hind legs. The purpose of the long chain was to keep the animal from charging at whoever was responsible for bringing the cows home. This safety precaution made it possible to outrun the animal if he charged. Well, it seems that one day all the cows came home to be milked, except the bull that had broken through the fence to graze in a hayfield near the pasture. This must have seemed like a good day for the two youngsters to play horses. They pulled their makeshift toboggan out to the field where the bull grazed, hitched it to the heavy chain dragging behind the animal, piggy-backed aboard the makeshift toboggan, and hi-dee-hoed for a half-mile ride over the grassy pasture all the way back to the barn.

CHAPTER 7

THE STORM THAT SAVED ME

MY graduation from the eighth grade left me feeling melancholy. Because we had not taken advantage of opportunities to share our fears and concerns with those devoted nuns, they would never know why we often ran to school in tears before Julia made us stay home to work. Why we rushed through re-doing our homework after Julia tore it up or burned it. Why our reading assignments weren't always completed because she wouldn't allow us to read in peace. Why the environment at home was never conducive to study unless she was gone. And surely no one told them how my brothers came home from school one day to find their clothes, beds, and bedding on the front lawn. Julia had evicted them. After all their hard work in the fields, with the horses, with the dairy, and in maintaining the farm, she decided they had no right to sleep in *her* house. The house built by my grandparents. So they moved their belongings to the old vacant house on the neighboring farm we were renting—the old house the neighbors used for storing grain and the haven for various rodents attracted to such storage.

The events of the previous ten years were beginning to overwhelm me. I needed to share my fears with someone outside the family, someone who could alleviate the fear and shame that was trapping me. But who could that be? The heavier this burden became, the less likely I was to talk about it. I found myself wanting to escape to another world, a safe refuge from the one in which I lived. To satisfy this need, I coped as best I could by secretly escaping to the tool shed, where I could make odd things out of the old leather scraps—leftovers from shoe and harness repair. But mostly, I would sneak away for what I recall as "ponderings in the woodshed." The smell of freshly split wood, like the smell of leather in the tool shed, seemed to provide an atmosphere for purging the worst experiences from my memory. Those mental pictures of Julia kicking my young brothers across the room; of Clarence being pinned to the floor as she held a butcher knife to his chest while she screamed she would stab him "right through the heart"; of the countless bloody noses, blows to the head, hot poker burns, hittings with wood sticks, and skull injuries; of locking the boys out of the house; of breaking down bedroom doors; of storming the front porch where the boys tried to play games, crashing furniture along the way; of unplugging the radio and throwing it on the floor—all accented with "I'm going to kill you." Then, as if to compensate for the anger building up in me, I would wander off to the buggy shed that housed the retired buggy and cutter. There, I would try to visualize happier days—those days of peace and plenty that my siblings remembered, days of Mother smiling as she brought home the boxes of Cracker Jacks from Lyga's Store. As I looked at the retired buggy and cutter collecting dust, pushed aside to make room for other farm machinery, I longed for those happy days. Oh, how I wished I could have been a part of those times.

The psychological abuse was no less damaging. My brothers were very conscientious about operating the rental farm along with our home property, and diligently maintained a well-managed schedule of work. Anton told me about the thirty-one cows on two farms that had to be milked by my father and five brothers. During the school year they had to get up especially early because they had to walk almost three miles to the high school. It was Ben who set this example for my brothers. Although my father made work assignments, Ben was the role model. They all seemed to go to Ben with their questions. The farm ran smoothly as we pulled through the Depression years. It would seem that my brothers would realize the benefits of our improving economics. Not so. Julia always managed to get her hands on the income from the farms. She believed that room and board was sufficient pay for our work. As if this weren't humiliation enough, when my brothers went out with our cousins, Julia would lock them out so they couldn't get back into the house. I recall the many times she would use table knives which she forced under the door moldings, to make it impossible to force the door open without tearing up the entire door frame. It was then necessary for my brothers to go around to the back of the house and come through the cellar door. And guess who would be waiting at the top of the stairs with a stick of wood to beat them?

Similar greetings would await my sisters after they came home from their dates. Julia would be waiting up to scream at them and pound them. She once tried to push Verna down the stairs for not dating her brother, but Verna was firm in her convictions. I hated these one-sided confrontations. They awakened me and left me very tired the next day. I was always expected to be up early to feed Julia's ducks and geese. She would yell from her bed downstairs to wake me up. Then she would go back to sleep while we all got up to do our chores. There was the cooking, the gardening, the housekeeping, and the milk house chores. Eleanore and I were responsible for washing and sterilizing the separator and various milk and cream containers. The separator, which separated the cream from the skim milk, was a bit complicated. I knew that disassembling and reassembling those many parts, especially those many disks, had to be exact, or the separator would malfunction and cause serious problems. It was a seven-day-a-week job, with no time off for holidays.

The chores themselves were not a problem. Our cousins and friends all had similar responsibilities. They too had beans, potatoes, cucumbers, and strawberries to pick. It was the fact that their efforts were appreciated and rewarded. Ours were not. And therein lay the basis for our resentment and anger.

Our older cousins were given the use of their parents' cars and money to spend for evenings out. My brothers had to rely on the generosity of their cousins, who actually enjoyed taking them along. With my sisters, there were always plenty of invitations. My brothers and sisters were all very popular, and I suspect Julia resented this.

These happy outings with friends and cousins probably offset Julia's lockouts and raging greetings when my brothers returned home. Each outing was a gamble on whether Julia would lock them out or be waiting to pound them. Ben seemed to be spared, but the younger brothers were her favorite targets. This situation neither deterred them, nor repressed their innovative plans. The oft-quoted expression, "hope springs eternal," could certainly be applied to their ambitious undertakings. And since Ben was not allowed use of the Chandler, it was only natural that the old Studebaker in the lean-to of the old granary would soon become the object for his serious scrutiny.

The old Studebaker was the classic touring car of the 1920s. A manually operated convertible top, folded in layers behind the back seat, covered its long body. Besides being manually operated, the top had to be secured to the body with numerous brass snaps, which must have been a real challenge during a sudden rain. Furthermore, its huge wheels with their round wooden spokes must have required a driver with very strong arms. I can see several reasons why my mother opted for the new Chandler in 1927. The safety of little children riding in the back seat of the Studebaker must have concerned her long before Verna gave her just cause for such anxieties by falling out. With Mother gone, and the three youngest family members living elsewhere, the Chandler became the family sedan, and the Studebaker was permanently retired. My brother Anton recalled the last license plate as number 1932.

Anton remembered the occasion in the summer of 1938, when he was twelve, that the old Studebaker was revived. It had been retired for six years and when Ben was eighteen, Adolph seventeen, Clifford fifteen, and Clarence thirteen, this group of entrepreneurs opened the old garage, the lean-to joining the old granary, to evaluate the abandoned Studebaker. Its dusty convertible top was stiff and rotting, and the jump seats were frozen in their retracted positions in the floor. They concentrated on work under the hood. After successfully getting the engine started, they had to deal with the problem of old tires. Neither tires nor inner tubes were available for those huge wheels. They resolved this problem by coiling rope inside the old tires and found this to work amazingly well. I was not at home to witness Ben as he drove the old Studebaker down Maule Coulee Road to the Maule farm. I would have been so excited to take that ride with him, especially since I missed all those happy trips to Joe Soldowski's Road House, where my father used to take my older brothers and sisters for ice cream during those happier days.

Ben enjoyed driving the old Studebaker to visit his friends, especially the Maule boys, up and down Maule Coulee Road. Since he was not allowed to drive the Chandler, he continued to ride with cousins to dances, parties, and other social events. It would seem that a twenty-year-old, hardworking son would be allowed to use his father's car occasionally. With Julia firmly entrenched in our family, this was not even a remote possibility. The Chandler never left the yard without her sitting in the front passenger seat.

If farm income had been more lucrative, my father might have been able to buy a car for Ben. Surely my father must have remembered how he courted Mother with the Studebaker touring car in 1917—the car he kept in the lean-to so long after her death. But with Julia, things would never be fair. My brothers, sisters, and I often talked about this unfairness among ourselves. It wasn't as if we had no outside opportunities to complain about mistreatment at home. It was that we just didn't take advantage of them. The stigma of embarrassing situations at home precluded our discussing them with friends or strangers. It is unfortunate that we didn't take advantage of the party line in our telephone system. This remarkable feat in engineering would have been an excellent tool for leaving clues about life at home. We knew that others who happened to be listening in more than likely, shared what we shared with the person on the other end of the line. Although this kind of eavesdropping was considered taboo, it was common knowledge that this taboo was regularly breached. And it really wasn't always intentional. The large oak box attached to a wall in each home housed the early telephone mechanisms. The little crank on the right side of each box was used to crank out the number of rings assigned to each home on the party line. I found it difficult to accurately crank two long rings, two short rings, a long and a short, a short and a long, two short and two long, or two long and two short. I would have to excuse anyone for picking up his phone for any ring I cranked. And what about those poor left-handed people using a right-handed phone? There were certainly plenty of reasons for picking up your phone when calls were intended for someone else.

Since private lines were not available in Maule Coulee, we learned to maintain some semblance of privacy by speaking in a sort of private code, usually agreed upon in advance. In other words, the code would be used to confirm plans made earlier in person—usually after church on Sunday. The use of codes sparked the curiosity of the true eavesdroppers, who probably picked up the phone every time it rang, regardless of two long, two short, or whatever. But even if they were not successful in breaking someone's code, they were definitely more informed by hearing both sides of a coded conversation than we were. Sometimes hearing only one side of Julia's coded conversations didn't make any sense at all. Eavesdroppers, however, often filled in the missing blanks for us. Regardless, I was too busy baby-sitting Julia's children and feeding her brood of ducks and geese to be bothered with gossip on the party line. As it turned out, the ducks and geese turned out to be the pivotal subjects upon which my freedom from Julia was eventually launched.

Chickens, ducks, and geese were always part of our farming experience. When nature was allowed to take its course, it was delightful to see some mature hen come out of hiding with her brood of baby chicks, or some duck or goose emerge in late spring or summer with her family of ducklings or goslings. I found it especially interesting to compare behavioral differences among ducklings, goslings, and baby chicks. Ducklings and goslings followed their mother figures in a very orderly fashion, usually in a single file. When their mother stopped, they stopped. Without any apparent training, they seemed very well behaved. Not so with baby chicks. When the mother hen decided to introduce her brood to the outside world, it was bedlam for her. Instead of the orderly single file adopted by their web-footed relatives, they jumped, hopped, and ran in front, in back, along side, and under her as she tried to lead them. Although she clucked enthusiastically, her hyperactive brood usually ignored her. It wasn't until she began scratching the dirt in search of worms, that some of them took note and attempted to imitate her. Little chicks just learning to walk were not able to stand on one leg and coordinate movements necessary for the scratching act, much less apply enough pressure to move enough soil to expose any worms hidden beneath. The result was an excited brood, cheeping and bumping into each other, with little wings flapping in their efforts to stay upright. More confusion followed and usually would be interrupted by the excited clucking of the mother hen, as she succeeded in pulling a sizable worm from the soil. Then, all the little chicks would instinctively pick at the worm and try to satisfy their needs for nourishment. After their feast, the mother hen repeated her scratching, as several more of her brood tried to stay upright during their attempts to imitate her.

The seasonal excitement of these scenes was

somehow lost when Man decided to improve on nature's tranquil ways. As a youngster, I recall several instances of Man's intrusion on nature's serenity. Egg layers, as adult chickens are often called, no longer hatched their own eggs. Instead, commercial incubators hatched hundreds of baby chicks for shipment to various farms. Orders were placed through stores, feed mills, and even catalogs. I can remember when a huge box of chirping chicks was sent by parcel post to our farm. In fact, the mailman delivered them. Along with the shipment and copy of the order form was an additional form to complete, a number count for replacements of baby chicks that didn't survive the trip.

Julia developed a strong interest in raising ducks and geese. The idea was hers. The cost of feeding and the responsibility of caring for them was ours. She had no problem acquiring "clucks," the setting hens that instinctively sat on anything resembling an egg. Clucks are very poor layers, and their owners welcomed ridding them from the hen house. Why feed a hen that doesn't earn her keep by laying eggs? Besides, their attitudes left much to be desired. No matter how kindly you approached them, how kindly you spoke to them, their responses were most ungrateful. They always seemed poised to attack. Feeding them did nothing to improve their attitudes, but it was one way of getting them out of their nests to retrieve any eggs, should they be inclined to lay any, although I wouldn't advise trying to retrieve an egg from a cluck without good gloves and protective arm covering. Out of their nests the clucks would puff out their wings, cluck assertively, and strut about as if ready to attack—a most unwelcoming sight around the hen house. The undesirable nature made it easy for Julia to acquire a number of clucks from neighbors for her ducks and geese business. Verna recalled the time when Julia sent her and Eleanore to a neighbor about a mile away to pick up some clucks. They each carried a gunnysack with the heavy clucks back to the farm, while Julia spent the day in town.

Because of the strong "sitting" instincts in clucks, they would sit on eggs of any species. Julia ordered my brothers to collect eggs laid by several ducks and geese in small sheds around the farm. Neither the ducks nor the geese were inclined to let anyone snatch the eggs beneath them, a challenge that brought out the adventurous spirit in my brothers. Stooping down and looking into the low shelters where ducks and geese nested could be hazardous. Snatching an egg while confronting the striking bill of a duck or goose at eye level was more of an adventure. Yet, unlike clucks that rarely left their nests, ducks and geese would cover their eggs carefully and wander off. Then even I would feel safe gathering their eggs. Some of the eggs were so well covered, we had difficulty finding them.

Thus, with help from Clifford, Clarence, and Anton, Julia went about setting up nesting boxes upstairs in the old granary. The clucks she acquired seemed content sitting on the eggs snatched daily from the ducks and geese. As we acquired more eggs, Julia set up more nesting boxes in the old granary, with a cluck for each box. After the eggs were hatched, the cute little creatures were separated from the clucks and fed hard-boiled eggs with starter feed. I don't recall the weaning process from the clucks. Perhaps the old clucks took one look at their hatchlings and decided to desert them. How did they feel about the results of their sacrifices in time and persistence? Good question. And did these sitting sessions, about three to four weeks for ducks, and four to five weeks for geese, satisfy their sitting instincts? I often wondered about that too, but not for long. The next phase of Julia's webbed-foot business made me forget the efforts of the poor old clucks. Cleaning sheds and feeding some 150 to 200 ducks and geese, in addition to helping with the housework and baby-sitting, left no time to be concerned about the old clucks.

Julia continued to bark orders from her bedroom downstairs for me to get up and feed her ducks and geese while she stayed in bed. I remember being tired and not wanting to get up, especially after a night when she stormed my sisters' bedrooms or awakened me during some tirade she had instigated. But we all dutifully got up to do the chores, cook the meals, clean the house, do the laundry, wash and sterilize the milking equipment and separator, and of course, feed all those ducks and geese in various sheds around the farm. I would mix the feed my father had bought and paid for with the skim milk my brothers had separated from the cream that was sold and carry it out to the fields where the ducks and geese were housed in small sheds. Twice a day, I repeated the process, carrying a heavy bucket of wet feed in one hand and a bucket of water in the other, rain or shine, hot or cool. Although the young were kept fenced in, the older ducks and geese roamed freely over the pastures where they snapped at butterflies and grasshoppers. It was quite a sight, seeing a streak of 150 to 200 white ducks and geese cresting the pasture hill and heading home to be fed. And I'm sure Julia watched as she planned how this large brood would be dressed and sold as her private income.

Julia may have welcomed the day for slaughtering and dressing this large web-footed brood; but for me, it was a day of mass tragedy. All those unsuspecting ducks and geese would be corralled in pens, from which they would be caught to have their throats slashed. Julia arranged to have extra men help with this gruesome process. With their heads wrapped to prevent soiling their feathers, they would then be placed on a gunnysack and firmly tied over a steaming copper boiler on the stove in the summer kitchen. The steam loosened the feathers, so they could be more easily plucked. Poultry buyers picked up the stacked carcasses at the end of the day, and the sound of 200 squawking ducks and geese was silenced for another season. The feathers were stored in large white sacks until January or February, when a "feather-bee" could be scheduled. Everyone in the family helped at the slaughtering because it was assumed that like other families, our entire family would enjoy the income from these poultry sales. We knew that Julia would get the income, and we would get the feathers, if we were lucky, for making soft pillows and warm feather comforters for those cold Wisconsin winters.

The feather bee was a social event that attracted many women from the village. Furniture was shoved aside as every available chair was arranged in a large circle in the living room. The women took their positions near large bags of feathers and began the tedious process of stripping. It didn't take very long before the storytellers began telling jokes. With each story came a round of laughter that naturally evoked a competition for the loudest response. Although I was expected to stay home from school to care for Julia's children, I found myself ignoring them and listening in. The day ended with bags and bags of soft down and stripped feathers, and the ladies who drove their own cars, took their passengers back home. For months after the feather bee, we found feathers in every nook and cranny around the house, a clear reminder that the cycle of clucks, ducklings, and goslings would be repeated again in a couple of months.

July 28, 1941, began as just another day of the usual work schedule. My father and brothers worked two large farms, with horses and farm machinery working various fields. After Eleanore and I prepared the noon meal and cleaned up the kitchen and dining areas as usual, we noticed storm clouds gathering over the hill in the southwestern sky. Julia came out of her bedroom and ordered me to check on the ducks housed in the sheds across the creek to the east. I could see the lightning and hear the thunder in the distance as I ran out to check on them. I found that at least a half dozen were missing. As I ran back to the house, I knew that Julia would have a tantrum, but I didn't expect the fury with which she reacted. By that time, the escalating storm outside was matched by the one taking place inside the house. As Julia came after me, she ordered me out in the storm to find the missing ducks. Eleanore and

I ran into the tool shed as the rain started to come down in torrents, with lightning flashing and thunder crashing. We could hear Julia screaming what she was going to do to me if I didn't find the ducks. I don't think Julia knew where we were, so I peaked out the tool shed window and saw her screaming and waving a butcher knife in the doorway of the front porch. Eleanore and I were both trembling with fear—of the bad storm and Julia—when I looked at her and said I couldn't take any more of these tirades. We both knew this was a bad one. Before I could tell Eleanore that I thought I should run to the Maule farm, Eleanore said, "GO." And before I could finish telling her to pack some clean clothes for me, she said, "GO!" again, so forcefully, I sneaked out of the tool shed and headed for the creek in the southeast pasture. By then the storm had subsided, and I had this sudden sense of relief as I walked barefoot, wet, and tearful down the creek toward the John Maule farm at the entrance to Maule Coulee. Because I followed the creek that ran through our pasture on to the Maule's farm, no one could see me. And if Julia did see me, she probably would have thought I was looking for her missing ducks. As I walked barefoot in the wet sand and shallow water, I felt terribly sorry for Eleanore, not knowing what was going to happen to her after she went back into that house. I felt sorry for everyone, my sisters, my brothers, and especially, my father. How is he going to deal with this? And what is going to happen to me now?

I continued down the creek, and was well into Maule property, when I saw Edmund Maule working in the pasture near their barn. As I walked toward him, his friendly smile helped as I told him what was happening at home. Before I could explain the situation further, he said I should go immediately and speak to his mother. Mrs. Maule, my grandmother's youngest sister, met me at the door with a most welcome smile. She undoubtedly guessed what had happened. She invited me in, and without questioning me further, began privately planning a course of action. She told me that she expected my father would be coming over and they would "talk about it." She knew my father would be coming, and she knew also what she planned to tell him. We ate supper, and while we waited that evening, she told me how she always worried about what would happen to me. Verna was already employed and away from the farm, and she and Eleanore would probably marry before long; but Mrs. Maule always worried about what would happen to me. The day's events more than likely relieved her of at least one worry. Nevertheless, we had to wait and see what my father had to say. And as I pondered the consequences of going back home, I recognized the lights and familiar sound of the Chandler as it drove into the yard.

Mrs. Maule suggested that I go to an upstairs bedroom and wait until she discussed the matter with my father. I waited upstairs, but I could hear my father's soft voice through the floor register in the bedroom. I listened intently as Mrs. Maule questioned him about the situation at home and the wisdom of my returning with him. I strained to hear his reply through the open floor register and in a barely audible voice I could hear him say, "I don't think so." Then, I heard the sound of the Chandler leave the yard. I was immensely relieved, yet very much saddened. My father had to give me away for the second time, the first time when I was two-and-a-half; and now, two weeks before my fourteenth birthday. I walked back down the stairs to meet Mrs. Maule, smiling as she held a paper bag holding the clothes Eleanore sent with my father. This time my father was able to leave me in good hands.

Meanwhile, as I later learned from Eleanore and my brothers, the scenario back at the farm grew more interesting by the minute. Secret communication moved among them and word of my whereabouts got around fast. Supper was planned as usual, with everyone seated around the supper table. Julia continued her usual tirade and no one let on that her abusive treatment was finally exposed. When my absence at the table was finally mentioned, she arrogantly said, "Oh, she'll come back when she gets hungry." Without hesitation, Ben looked at her and said, "She isn't coming back". Whether it was the shock of Ben's very first retaliation in ten years, the realization that I was out of reach, or the fact that she was finally exposed, Julia knew she was in trouble. She left the table and ordered my father to bring me home. Later, when he came home without me, she ordered him to call the doctor because she was ill. The doctor visited and told him there was nothing wrong with her. Mrs. Maule chuckled over this story. How did we learn all of this? The party line. I never liked to answer the telephone at home. Suddenly, I was monitoring every call to the farm from the Maule's telephone.

I felt safe with Mrs. Maule, my great aunt, but she was afraid Julia would convince my father to come back to get me. To keep me out of reach, she immediately arranged for my Aunt Anna, mother's younger sister, to come and get me. Julia hated Anna, because Anna was beautiful and bright. I feel also that Julia was jealous of Anna, perhaps because my father liked her. Anna lived about thirty miles away in another county. She was a kind and wonderful lady with a delightful sense of humor. She never seemed to lose her temper and I appreciated that. I felt her children, my cousins, were fortunate to have her as their mother. Mrs. Maule was her aunt, and they were very close.

Eleanore arranged to send more clothes to me, and before I had time to wonder about who took over my chores at home, I was in the car and off to Aunt Anna's farm in Dodge, Wisconsin. Aunt Anna wasted no time in contacting the District Attorney, Mr. Kostner, who arranged a meeting with my father. Meanwhile, after threshing was completed in Maule Coulee, Ben left for work "out West" and was not available as a witness at the meeting with Mr. Kostner. Verna, Adolph, Eleanore, and Clifford, however, were called upon to tell about abuses sustained during Julia's rages, as she and my father listened. My brothers and sisters were surprised to hear my father add to their complaints. Up to now, he never said a thing in our defense. After each one recited a litany of abuses, Mr. Kostner spoke to Julia. He didn't mince any words when he said, among other things, "You are the meanest woman in Trempealeau County."

I was at Aunt Anna's in Dodge about a month, enjoying a normal family life. I helped with the housekeeping as Anna made delicious food and desserts for her family. They had a large house in the country. Everything was fine. But when an opportunity came along for a job near the high school back home, I decided it would be nice to be back with the relatives and friends I had known since my first grade. At first I was worried that my father would make me return home, but my anxiety about what he might do was short-lived as I began to think in terms of life on my own—a life completely free of Julia.

CHAPTER 8

HIGH SCHOOL AND WORLD WAR II

On Labor Day in September 1941, Aunt Anna brought me back to Independence, where I would be enrolled in the ninth grade. I settled in with the Joe Roskos family in a comfortable home just two blocks from the high school. I couldn't believe I would no longer have to walk almost three miles to school. No more long walks in the dark, on cold mornings; and surely no need to worry about transportation to and from school activities. Unfortunately, my two older brothers, Anton and Clarence, had to walk the three-mile distance from the farm after completing all those chores. I couldn't believe how lucky I was.

Nevertheless, I still felt displaced. There was no official declaration of my status in my family and I realized I was completely on my own. I tried to maintain contact with the situation at the farm by talking with Anton, who sat behind me in study hall, but we got in trouble with the teacher in charge. I had only fleeting contacts with my brothers before and after school because they usually were with friends, and we weren't going to discuss home problems in their presence. I'm sure some of our friends knew about the circumstances leading to my leaving home, but they preferred not to pry into the matter, perhaps understanding that this situation was a deeply painful matter for me. Anton managed to relay the important news from the farm to me.

In one case, it was news that Ben was called home from his job out west to report for army duty. We lived in a community settled predominantly by Polish immigrants, and the news of Hitler's invasion of Poland was met with alarm. Many of the finest young men in the area signed up to "get Hitler." Little did they realize that the localized invasions in Europe would escalate to become a worldwide major conflict. I remember thinking how worried my father must have been.

I recall Anton relaying another message about an event on the farm, occurring about the same time. I wasn't sure about the details, but Anton gave an account of the last day of the old Studebaker in action. On Saturday, October 25, 1941, Ben and Anton decided to pick up the county road grader parked about a mile up Maule Coulee Road and bring it to the farm for some road repair. They drove up the road, attached it to the Studebaker, and with Ben at the wheel of the Studebaker and Anton sitting on the grader, they started back to the farm. About halfway home, the rope in one of the front tires broke through the rotting rubber. It unwound from the rim, coiled around the tie rod of the steering mechanism, and pulled the wheels sharply to the right, causing the Studebaker to nosedive into a ditch along the side of the road. Fortunately, neither Ben nor Anton was hurt. Ben climbed over the hood to safety, and the two of them walked home to harness four horses to rescue the old Studebaker.

The real challenge was yet to come with the horses who do not like displacements or weird changes in their environments. The sight of the grader attached to the up-ended car fit these criteria perfectly. Ben cautiously drove the horses, four abreast, toward these weird displacements and was prepared for the inevitable—four frightened horses ready to bolt. This experience, along with many others on the farm, must have conditioned Ben for his brilliant performance in the Army. He managed to get the four frightened horses to pull the old car out of the ditch. Four horses pulling the car and attached grader down Maule Coulee Road was a sad ending for the old Studebaker. A month later, November 26, 1941, Ben was off to the Army.

This was the kind of story that brought back old memories of happenings on the farm—the faithful horses, the threshing season, the long walks to and from Maule Coulee School, and the beautifully tilled fields and hills. Because of Julia, I was afraid to visit the valley from which I felt estranged. On a nice warm Thursday, about a month into my freshman year in high school, I decided to walk up to the church on the hill to make my confession in preparation for my

"First Friday" communion in October 1941. Our parish priest and the nuns at the parochial school encouraged this practice. I found it to be a helpful practice during my years with Julia—.confessions on Thursday afternoons, followed by communion on Friday mornings. I always felt better after these First Friday communions. On this particular Thursday after school, I was walking down the hill from the church when I met the Mother Superior, who had been my eighth grade teacher. She looked directly at me, and I will never forget the agonized look on her face. She had heard of the incident that caused me to leave the farm and questioned me further about the episode. After telling her about the storm, the lost geese, and Julia threatening me with the butcher knife, I could see she was at a loss for words. She just kept shaking her head from side to side. When she finally found words to respond, she encouraged me to do well in school, as if she knew I could. The nuns finally had their answers to earlier questions about our school attendance. I wondered how they felt now that they knew. How could they have known what to do back then if we kept our secrets to ourselves?

Ben's leaving for the Army on November 26, 1941, was a major loss for my father and must have sent him into a deeper depression. Along with losing control of his farming business, with Julia taking most of the income, he was now losing the mainstay to his family. Verna and Adolph were temporarily employed elsewhere, leaving three younger school-age boys to farm and Eleanore to do the cooking and housework. It was a bleak December indeed. Ben spent a year in basic training, had a short weekend furlough visit to the farm, and was shipped to North Africa. He landed in Casablanca on Christmas Eve, 1942.

Things had begun to change rapidly on the farm. On March 23, 1942, my father had an auction on the nearby rental farm. He sold off cows, several horses, and miscellaneous farm equipment. It all seemed so sad. Although people attending the auction told me that prices went very high, considering the times, it was common knowledge in our family that my father didn't see any of the money. It was also the year that Verna and Eleanore both decided to get married. Each had large weddings at the big church, with receptions on the farm in Maule Coulee—Verna on April 8, 1942, and Eleanore on October 28, 1942. Now Julia found herself in charge, more so than when Verna and Eleanore were in charge of housekeeping. This change was to create a serious problem for Clifford, Clarence, and Anton, who continued to work the farm. With Verna and Eleanore both gone, Julia usually had one of her younger sisters stay with her "to help." There were no bets on whether there would be a wholesome meal on the table for my brothers when they came in from doing the farm chores. And they knew my father was not inclined to complain about the food, or anything else for that matter. Free room and board for Julia's sisters had always been his marriage gratuity, even when my sisters and I were at home.

I continued to keep informed about happenings on the farm through conversations with Anton at school. Verna's husband, Aloysie Halama, purchased a farm about six miles north of town, and they were planning on my living with them. I was looking forward to being settled somewhere, but at the same time, was concerned about the distance I would have to travel to school. I moved out to Verna and Aloysie's farm at the end of my freshman year. Fortunately, they now had school buses to pick up students in the county. Unfortunately, I would have to deal with paying the bus fare, since school buses were privately owned. Verna had already figured out a way to solve this. We would plant pickles and strawberries, and sell them. The income would more than pay for the bus fare if the crop were good. It wasn't. But I supplemented my income by picking strawberries at the neighbors—for 1 to 2 cents per quart. Times were not good. Gasoline, sugar, and other items were rationed. Because we learned to be resourceful under Julia's dominance, we now knew how to be frugal and still live comfortably. My big hurdle at Verna's farm was learning how to milk cows, morning and evening, school or no school. Also, there were no brothers to bring home the cows from the pasture. I rather enjoyed the walk in the pasture, especially since there was no bull to frighten me. In any event, I didn't let farm work interfere with my schoolwork, and I managed to complete another successful year in high school.

Other events on my father's farm during my high school years must have made him very sad. His fondness for horses was shown in the kindness with which he trained them. Now they were growing old and were unable to do the heavy work on the farm. Tractors replaced them, as they were gradually sold or put down. Only one of them, Prince, died as a young colt and is buried on the farm. Many of them were sold to the fox farm where they were put down and used for fox food or mink food. King, one of the oldest, the teammate for the young trainees, was probably one of the first to go. Colonel, who always gave a nod when addressed, would be missed for his cooperative "yes sir" nodding. Although Florie was known to be a quitter when it came time to pull a heavy load, she had a series of beautiful offspring. It was especially sad when Robin, the workhorse and family pet, was struck by lightning and had to be put down before his time. But the saddest loss of all was Nance. She had three foals before she was sold. About two years after she was sold, she foundered. Her new owner decided to sell her to the fox and mink farm. When he delivered her there to be put down, there was no one there to accept her, so he tied her to a tree and left her. She managed to untie the rope, and instead of returning to her new owner, she walked two miles down the road to our farm where she waited at the barn door to her former stall. This long, painful walk to say her "last good-bye" must have been very sad for my father and brothers, and empty stalls, no less saddening. Although I was no longer at home to witness these events, I still choke up at the thought.

The summer of 1943 brought the war closer to home in tragic and exciting ways. Several of the young men who enlisted in the Army were now missing in action or confirmed dead. It was no wonder that anxiety peaked whenever word of the fatal telegram was spread. But when the phone call came to my father during the invasion of Sicily relating the news of Ben's heroic accomplishments, he was so unnerved he was unable to tell the family what actually had happened. We knew Ben was safe, but details of his involvement in the surrender of the Germans at Palermo weren't understood until we read them as front-page news in the western Wisconsin newspapers. I recall the goosebumps on my arms as I read Ben's words, quoted exactly, during his destruction of a large German tank and the ammunition dump fortifying the city of Palermo. Ben had been assigned to the Second Armored Division, led by General Patton, during the North African campaign. After the success of that campaign and the fall of Sicily, he went on to England to become part of the Normandy invasion—D-Day at Omaha Beach, on to St. Lo and to the Battle of the Bulge. In one letter to Clarence, Ben expressed his feelings about the war. He said, "When things really got tough, I thought of our life at home, and I figured I had it pretty good in the Army." This remark, by a man who earned seven battle stars and two Purple Hearts, pretty much tells the story of our life at home. He had two tanks "shot out from under" him and was hospitalized once in Sicily, and again in Belgium. In Sicily, he had the good fortune of being in the hospital during Patton's "slapping episode"—the incident that brought on a storm of criticism of the general. I recall Ben's downplaying the incident, saying that no one in the hospital made much of it. Hah! Patton's critics never met Julia. I learned later that after all the attention Ben received in the newspapers, Julia wrote to him and asked him to write a nice letter about her so she could publish it in the local paper.

My junior year in high school was another anxiety-filled time. Social life was often overshadowed by news of sons, brothers, and boyfriends missing in action, being held as prisoners or war, or being killed. Nevertheless, basketball games, the junior prom, class plays, and school picnics went on as usual. Farmers were able to get gasoline for their tractors, and I expect some of it went off course since farmers had farther to drive for necessary supplies and repairs. Why not make the trip worthwhile and add a social call—rather, a bereavement call on a family mourning the loss of a son in battle? This also was the year Julia went on several rampages on the farm. When my brothers were out of reach during one of her rages, she decided to attack my father. Word of his plight spread to someone who had advised him to get a divorce. He was finally ready to move forward on the matter when something, or someone, changed his mind. Julia was pregnant again—her fifth child with my father. And so the matter was dropped. We were all disappointed.

Through all the chaos at home and abroad, I managed to enter my senior year in high school determined to make a success of my life—in school and after graduation. I decided to leave my sister's farm to take a job as cook and housekeeper for the editor of the local paper, Mr. Kirkpatrick, and his daughter, Eileen. They lived in a large, Tudor-style home just a few blocks from the high school. Cleaning the big house every weekend and cooking the evening dinner every day were time-consuming, but I managed. Nothing could be more difficult than life on the farm. Furthermore, chances for earning outside income by baby-sitting were greater. I also had more time to reflect on the many changes in my life. My older brothers had graduated from high school, but I had a younger brother, Ed, who was a year behind me. He was one-and-a-half years old when our mother died and was brought up in the Uncle Louie household. He often referred to himself as the lucky one. And indeed he was. He was spared the chaos on the Maule Coulee farm. We more or less got acquainted during our high school years and it was gratifying for me to finally enjoy an occasional chat. My brothers were all good students and I was proud of them. I was always competitive, but my senior year I decided to go for broke. It paid off.

Now that Anton and Clarence had graduated, I had no lifeline to the happenings on the farm in Maule Coulee. I missed Anton at school. He had kept me up to date about things on the farm. It was he who told me about the auction on the rental farm; how the tractors replaced the horses that grew too old to work; and how Adolph, Clifford, and Clarence found jobs in Milwaukee. Anton found work locally while he waited to join the Marines. My father watched sadly as the offspring of his first marriage left him with Julia and the pampered second family. In a letter dated July 18, 1999, Clarence describes an especially poignant scene. Before he and Adolph left for Milwaukee, my father came to them and told them to borrow some money from a businessman downtown, because he had none to give them. Obviously, the money from the lucrative auction less than six months earlier was not available to him. He was deeply depressed as he left to drive Julia and their children to visit her mother that Sunday afternoon. When he returned, Clarence and Adolph were gone, thanks to the generosity of a distant cousin who opened his wallet and lent them money; Ed

Maule had arranged for the two jobs and drove them to Milwaukee. Clifford also joined them later, but he had to return home after becoming seriously affected by rheumatoid arthritis.

Verna and Eleanore had homes of their own on large farms about five miles from each other. My brothers were always welcomed when they came home from Milwaukee. Julia was not disposed to feeding them when they slaved for her, and she surely didn't welcome them now that they worked elsewhere. It was only natural that Verna and Eleanore provided food and lodging intermittently. Meanwhile, I was involved seven days a week with my job and schoolwork. Weekends were baby-sitting times for me, so I really didn't see that much of any of my brothers and sisters. I actually felt that the cohesiveness we had earlier at home in Maule Coulee was breaking down. We were all becoming independently involved with our own lives. When quarterly report cards were distributed in high school, I didn't know where to take mine to be signed. I wouldn't risk sending it home to my father for fear Julia would destroy it. Besides, I never got to see my father anymore. So I did the simplest thing I could think of—I forged his signature.

In early April 1945, the fields around Independence were turning green, and signs of spring were everywhere. The wars in Europe and the Pacific were not letting up. And to add to the anxiety about the outcome in either theatre, our president, Franklin D. Roosevelt, died. On April 12, 1945, the entire nation went into mourning. The somber music played on every radio station was interrupted only for announcements regarding the circumstances surrounding his death and for occasional news about the continuing wars on opposite sides of the globe. The streets seemed deserted as I walked to the post office to check the mail. Posted on the bulletin board of the old post office was a stack of applications from the U.S. Civil Service Department for positions with the U.S. Treasury Department, War Bond Division, Merchandise Mart, in Chicago. I took two copies, hoping to find another interested classmate. I really wasn't sure I was ready for Chicago, and I couldn't find another classmate who was interested, but I typed in the appropriate information and mailed it without discussing it with anyone.

A couple of weeks later, I was called into the principal's office. With several teachers present, a fellow classmate and I were told that we were to be the commencement speakers. Although I was not altogether surprised, the reality of the situation left me very anxious about the responsibility I now had. We were told to write our own commencement speeches, and our English teacher would edit our work. As I walked back to the study hall, I looked at my fellow classmate and asked him what he planned to say. He seemed at a loss for words also. He was an excellent student and had his college plans made well in advance. My plans for college were pretty dim since there was no way I would be able to afford even the tuition. Nevertheless, I put my heart and soul into preparing my speech.

On May 8, 1945, I was well into writing my speech when I took a break and walked up the hill to church for the Holy Day evening service on Ascension Day. After the service, I noticed a large crowd gathered around in a circle on the plaza in front of the church. I was alone and unaware of the reason for all the excitement. I asked someone nearby what was happening. This person, who apparently didn't know who I was, excitedly told me, "Ben Kulig is home!" I couldn't believe my ears as I tried to break through the crowd to talk to him. The scene was so hectic I was unable to get a word in as people shouted questions about his last three years in the major campaigns in Europe. I hadn't seen Ben for three years, and the news releases quoting him verbatim from the battlefields as he fought, rushed through my mind. I was disappointed in not being able to talk to him, but it seemed like my brothers and sisters politely stepped aside as the excited crowd took over. We knew we would have our chance to visit in private. So I ran down the hill, rushed the half-mile through town, and went directly to the newspaper office where Mr. Kirkpatrick and Eileen were still working on the next day's issue. They both were surprised, and naturally concerned about my unscheduled visit, and before either of them could speak, I blurted out, "Ben is home, Ben is home!" They had no idea how excited I was. I told them he had left for the Army just as I was entering high school as a freshman, and he was back for my graduation—to hear my commencement address. His four-year absence earned him two Purple Hearts, a Good Conduct Medal, the American Defense Service Medal, American Campaign Medal, European-African Medal, Middle Eastern Campaign Medal (one Bronze, one Silver, one Arrowhead), World War II Victory Medal, Belgian Fourragere, Honorable

Service Lapel Button WWII, and the Silver Service Star, awarded in lieu of five Bronze Service Stars. During the same four years, I had earned *one* commencement speech.

After reviewing and editing my presentation with my English teacher, I prepared for my graduation and the job interview to be held two weeks later. The graduation ceremony was overshadowed by my nervousness over the speech I had to present. With my father, Julia, Ben, all my brothers, and my sisters and their husbands in the audience, I spoke as if my goals would be reached in spite of barriers in my path. I wasn't exactly sure of what my goals were going to be, but I knew they would be appropriate and attainable. I left the stage, unable to see my family in the dimly lit auditorium, and found my seat among the other graduates. As the other speakers, along with my fellow classmate, gave their speeches, I found it difficult to absorb their ideas, congratulations, and good wishes. My mind somehow kept wandering back to that fateful day in July, four years earlier, when I tearfully escaped tyranny as I walked barefoot down the creek to Mrs. Maule's. I thought of the wonderful high school teachers who made this night possible, but most of all, how I must never let these people down. A couple of days later, Mr. Kirkpatrick came home from his newspaper office to give me a cash gift from my father. How did my father ever manage to secretly get this money to Mr. Kirkpatrick?

The author's father and mother, William Kulig and Elizabeth Wiench, were wed on October 16, 1917.

In 1928, the William Kulig Family enjoys the Chandler. Ben, Verna, and Adolph sit on the running board, while Eleanore, Clarence, Clifford, and Anton sit on the grass. Their mother, Elizabeth, holds the author, the baby Adeline.

The author, Adeline Kulig, at age three. This is the only photo taken of her as a child after her mother's death.

Verna and Ben (second row top left) and Clarence and Clifford (second row bottom right) attend Maule Coulee School (about 1931).

Below: The Maule Coulee School was closed in 1942.

Doris Anderson Hanson taught the author at the Maule Coulee School in 1932 and 1933. This photo was taken when Mrs. Hanson was 85 years old.

Anna Wiench George, Elizabeth Kulig's younger sister, rescued Adeline Kulig from her abusive stepmother when the author was 13 years old. Aunt Anna also reported the abuse to the District Attorney.

CHAPTER 9

CHICAGO: A WHOLE NEW WORLD

WHAT should have been an exciting adventure into a new world of freedom actually began as an anxiety-filled experience I would rather have avoided. The sudden change from a secluded life in a small town to the hustle and bustle of life in a large city was a real culture shock. Besides, it was heartbreaking to think that while Ben, our role model, was finally home safe, I was about to take off on an unknown journey, all alone. It would have been less traumatic had I found work in Milwaukee, where brothers and relatives lived. Instead, I decided to fulfill my commitment to the Civil Service position I had applied for.

Before my high school graduation plans had fully materialized, I knew I would have to get a job. This meant forfeiting the one-year scholarship I would have been awarded had I enrolled at a branch of the University of Wisconsin. I believed there was no way I could afford college. I moved out of the Kirkpatrick's house and spent a week with my sister Eleanore on her farm before finalizing my trip to Chicago. My brother Adolph, who was working in Milwaukee, arranged to come home and accompany me on the train as far as Milwaukee, from where I went on alone to Chicago. I will never forget the worried look on his face as he stood on the train platform in Milwaukee and watched me leave all alone to a city none of us had ever visited. There was no one in Chicago even remotely known to our family. I was seventeen years old, all alone, with two suitcases and the cash gifts I had received for my graduation. Not only was I terrified of what lay ahead, I was exhausted because of anxiety and lack of sleep. I sat alone on the train after Adolph got off in Milwaukee, afraid to talk to anyone except the porters. It would have helped if there had been a friendly lady to speak to. Instead I was alone with men who seemed to be completely engrossed in the day's paper. The train pulled slowly out of Milwaukee and the flat countryside of northern Illinois came into view. To add to my loneliness, the song "Sentimental Journey" kept repeating in my mind. My fear and anxiety made the ride from Milwaukee to Chicago seem endless. In fact, I was so scared, I remember little about the trip after Adolph got off the train. When the train finally moved slowly through the tunnel-like canopies of Chicago's Union Station, my heart was beating so fast, I could hardly breathe. The strains of "Sentimental Journey" dissipated in the smoke of the tunnel as we screeched to a stop. I grabbed my two suitcases and headed for the Travelers' Aid counter where I was to make contact with a woman from the Treasury Department.

The War Bond Division of the Treasury Department must have had a dire need for clerical help, because their personnel department arranged to meet my train and direct me to a small apartment on the near North Side of Chicago. I looked on with admiration as the attractive young lady who met me efficiently arranged for a taxi and saw me to my new residence, a small apartment near the Gold Coast beach. As we rode, I felt great relief in being safe and soon to be settled in. After giving me directions on where to report for work the following morning and how to get there, she bade me and my new landlady good-bye and left. I never saw this lovely young lady again.

After my new landlady showed me to my apartment, she left me to my unpacking. I looked around the tiny apartment and decided I could manage all right in the small quarters. I don't remember eating that evening. All I remember is that I was exhausted. My fear and anxiety were now replaced by extreme loneliness. I don't recall if there was a telephone in the apartment; if there was, it very likely would not have been connected anyway. And if this wasn't enough of a handicap, I probably could not have afforded a long-distance phone call, at that time a luxury for the elite—and I fell far short of that. So I sat down and started to write a letter to my sister Eleanore, telling her I was safe, well, and looking forward to starting my new job the next morning. I knew she would make the necessary calls to the rest of my family. I finished the letter and relapsed into a dreadful feeling of loneliness, thinking I had made the biggest mistake of my life. I missed everyone: my family, my high school friends, my teachers, everyone I ever knew. I sat down on the bed, pondered my new circumstances, and without checking the time, bathed and dressed into my pajamas. Too tired to contemplate what the next day had in store for me, I set my alarm and pulled the sheet over me, hoping my family was not as worried and lonely as I was.

Sheer exhaustion had overtaken the effects of anxiety, fear, and loneliness as I dozed off to sleep. What happened next might have sent the entire staff at the personnel department into a quandary-like panic, had I told anyone there. About 2:00 a.m., I was awakened by a male voice in the dark as he was feeling the bed with both hands. I will always remember the surprise in his voice as he said: "Oh. Is there someone in here?" I answered him, of course, and without turning on any lights, he left. I couldn't believe what had just happened and began to seriously wonder what other frightening experiences were in store for me. What kind of city was this? Was I too naive to handle life here? I must not have wondered too long because I went back to sleep, without checking the door or the lights, and the next thing I knew, my alarm went off and I was getting dressed for work. As I went out into the warm sunny street, I was overwhelmed by the hustle and bustle, especially the noisy streetcars and traffic. I had hardly boarded the streetcar when it took off and would have sent me sprawling to the floor had not some nice man lent his support. I was terribly embarrassed, until I noticed that the incident was completely ignored by other passengers. It wasn't long before my next hurdle was conquered. I found my way to work.

I followed the printed instructions mailed to me earlier, and after my first elevator ride, I found my way to the room designated on the tenth floor of the Merchandise Mart in Chicago. Actually, the room was easy to find. There were literally dozens of young, happy, chatting girls heading for the same room. I heard them discussing their reasons for being there, so I just followed them. They all seemed better prepared for this venture than I was. As we were more or less herded into one large room, the chatting stopped, and we were given instructions for the procedures to be followed. I spoke very little to the girls sitting near me as we waited for our names to be called. For the next three hours, three ladies worked in relay, calling name after name. Some names were called in groups. I was very disappointed when the lunch break was announced and I hadn't been called yet. Was I going to be shuttled to some little corner of this huge building where no one would ever know me? Would all the good positions be taken before they called my name? I was beginning to feel very discouraged. I was not used to being shoved to the bottom of the list; but then, this was Chicago. Anything can happen here, I thought, remembering that last night's intruder was proof of that.

During lunch in the huge cafeteria, I spoke with several of the other applicants. None of them seemed to be worried. If they were, they didn't say so. Some of them even felt brave enough to criticize the food and hope future dining opportunities would be an improvement. I was just glad to have affordable food. I felt rejuvenated after lunch and expected to be included with the next group to be called. No such luck. I was really beginning to feel discouraged as group after group left the large room. I assumed that I could just come back the next day. Surely they must have a job for me or they would not have notified me to report for work. I was pondering the various activities taking place around me when a new lady walked into the room holding a manila folder. It was 3:00 p.m. I was stunned when she called my name–Adeline Kulig. I rose to meet her and waited for her to call the rest of the group. She didn't call anyone else. This worried me at first. Then she looked directly at me and asked me to follow her to the personnel office. She introduced herself as Mary Baratta and asked several questions, none of which I remember. After the interview, she introduced me to a private investigator, whose name I have forgotten, and told me I would be his private secretary. Four other girls were eventually added to the personnel staff. I didn't understand why I was chosen to work as a private secretary, while the rest of those happy, self-confident girls ended up in typing pools. I was given a desk near the private investigator, who seemed to be professionally friendly. It was after 4:00 p.m., on June 12, 1945, and I now knew I would be working in the largest building in Chicago for $146.00 per month.

When I left the Merchandise Mart, I didn't remember which streetcar to take back to my apartment on North State Street, so I took out a map of Chicago and walked the twelve blocks. As I reached the front door, I found a very concerned landlady waiting for me. Before I could say *hello*, she began apologizing for the incident at 2:00 a.m. that morning. Her son didn't know the apartment was occupied when he came in late. I was relieved to learn I did not have to *tell her* what had happened. As the embarrassed son stood behind her, I could see their concern was obvious and understandable. They counted on the good graces of the Treasury Department to continue referring future tenants to them. An incident like this could seriously affect their livelihood. After reassuring them that I understood this unfortunate episode, which I really didn't, I noticed that the door to my apartment was already open. Inside were two happy young girls with suitcases spread all over the floor. They were planning to report to the tenth floor of the Merchandise Mart the following morning.

I walked into the small living room of the apartment, hopscotched around the open suitcases and headed for the tiny bedroom where I had slept the night before. I sat on the bed, removed my high-heeled shoes, and tried not to show my surprise at sharing the apartment with two additional tenants. After all, the place had only one single bed, and this certainly was not the spacious Kirkpatrick's house. Without further ado, we set out to learn all about each other. Both girls—Muriel and Scotty—were extremely outgoing and wasted no time trying to learn all about me. I was fascinated by their southern accents—southern Illinois, that is. What must I have sounded like to them? I came from a bilingual home in Wisconsin and had never been further from my birthplace than the two small cities approximately

30 to 40 miles away from the farm. And those day trips were the highlight of my life for seventeen years. Having visited Chicago before, both girls had many exciting ideas about what they wanted to do during their off-work time in Chicago—visiting the parks, the zoos, and the museums, to name a few. I was impressed. I really didn't know much about "off-work" time. I didn't have much experience with that. Therefore, I was "all ears" as they talked about the wonderful sights to see in Chicago. The two of them sat on the floor near their opened suitcases, and I could see they were going to be a lot of fun. One of them had difficulty remembering my unusual name—Adeline—so she just decided to call me "Jo-Jo."

We chatted for a long time before it became apparent that we needed to discuss more serious questions such as, where do we sleep? What do we eat? How do we get to work the following morning? The first two problems were happily resolved. The sofa they were leaning against opened into a double bed, where they planned to sleep. And their mothers had sent a supply of easily prepared quick meals with each of them. They were happy to share their food with me until I could find a grocery store where I could purchase food to add to their supply. I couldn't believe my good fortune. They already knew how to get to work, which turned out to be a better route than the one I took on my first day. They were going to introduce me to the elevated train, which would let us off on the second floor of the Merchandise Mart. This sounded too good to be true. I was looking forward to the trip, which would cost me ten cents each way.

We ate our first meal together, with two of us sitting and the third standing in the small dining area. Then they decided to walk to the beach a couple of blocks away. I didn't have any beach clothes, so I offered to clean up the kitchen while they were gone. They came back very excited about the huge breakers hitting the rocks. I reacted equally excited. I didn't want them to know that I didn't know what "breakers" were. I had seen the Trempealeau and Mississippi rivers, and as far as I knew, they didn't have "breakers." It wasn't long before it was time to take our turns in the small shower. I suggested they go first. After I showered, I came out of the bathroom to find I could not get to my bed. The opened sofa bed on which they settled for the night cut off the passage to my cot. Their bed had completely filled the living room and I had to crawl over them to reach my cot in the tiny alcove. We started our tenancy together laughing hysterically. We each paid $4.00 per week rent and the location was superb. At approximately $12.00 per month each, it may not have been the Kirkpatrick's house, but it was a pretty good deal, considering Chicago and the times.

The next morning, Muriel and Scotty were up and eating breakfast before I awakened. Thank goodness. The sofa bed was folded back into its casing, and I could walk through the living room to the bathroom without crawling over it. Like the living room, the kitchen was too small to accommodate three people, so we ate in relays. The tiny bath served our purposes, provided we scheduled its use wisely. Both the plumbing and the kitchen appliances could be temperamental. When we showered or flushed the toilet, the plumbing seemed to groan in agony. With each bathroom flush, the kitchen plumbing on the opposite wall answered with a louder groan followed by an agitation that would stop abruptly. The noise worried me. I had never seen plumbing act that way. Muriel and Scotty saw my concern and broke into uncontrollable laughter. These two had been to Chicago before. Noisy plumbing was of no concern to them as long as we all managed to be ready in time to make it to the "L," the elevated train that took us to work at the Merchandise Mart.

Our ride on the L was only the second time I had been on a train. I was fascinated by the elevated tracks, which curved around second-floor levels of red brick buildings and took us directly to the second-floor platform of the Merchandise Mart. I bade good luck to Muriel and Scotty as I got off on the sixth floor and expressed hope that their day on the tenth floor would be exciting. On my walk down the long hall to the personnel department, I realized I was a maverick amongst the herd. It seemed that everyone I met since my arrival had come with a friend or with a group. I had come alone, and it would take a while for me to adjust.

I went directly to my desk, set up my clerical equipment, and waited for the private investigator to report for work. With my typewriter uncovered, stenographer's pad and pencil in hand, I sat poised to go to work. I could see Mary Baratta in her office next to the man in charge of this entire operation, which included the *ninety* clerical workers hired the day before. Around me were the three women I had also seen the day before. As they left to sort out the new applicants on the tenth floor, I hoped they would assign Muriel and Scotty to my department. I began to understand how I fit into this huge constellation. Just about then, the private investigator walked in with his briefcase and pulled out a bunch of folders. This is it, I thought, as I grabbed my steno pad and pencil. He greeted me and told me he would have some reports for me to type later that day. I was glad when one of the personnel staff asked me to do some typing for her. It would have been very boring sitting there for hours, holding a steno pad and pencil.

I joined four other girls during our lunch break that day. The two who lived in Chicago were very outgoing and seemed curious about our backgrounds and plans for the future. I volunteered very little and was happy to see the other four take over the conversation as I listened. I learned they all were taking this work at the Treasury Department as a temporary assignment until they made up their minds about college. The most outgoing and most attractive of the four young women knew exactly what she wanted to do. She was going to be a nun. She was merely waiting to be accepted and had already decided on her new name: "Sister Mary Frances." She was so vivacious and self-confident—the antithesis of what I considered myself to be.

While I waited for my dictation session with the private investigator, I helped the woman in charge of making identification badges for the new people in our department. This was fun. People would come in to be photographed, we would develop the pictures, choose the best pose, and put them into silver metal frames, stamped out by a hand-operated gadget. Strange work for a stenographer, I thought, but kind of fun and kind of nostalgic. It was like the photo booth at the county fair in Wisconsin. And the photo-framer reminded me of the sausage-maker I operated as a child on the farm. Who would have guessed that the sausage-maker was preparing me for a future position with the Treasury Department of the United States. In the middle of one of these nostalgic moments, I was called by the private investigator to type his reports. Before I could grab my steno pad and pencil, he handed me several sheets of paper, with several handwritten letters and reports. He preferred writing them instead of dictating them. This was going to be easy, I thought, and was pleased that his handwriting was legible.

Instead of going directly home that day, I stopped at a department store not far from the office and bought a pair of shorts and a halter for the beach. What a different approach, I thought. On the farm we did everything we could to protect our skin from the sun. Sun tanning was not considered chic. But here in Chicago I was determined to see those exciting breakers, and I intended to dress the part. I got home to find Muriel and Scotty completely exhausted—too tired to eat, and most certainly too tired to go to the beach. I showed them my new purchase, and we made plans to go to the beach the following day. This day they could only tell me about the grueling day they had had on the tenth floor of the Merchandise Mart and of their assignments to the typing and steno pools. Before long, we were talking about all the exciting things to do in Chicago. That weekend, Count Basie would be appearing at the Chicago Theatre, and we simply would have to go.

We followed our usual routine that evening, but this time I was in my bed *before* they opened that sofa bed and cut me off. The next morning, we were up, organized, and on our way to work as if we had been doing it for months. I had a normal kind of day and was making more friends. Muriel and Scotty didn't have much to say about their work. To them it was something to do when they weren't having fun. We arrived home about the same time, changed clothes, and walked the two blocks to the beach. The water seemed relatively calm, and those "breakers" were nowhere to be seen. I was too awestricken by the vastness of Lake Michigan to be concerned about breakers. I had never seen a body of water this large. I had never seen any water that didn't have a bridge crossing it, or that was so vast I couldn't see the other side. I just stared speechless. Muriel and Scotty were amused. They were determined to accompany me to the beach at every opportunity. The walk in the sand back to our apartment was exciting for them. For me it was a reminder of my escape from Julia, that barefoot walk down the creek on our farm in Maule Coulee.

The regimen for our lives in the apartment was necessarily determined by the size and arrangement of our quarters. And I expect this, in turn, was a result of the economy during the last decade before World War II. It was easy to see that the apartment building was once a very elegant home on what was referred to as the Gold Coast of Chicago. Like life on the farm during the 1930s, the Depression years took a similar toll on Chicago's affluent. I could visualize the beautiful staircase leading to a spacious bedroom and private bath. This bedroom was now an apartment and home to three Civil Service workers. Two other doors on the landing at the top of the stairway opened into two similar subdivided quarters. And so it was. Decadent aristocracy made way for affordable housing for Civil Service employees.

What we lacked in living space, we made up for in enthusiasm. Muriel and Scotty talked excitedly about going down to the "Loop." This was an area of Chicago encircled by the elevated train, which, like the Merchandise Mart, had convenient stops with platforms leading directly into the major department stores in Chicago. I was fascinated by this kind of direct accessibility. Chicago city planners certainly were on the ball and way ahead of their time. But our first goal was to see a movie followed by the Count Basie show at the Chicago Theater. For this, we merely walked a half block to the streetcar at Division and State Streets, which dropped us off directly in front of the theater. I remember enjoying both the movie and the band performance. I remember also thinking that a dollar for that performance was a bit high; movies at home cost a quarter, and I couldn't always afford that. After seeing that night's performance, however, I believed it was money well spent. I didn't even mind spending twenty cents for the round-trip streetcar fare.

I didn't get down to the Loop and State Street for several weeks after that. On August 6, 1945, the atom bomb was dropped on Hiroshima, and three days later, August 9, on Nagasaki. Japan surrendered and World War II was over. We were allowed to leave work early because personnel decided that the impending celebration was best carried out in the street. The hallways of the Merchandise Mart were beginning to erupt with revelry. I headed for the elevator and the L train, somewhat concerned about the course this revelry was going to take. I arrived at the apartment to find Muriel and Scotty waiting for me. "Come on, Jo, lets go down to State Street and join the celebration!" they yelled. So off we went to catch the streetcar at Division and State. We rode a few blocks with other merrymakers when the conductor announced that the street ahead was closed and we would have to walk the rest of the way. We barely walked another block when we ran into wall-to-wall people—merry-makers, the likes of which I had never seen before. I told Muriel and Scotty not to leave me, to stick together, as everyone hugged, kissed, yelled, and sang until we were hoarse. I don't recall any drinking, and certainly there was no vandalism, just a lot of noisemakers and whistles, like New Year's Eve on a hot August night. What an experience. New Year's Eve on Times Square in New York five years later was mild by comparison. State Street in Chicago on the day Japan surrendered was an experience I will never forget.

We were not sure about our status at work the following day, so we all reported as usual. Not long after we arrived, we were told we had the day off. What did I do? I went to the nearest department store to shop, and the place was practically deserted. Everyone went home to listen to their radios. I didn't have a radio, so I changed clothes and walked to the Oak Street Beach. It, too, was somewhat deserted. I sat down on my towel and looked at the never-ending expanse of water. What was it like for Ben to cross the Atlantic, the Mediterranean, and the English Channel; first to Morroco, then to Sicily, Omaha Beach, and on to the Battle of the Bulge. As I pondered, it all somehow seemed so unfair that the Oak Street Beach was filled with happy throngs on D-Day, while Omaha Beach was strewn with fallen heroes.

The next day we went to work as usual. But work was not "as usual" as we expected. Would the War Bond Department continue selling War Bonds? There seemed to be more anxiety about this among our superiors than among us underlings. We just did what we were told and went on our merry ways. One day I asked the private investigator if he knew that I was a stenographer and if he would prefer dictating his letters and reports. He smiled, saying he could think better with a pen in his hand. I understood, but fearing I would lose my stenographic skills if I didn't use them, I practiced them on my own.

With the huge crowds filing out of the Merchandise Mart each day, I rarely saw Muriel and Scotty on our way home. On one particular day I saw them leaving the L and joined them on our walk home. As we neared our apartment, Muriel became very excited. Just ahead of us, also walking, was K. T. Stevens, the star of the play *The Voice of the Turtle* playing at a theatre down in the Loop. She was staying at the elegant Ambassador East Hotel, just one block from our apartment, and I wondered what kind of plumbing she had in her suite. Several years later, after brunch in The Pump Room of that hotel, I remembered that moment and decided to check out the plumbing in the Ladies' Lounge. Elegant—and quiet.

Work took on a different meaning after V. J. Day, September 2, 1945. The War Bond Division became the Savings Bond Department, and employees were relocated to various new divisions in the reorganized Treasury Department. My job hadn't changed. Those of us who stayed in personnel bonded more closely as our group became smaller. It wasn't until some of the temporary employees were making plans to leave for college later in September that I suddenly felt deeply saddened. On their final working day, amidst the good-byes and good-lucks, I was so overcome, I went into a back workroom, sat down at a work table, buried my head in my hands and cried. Before I could compose myself, my friend Ethel Wood, another secretary, joined me at the table and broke down also. She too had no money for college but was determined to save enough to start college the following year. She went on to say that she talked to a couple on the North Side of Chicago, acquaintances of the friend who came to Chicago with her. They assured her she could go to college if she managed her finances well. I was too distressed to absorb what she was saying. Actually, I was only half listening. But she persisted by saying she planned to see them that weekend. She would call them and ask if she could bring me along to visit them. The next day at work she told me I was invited to join her on the visit.

For the next three days, before the scheduled visit, I remained skeptical about the feasibility of saving enough for college in one year—at $146 per month. Nevertheless, I did not renege on my promise to join Ethel on her weekend visit to the "wonderful couple" she knew. We took the elevated train north, continued beyond the Thornedale stop where she lived, and went directly to Jarvis Avenue. We got off the elevated and walked about a block to the home of Betty and Lyman Dunn. They answered the door with what I remember as the most delightful and enthusiastic welcome I had ever received. This attractive couple had no children of their own; they welcomed us as if we were old friends returning from a long trip. I couldn't believe the sincerity with which I was welcomed. After formal introductions, we were seated at a formally set dinner table with lovely sterling, china, and many candles. Lyman served the main course at one end, and Betty served the vegetables at the opposite end. I watched carefully to make sure I picked up the silver in the right order, as Ethel chatted on happily with them. They asked how she was doing with regard to saving her money. I waited for the usual questions. They knew I hadn't yet made up my mind. I was still thinking college was beyond reach for me. Before I could even mention affordability, they went on talking as if my course of action was predetermined. In their minds, college definitely was to be my goal.

I was still in a bit of a quandary when Betty announced that it was the maid's and the butler's night off and we would have to clear the table for the desert course. Lyman added to Betty's remark by saying that the maid and butler have been "off" for over fifteen years, ever since they were married. We all gathered around the kitchen sink with our dishes and felt comfortable with each other. It was in the kitchen while Betty was rinsing the plates that Lyman told of his courtship with Betty. I realized then that she was definitely born privileged. She grew up in a large home in Bloomington, Illinois, the only child of wealthy grandparents and prominent parents; and yes, there *was* a maid, a butler, a chauffeur, and a private nurse. Lyman, on the other hand, was orphaned as a child. His parents died during the flu epidemic in 1918. He met Betty while they were students at the University of Illinois. He was working his way through college during the 1920s.

We returned to the dinner table with our desserts and more silver. They talked at length about their years at the university. Betty had been president of her sorority. Lyman had been the president of his fraternity, planned to go to medical school, and worked on campus, cleaning the chemistry building. I was fascinated by how he managed to get through college without help from anyone. Betty went on to tell about her mother's life as a debutante, her marriage to a very prominent attorney, her private education in Illinois, and high school in Florida. She seemed very interested in hearing about my childhood and early education, but I did not tell her about Julia. The evening was too beautiful for that. As the candles in the candelabra were burning down, and the maid and butler were not about to reappear after all these years, we quickly cleared the table, washed the dishes, and retired to the living room to make future plans. I would be moving in with Ethel, so that we could get together on weekends with the Dunns, and we would seriously save a portion of our salaries each payday. With that, Lyman drove us to Ethel's living quarters where I spent the night.

After I returned to my apartment the following day, I immediately wrote to my sisters to tell them about the wonderful people I had met. We had been corresponding regularly, and they were looking forward to the week when I planned to take my first vacation, a trip home in October to see them. Before that trip, I would have to say good-bye to Muriel and Scotty and move to the house much further north of the city. Betty came to pick up my belongings, and we took the beautiful outer drive north along Lake Michigan to the house where Ethel lived—only a couple of L stops from Betty and Lyman's apartment.

Ethel's quarters were simple—a large well-furnished bedroom, a bathroom, and ample closet space in a large home. Like the subdivided home I had just vacated on the near north side, my new quarters also seemed to have evolved as a result of the Depression. Room rent provided badly needed income for the owners of large homes. The room was more than adequate for Ethel's and my limited possessions and we really didn't miss the kitchen. We ate most of our meals in the cafeteria at the Merchandise Mart and spent every weekend with Betty and Lyman.

CHAPTER 10

BETTY AND LYMAN: MY MENTORS

At first I questioned the wisdom of moving so much further from work, although the L price, 10 cents, was still the same. In 1945, a person could ride all over Chicago for 10 cents and a transfer slip. It didn't take long for me to understand Betty and Lyman's rationale for my move closer to them. Ethel and I would be spending much of our time on weekends with them, instead of spending our salaries foolhardily around Chicago. There certainly were plenty of such opportunities for one whose patience with poverty was pretty much exhausted. Ethel and I began having wonderful times during those weekends with the Dunns. We followed them around the golf course. We visited all the parks, museums, and exhibits. In fact, we took advantage of all the "freebees" around Chicago. I didn't realize one could do so much and have so much fun in that city, while spending so little money. With suggestions and guidance from Betty and Lyman, Ethel and I were becoming quite sophisticated and informed. They invited us every weekend, and we were delighted to spend our time with these "master planners." Dinner table discussions were always inspiring. Lyman told us about life in Arkansas and his boyhood on a farm near St. Louis. Betty talked amusingly about her family and how her father's ideas about marrying for money and position were foremost in his mind, which was what he believed and what he did. Betty did exactly the opposite; Lyman had neither money nor position when they married.

It was early in September 1945, while I was still getting acquainted with the Dunns that my brother Adolph quit his job in Milwaukee and joined the Navy Reserves. I would miss seeing him at home in Wisconsin during my October visit, but he was stationed not far from me in Chicago. This location made it possible for him to visit me before he was shipped to the San Francisco area. Not long after that, I boarded the train to visit my family in Wisconsin. By then, the loneliness, nostalgia, and anxiety I had experienced four months earlier were pretty much gone. Betty and Lyman seemed to take care of that. Their upbeat natures seemed to inspire me more with each weekend visit. Yet I couldn't fully understand why they were so interested in my welfare. Why were they investing so much time and energy in me? Was I worthy of their efforts? On the long train ride back to visit my family, these questions kept creeping into my mind. During my high school years, I felt I was completely on my own. I wasn't accustomed to having anyone care this much about me. My weekends with the Dunns seemed too good to be true, and I was afraid to be happy about it. This uncertainty did not interfere with my commitment to them, and I welcomed the sacrifices I would have to make for college to become a reality.

I enjoyed a marvelous visit with my brothers and sisters. I stayed with Eleanore and her husband, Art, on their farm in the country. They made sure I got to see everyone in the family. I learned on this visit that Anton planned to join the Marines and would be leaving the following month, November 1945. Ben and Clarence had found jobs in the area. That left Cliff at home on the farm, helping my father. We did not visit my father at the farm. Julia did not invite us, and we did not feel welcome there anymore. It was my sisters who invited him, Julia, and their children to their homes. My father seemed pleased to see me, but I could see he was not happy. He was quiet and withdrawn. It was as if he didn't know what to say to me. I felt sad leaving everyone and taking the train back to Chicago, but somehow I knew I would be happy when I saw Ethel and the Dunns.

Not long after I returned to Chicago, I received a letter from my brother Cliff telling more about Julia's abusive behavior. Verna and Eleanore also wrote, confirming Clifford's remarks. It seems Julia was back to her old habits. She didn't allow Cliff to play the radio. When he came in from doing the chores, he would turn on the radio. Julia would become so infuriated, she would turn it off and throw it on the floor. When Cliff turned it back on, she went for the iron poker and hit him across the back. Julia actually would beat her own sister, who was living with her at the time. But it wasn't until Cliff, Eleanore, and Verna wrote to tell me that Julia had attacked my father and beat him up, that I became upset. After reading the letters, I joined Ethel for the short L ride to the Dunns. I tried not to let on how I was feeling and went about setting the table for dinner. Betty sensed something was wrong and asked about it. Ethel already knew and may have mentioned it to her. I remember going out into their solarium, sitting down on the sofa, and breaking down completely. When Betty came in, I began telling her all about Julia, how she abused us, and how she was now abusing my father. Betty was very understanding, and in the midst of her consolation, I was surprised by the spontaneity with which she asked the next question: "Would you like to be adopted?" I was caught off guard and in no state for making a decision like that; however, I thought of my brothers and sisters and knew they might be hurt. My response was more like, "I don't think so," without any offense. She understood.

We had our usual happy dinner conversations and discussions without any mention of my upsetting mail. I could tell that Ethel, Betty, and Lyman were all doing their best to keep the dinner topics light-hearted. Before Lyman drove Ethel and me back to our living quarters, Betty took me aside and told me I should write a letter to my father, telling him about my plans to go to college, and asking if he would be able to help me financially. I promised her I would. In fact, it was on her typewriter in her home office that I typed the letter, and I mailed it immediately. I didn't have much hope for getting a response; therefore, I wasn't disappointed when I never received one. I knew there was no way Julia would allow him to help me financially. In fact, I doubt if he ever saw the letter.

On our next weekend visit to the Dunns, they had exciting news to share. An earlier protégé of theirs, Norma Dotson, would be ending her tour of duty with the American Red Cross and was planning to return to the Chicago area. She wanted to pursue a master's degree in the field of education at one of the local universities. Betty, who knew Norma as a student at a university near Bloomington, Illinois, said she was talented and outgoing. After Norma returned to Chicago, she, Ethel, and I became very close, like sisters. With Norma's ideas for parties, the Dunn household became one long celebration. Norma could think of numerous reasons for dinner parties, enhanced by her handmade, artistically decorated place cards and special flowers. Betty and Lyman began inviting their old friends to join our unusual "family." And invitations were returned. Ethel and I would bring the flowers. Dinner party conversation always made it back to discussions on how best to afford college, especially now that there were three of us with the same goals.

Our college-bound trio soon increased by two more members. Betty had heard from two of Lyman's relatives, Jay and Willard Payne, who were in the service and would soon be discharged. Before either of them had returned from the Navy and Army, respectively, Lyman had already made connections for jobs for them. Jay would be combining night school and work, while Willard would be concentrating on employment. Thus, the Dunn household went from empty nest to home base for five prospective working students. The activity and focus of the household and the people greatly inspired me. We were all "going for it." The weekend dinner table became an event to look forward to. With Norma and Betty at the helm, how could it not be. This experience was excellent food for my soul and psyche.

I kept my brothers and sisters posted on my activities. I heard nothing from my father and his silence hurt me, although I tried not to show my feelings. Betty and Lyman never brought up the subject again, sparing me further heartache. Instead, they discussed Ethel's and my need to get our transcripts from high school and to begin applying for college admission. Betty also advised me to get a couple of letters of recommendation—one from my high school principal and another from a responsible citizen back home. I immediately typed two letters—one to my principal and one to Mr. Kirkpatrick, the owner and editor of the local paper for whom I worked during my senior year in high school. Both responded immediately, with notes of encouragement attached.

Betty and Lyman's efforts on our behalf were inexhaustible. They reviewed our transcripts and decided Ethel and I needed to study a foreign language. They found a night school within walking distance from our jobs, where we immediately enrolled for two semesters of Spanish. I rather enjoyed it, even if it took away much of my free time. We both applied to the University of Illinois, where Betty and Lyman had been students. I expressed concern about being from out of state, but Betty and Lyman said it would not be a problem. They would be my parents, they said, if that were what it took to get me enrolled. Betty also decided I should apply for a scholarship to the University of Illinois. I completed the necessary paperwork, and while I was at work, Betty took it, along with my high school transcripts and letters of recommendation, to the Law Offices of Arrington, Fiedler, and Healy on South LaSalle Street in Chicago. She knew Mr. Arrington was the Representative to the General Assembly of Illinois for the Sixth District. On May 10, 1946, Betty received a letter from Representative Arrington advising her that I was designated as his appointee for a four-year tuition scholarship to the University of Illinois. On July 12, 1946, the University of Illinois was advised of my appointment. Soon afterward, a letter from the University of Illinois confirmed my appointment. I was elated. Norma immediately began designing the place cards for our next dinner to celebrate the good news. Ethel and I enthusiastically continued our night school classes. We expected to hear about her acceptance at the university any day. We did, and Norma designed another set of place cards for another dinner bash.

Just who were Betty and Lyman, these two wonderful mentors whom we relied on for advice? Over the many weekends spent with the Dunns, I learned much about their lives. Lyman was orphaned as a child during the flu epidemic in Arkansas around 1918. Grandparents on a farm near Alton, Illinois, brought him up, along with his younger brother. At school, teachers recognized his special talents, and in high school, his brilliance in math and science amazed his teachers. It was only natural that doors would open for him to attend college. He found jobs on campus, and never apologized to anyone for cleaning the chemistry building. Because of his superior talents as a student, he became an asset to any dormitory or fraternity on campus. His colleagues often relied on his help, especially before exams. His plan to go to medical school naturally drew him to the medical fraternity on campus. He became house president and enjoyed all the social benefits of fraternity life. He left the University of Illinois in Champaign-Urbana before he completed his senior year because of his early acceptance at the University of Illinois Medical School in Chicago.

Betty, on the other hand, grew up privileged. Her grandparents in Bloomington, Illinois, owned lucrative businesses locally and in Florida. Her mother was a debutante, a member of the highest social strata, brought up with all the social graces of the times. When she reached marriageable age, word of an eligible, prominent attorney in Peoria reached the social circles in Bloomington. Betty never discussed how her parents met, but it was evident that her mother's social position was a real asset to her father. They lived in Peoria after their marriage, and eventually moved to Bloomington, to live with her widowed grandmother in the large home built by her wealthy grandparents. Betty's father was a prominent criminal lawyer, and to her knowledge, never lost a case. She described him as a brilliant attorney with "a steel-trap mind." I always saw Betty as a perfect blend of what she described in her parents. She had the beauty, charm, and elegance of her debutante mother combined with the no-

nonsense legal mind of her father. From her mother she inherited the charm and social graces for successful entertaining, from her father, the understanding of the need for a woman to have a career. The former came naturally. On the latter, she was way ahead of her time.

Betty's father, Luther Hinckle, was a contemporary of Clarence Darrow and Betty described how they competed for Illinois prominence. Her father was as prominent and successful in central Illinois, as Clarence Darrow was in northern Illinois. As Betty described it, they learned from each other. To instill in Betty the importance of women having careers, her father thought it would be wise for her to accompany him on his law circuit. This meant sitting through the not-so-delicate trials of his criminal clients. Though she never discussed these courtroom sessions, she told me about the drives back home when the chauffeur lit the carriage lamps. Perhaps that is why Betty always loved lamplighting time. She would often drive up to the North Shore suburbs of Chicago to catch this hour by driving along the large estates there. This activity may have been a throwback to her life with her grandparents in Bloomington, where the family's chauffeur drove them around after dinner. I loved these North Shore drives with Betty. It was as if we both wafted into another world as she drove.

Betty's marriage to Lyman must have caused a real dilemma for her mother. She liked Lyman very much. But the "money and social position" criteria set by her father posed a big problem for her. Not so for Betty. She knew her mother and the social set of

Bloomington would naturally be expecting an elegant affair, but this was *her* wedding and would be done *her* way. Betty planned a simple wedding in her lovely home. Since her father declined giving her away, she told me many years later, "I came down the staircase by myself to meet Lyman at the foot of the stairs, where the minister married us." They were college sweethearts who had completed their undergraduate work at the University of Illinois—Lyman in the premedical program and Betty in journalism—and they believed in themselves and each other. Betty told me she knew the first time she met Lyman that she was going to marry him, and she did. On this issue, she was her father's daughter. No nonsense.

The Depression took its toll on Lyman, Betty, and her family. Lyman was forced to drop out of the University of Illinois Medical School in Chicago, and Betty's family lost a fortune as their lucrative businesses suffered major losses. Betty and Lyman were intelligent, educated Illini, the fighting Illini from the University of Illinois, and they knew they would make it through the hard times. They both found employment in Chicago. By keeping in close contact with Illini friends, they realized that pooling their combined resources helped to get them through those difficult years, while still having a lot of fun. It was early in the Depression years, after Lyman dropped out of medical school, that he had a position with Bowman Dairy Company in Chicago. He made many discoveries in the Bowman chemical laboratory, but the times were not right for his innovative research. It would be many years later before his research and experiments would pay off.

From the stories Betty told me about her work as province president of her college sorority, Alpha Chi Omega, it was obvious that she enjoyed working with college students. When she became active in Theta Sigma Phi, the national fraternity for women in journalism, she combined her journalistic studies with lecturing. She traveled all over Europe in the late 1930s, after which she gave lectures in the auditorium of the Art Institute of Chicago. Her topics relating to the coming crisis in Europe seemed to be falling on disinterested ears, and she became disillusioned with the lack of American concern. She stopped lecturing, and when Hitler invaded Austria and Poland, she knew her audiences should have been paying closer attention.

At the time I met Betty and Lyman in 1945, she was 36 years of age and Lyman was 38. Neither had found the professional niche they both kept searching for. What they both had in common was a deep interest in helping teenagers further their education. We all experienced poverty, and we all knew how to overcome it. Betty went from a life of wealth to a life in which careful management of her income was crucial. She learned how to cook and manage a home. Lyman didn't like working for other people, but he knew that his promotional ideas would eventually pay off. We all had unfulfilled dreams. Yet Betty and Lyman kept inspiring us so that we would never give up hope. Our days of hard work and night school were followed by weekend dinner bashes, after which we often put on a stack of 78 rpm records, rolled up the living room oriental rug, and jitterbugged. All of us, Betty, Lyman, Norma, Willard, Jay, Ethel, and I, tried to outdo each other. And to keep the neighbors upstairs happy, we invited them to join us.

In early September 1946, the time had come for Ethel and me to quit our jobs and move down to the University of Illinois campus in Champaign-Urbana. I made one trip home to Wisconsin before leaving for college. My brother Clarence was getting married, and I was to be a bridesmaid at the wedding. It was a lovely affair, and I was happy to see everyone in my family doing so well. Only Anton, who was serving with the Marines in China, was missing. I saw my father during the wedding festivities but I could not bring myself to ask him if he received my letter asking for his financial help for college. He seemed happy to see my brothers, sisters and me and I didn't want to spoil this day for him. So I never mentioned the letter; in fact, I wasn't disappointed because I knew all along that I wouldn't hear from him. After the wedding I went back to Chicago to pack for college and the trip to Champaign-Urbana.

On a bright, warm day in mid-September, Ethel and I loaded Betty's car with our belongings and Betty drove us down to the university. We had visited the campus earlier for a weekend; therefore, it was not a completely new experience. Betty stayed with friends while we got settled in our dorms, took our entrance exams, and registered for our courses, all under her guidance. Ethel and I were finally at the starting gate, about to take off "on course" to fulfill the dream and keep the promise we pledged to each other on the sixth floor of the Treasury Department in the Merchandise Mart one year earlier.

CHAPTER 11

COLLEGE

AFTER Betty left us to begin the four-and-a-half hour drive alone back to Chicago, I began the settling-in process. As I organized my desk and bookshelf with the newly purchased texts and notebooks, I thought about the events of the past year and how Betty and Lyman had helped organize our lives, how they made sure we managed our money well, but most of all, how they kept us from becoming discouraged. It was as if they trained us to ride our own special horses that would eventually take us to the starting gate. Once at the starting gate, we listened for the countdown, fully committed to respond to the word, "GO!" Ethel and I were ready for take-off, across ditches, fences, coops, and other obstacles and hurdles "on course." We gave no thought to withdrawing or turning back. Betty always told us,

"We will open doors for you, but you must walk through them." There was no way I would disappoint her. Furthermore, others were counting on me to see the course: the representative from the Illinois General Assembly who appointed me as the recipient of the four-year scholarship, the principal of my high school, my high school teachers, Mr. Kirkpatrick, and especially my family. For all of them, I was determined to "gallop the course and jump the obstacles."

It wasn't long before Ethel and I became aware of some of the hurdles and obstacles we would face. In the fall of 1946, World War II veterans were returning to civilian life to begin their college careers. College campuses all over the country were overcrowded. Because of its excellent reputation, the engineering school at the University of Illinois was especially attractive to returning GIs. The good news: There were eleven men for each girl on campus. The bad news: It would be necessary to "flunk out" 3,000 freshmen to accommodate students and reduce class sizes, putting a damper on campus life. I would have to restructure those happy tales told by Betty and Lyman about campus life during the 1920s. Besides, how could I enjoy my quota of eleven men when I had to work fifteen to twenty hours each week while carrying a full load of courses?

Ethel and I were all set with our campus jobs. It didn't matter that we gave up our Civil Service positions, which paid 91 cents per hour before taxes, to work on campus for 50 cents per hour. That was the going rate for campus jobs. It had its advantages, however, since we could arrange our work hours around our classes, which were always given priority.

Our experience with clerical work in Civil Service gave us a definite advantage. After some time with menial office work around campus, I was able to get a secretarial position in the Landscape Architecture Department, which I held until my senior year.

Betty wasted no time in getting back to her typewriter. In fact, it seems she had no more than unpacked after her drive back to Chicago, before she typed each of us a letter. Along with her usual encouraging "not-to-worry" letters, she told of her latest work with Theta Sigma Phi, the professional fraternity for her journalism major at the University of Illinois. She wrote faithfully every week and encouraged us to write and to keep her and Lyman informed about our activities. Writing letters to the Dunns was as important as doing my class assignments.

Even though Betty and Lyman would be visiting on campus for the upcoming homecoming activities, it was difficult for me to get caught up in the excitement over the annual event. Parades and rallies had their place, but I was more concerned about the 3,000 freshmen who would have to drop out at the end of the year. I came from a small high school and had no idea how I would rank at this enormous university. To monitor the status of freshmen on campus, the university assigned an advisor to each dormitory. She would be the first to know if we were failing. Midway through our first semester she would receive our grades from the registrar and discuss them with us. On the day she notified me to meet with her privately, she was all smiles. When she gave me my mid-semester grades, I gave a big sigh of relief. I was definitely "in the hunt."

When Betty and Lyman arrived for homecoming, they took us out to elegant dinners at local hotels and restaurants. We were the envy of our roommates. The next day we went to the football game together. I had earlier been chosen to sit in "Block I," the Illini cheering section, where I learned how to flip cards synchronized with the cheerleaders' cheers. My seat on the fifty-yard line gave me an excellent view of the playing field. Unfortunately, I knew nothing about football. We didn't have football at my small high school, and after-school farm chores precluded having time for football practice. Betty and Lyman understood everything about college football and had a wonderful time.

Betty encouraged me to do more socially. She thought I worried needlessly, and she was probably right. I began socializing more with my dorm residents. I no longer felt I was going to be one of the 3,000 unable to jump the freshman obstacles and hurdles. I began accepting dates for weekend dances, movies, and the Christmas formal. We all lived close to campus and walked to all of these events. Undergraduates were not permitted to have cars, and we didn't miss them. There were buses to take us wherever we needed to go.

When it came time for our Christmas vacations, Betty and Lyman arranged to pick us up and drive us to Bloomington, Illinois, for Christmas at Betty's parents' large, beautiful home. Norma joined us and helped prepare the food. We all helped setting up the dinner table in the huge dining room. The fire in the living room fireplace was burning brightly as we dimmed the lights, lit the candles, and sang Christmas carols. Because of limited space in the car for all of us—Betty, Lyman, Norma, Ethel, and me—and the trunk filled with baggage for our vacations in Chicago, Christmas gifts were limited to small items, many of them in envelopes on the tree. In one envelope on the tree for me were two tickets to the Chicago Symphony at Orchestra Hall and a ticket to see "Song of Norway" at the Schubert Theatre in Chicago.

My sisters in Wisconsin had written to ask about my Christmas plans. I wrote a short note to them, briefly describing my Christmas vacation activities. In a long letter to Mr. Kirkpatrick, I described my vacation activities in Chicago—the symphony, the theater musicals, the Christmas window scenes in the department stores, the Art Institute, the museum trips, and the elegant Christmas brunch at the Edgewater Beach Hotel. I wasn't surprised when he published it on the front page of the local paper. It was an efficient way for me to get word to my family and relatives. It would also answer many of those questions they were saving for my visit the following summer. Before we knew it, it was time for Ethel and me to take the train back to campus where we had to take our semester exams and our first semester would be over.

The train ride back to the Champagne-Urbana campus seemed long, much longer than the drive from Bloomington to Chicago two weeks earlier. The Illinois Central Railroad added extra cars to accommodate returning students to campus, and these extra cars were often sidetracked to allow the speedier trains to pass. Consequently, this four-or-five-hour trip taken by car could last as long as six hours by train. Most of the passengers in our car were students who were sleeping off the revelry of the holiday break. Ethel and I were quietly reflecting on the events of the past two weeks. Quite frankly, I was missing my family in Wisconsin. The Christmas cards and photographs from home were reminders of the changes taking place there. I only hoped my letter in the paper made them proud. I began looking forward to seeing all of them on my next visit. The train going south was taking me further and further from them and nostalgia was setting in. Then, as I spoke to Ethel, we both realized how lucky we were to know Betty and Lyman and how lucky we were to be freshmen at the University of Illinois.

During our second semester, it was time to start thinking about summer jobs. Betty knew of summer resorts that were hiring summer help. She sent me the address of a nearby resort where I applied for work as a waitress. I had never worked as a waitress before, and I quickly discovered that this new experience was hard work. I met other college students trying to earn money for college. We worked hard, and we played hard. It seemed we never got enough sleep. The resort work schedule made it impossible for me to visit my family before I started work, but I was looking forward to seeing them before returning to the university for my sophomore year. Before my visit, however, my sister Verna was pleasantly surprised by a call from the La Crosse, Wisconsin, newspaper, which had received a press release about my freshman year at the University of Illinois, and needed my photograph to accompany the article they were preparing. Verna obliged with a portrait of me in a hand-me-down suit from Norma.

When I visited my family at the end of the summer, I learned that my younger brother Ed had enrolled as a freshman at La Crosse State College, now a branch of the University of Wisconsin. For the previous year he had been working as a bookkeeper for Warner Brothers Farm Equipment and Feed Supply in town. A friend of his had just returned from the Army with GI benefits, and together, they decided to get their college degrees.

While I was visiting my family in Wisconsin, I received the sad news that Betty's mother had died. I was unable to make it for the funeral, but Lyman, Norma, Ethel, Jay, and Willard were there for Betty's support. Her mother's large home in Bloomington would now be sold. With its location adjacent to Illinois Wesleyan University, it was an appropriate building for that university to acquire. While Betty's home in Bloomington became Adams Hall—and later, English House—Betty and Lyman moved from the small apartment on the far north side to their newly purchased spacious flat near Lake Shore Drive and Lincoln Park. She shipped her mother's beautiful furnishings to their new home in Chicago where we all could enjoy them.

I returned to the University of Illinois, enrolled as a sophomore, and resumed my 15-to-20-hour-per-week job with the Department of Landscape Architecture. During the previous year, I became interested in the speech correction courses and clinical practicum taken by a senior student in my dorm. We discussed it in detail and I continued to think about this new program at the university during my summer break. When I returned to campus in fall, I was prepared to declare my major in "speech correction," now known as "speech and language pathology." When Betty and Lyman came down for homecoming that fall, they took Ethel and me to the Urbana Lincoln Hotel for an elegant candlelight dinner. I decided to announce my "major" decision just before dessert. Betty was pleased and delighted as she turned to Lyman to tell him how wonderful the idea was. Then she turned to me with her big smile and said, "Oh, by the way, what *is* speech correction?" My chosen field was so new that she, as a national officer in the field of journalism, had never heard of it. I didn't need to explain much about the field, because she was a journalist, and as such, would now find everything published about my field and mail it to me. I felt a sense of relief to have found a major I knew I would enjoy. I could now concentrate on the special courses required for my major. Declaring a major had several bonuses, including the opportunity to become a member of Zeta Phi Eta, the national professional speech arts fraternity, and to establish relationships with other members in my field. We became a closely knit group with similar goals.

After my sophomore year, I spent another summer working at a resort in northern Wisconsin. My sisters and their husbands visited me there and brought me up-to-date on happenings back home. Ben had bought a farm and would be getting married that fall. Adolph would be working in La Crosse. Cliff had left the farm and was working in Milwaukee. Clarence and Anton had lucrative positions in Whitehall, and Ed had successfully completed his freshman year at La Crosse State. Julia became a topic my sisters avoided, and I was not going to spoil their visit by asking about her. Nevertheless, we were all concerned about my father's welfare. My brothers and sisters had left him in the care of Julia and their five children, ages 4 to 12. We didn't hear of any episodes of violence; but then, how were we to know?

My junior and senior years were career oriented. Betty suggested that instead of waiting tables during summer vacations, I should take a position with Houghton-Mifflin Publishers. They had positions open for correspondents during the summer, when the bulk of school textbook orders took place. With my clerical experience, this work would be easier than waiting tables. I would be living with Betty and Lyman in their spacious flat near Lake Shore Drive and Lincoln Park. Comfortably settled with the Dunns, and with the manager of the Houghton-Mifflin Chicago office living next door, all I had to do is walk down the back stairs to his garage for the ride to work with him.

My working through the first two years of college seemed hardly more than a minor inconvenience compared to my brother Ed's situation at La Crosse State. While I was able to enjoy campus life on weekends, he and his roommate would hitchhike sixty miles home, where he often would work Saturdays at Warner's Farm Equipment and Feed Supply. On cold winter days hitchhiking home could be especially trying. He recalled many rides crowded into old cars. A ride home in the back of a pickup truck, which he shared with parts of old barn cleaning equipment remains memorable, probably because of the way he smelled when he walked in the door of Uncle Louie's house. Nevertheless, he was proud to tell me he was living on $7.00 a week—$4.00 for rent, $1.08 for bus fare back to campus, and the rest for food, which they cooked on the gas burner in the shared room. The meat and eggs they took back from our farm community also served them well during the week at college.

After his first two years at La Crosse, Ed and his roommate transferred to Marquette University in Milwaukee. While there, he was able to visit me during our college breaks. We would meet at the Dunn's, where Betty and Lyman took an immediate interest in him. The Dunns always opened their doors to students, especially working students.

These times with the Dunns were inspiring for Ed and me. Lyman was busy introducing new ideas and methods to his employers and their companies, while Betty was establishing her position with Theta Sigma Phi. She would be running for national president of the organization. I would accompany her as she went around Chicago, arranging for Theta Sig national conventions and headline speakers. Even more exciting were the times Betty threw dinner parties to entertain the fraternity's successful women—society editors of large newspapers across the country and authors of various books, usually bestsellers that were made into movies. I was exposed to successful women from across the country, and if I didn't learn from listening to them, I should have absorbed success by osmosis.

While Betty was busy laying groundwork for her rise to the top in Theta Sigma Phi, Lyman enjoyed being innovator, promoter, and entrepreneur for various companies in Chicago. As word spread of his fine skills in food chemistry, he became a popular consultant for many companies. I remember taking a call from the CEO of a major food company who was concerned about a massive recall of a food product on the market and who was eager to have Lyman return his call. When Lyman returned the call, he explained the problem to the man and told him how to solve it all in less than fifteen minutes. Betty often laughed about the way Lyman "made a million for other people." Such remarks prompted Lyman to bring some of his food ideas and inventions home, instead of running tests in the laboratories of the companies, where others often surreptitiously took credit for his ideas. We often asked him, "What experiment are we having for dinner tonight?" Boyfriends and girlfriends were always welcome to share the results, often joining us in critiquing some new concoction. It was these kinds of sessions that led to Lyman's patents for meat substitutes used in poor countries, numerous frozen fruit desserts and drinks, and the popular soft-serve frozen dessert formulas used by major brand names. He became a world authority on frozen food products and made many trips out of the country to help others improve their food and dessert menus. The World Health Organization repeatedly called for his services. It was in this environment that I was nurtured.

Before leaving campus at the end of my junior year, the director of my department told me it would not be possible for me to hold my campus job while completing my clinical practice requirements during my senior year. She advised me to apply for another scholarship. I applied and received the good news of a one-year cash scholarship before returning for my senior year, and felt confident that I would make it financially. It would be the first time since entering the eighth grade that I hadn't worked while attending school.

During homecoming weekend in October 1949, Betty and Lyman arranged a special dinner at a restaurant near campus in Champaign. That evening in the candle-lit dining room of the restaurant, Betty presented me with a beautiful diamond and emerald dinner ring, with a matching watch, made from her family's jewels, her high school and college rings, and a tie pin belonging to her grandfather. She had it all specially designed by her jeweler. I was speechless. She told me to wear the watch and ring all the time, rather than take a chance of losing or misplacing them. So there I was, going to class in cashmere sweaters from I.Magnins, given to me earlier by one of Betty's friends, and the diamonds and emeralds from her family's jewels. And with no campus job to interfere with campus activities, I had no excuse for not doing well.

Our "Chicago Family" remained close. I had another wonderful Christmas with Betty and Lyman that year. Norma and Willard who were married two years earlier, Jay and his new wife, and Ethel who had a good job on campus and would be marrying soon also joined us. Betty and Lyman's home was a natural gathering place for everyone to share experiences, along with Lyman's "experiments." My brother Ed often would come down from Marquette to join us. When we went our separate ways after Christmas, I realized how Betty and Lyman touched all of our lives. On the train back to the university, I thought about the new luggage Betty gave me, along with a note about how important it was to travel. Of course I would not disappoint her.

I completed my last semester with a strong indoctrination in career and professionalism. I was excused from some of my final examinations by taking oral examinations for class honors presided over by staff members and department heads. Betty and Lyman, my brother Ed, Norma, Willard, and other friends came to my graduation. My graduation ceremony on June 18, 1950, with Senator Adlai Stevenson as our commencement speaker, had a mid-century theme. As he spoke, I remembered the early obstacles, the hard work, the social activities, and the wonderful friends I had made and hoped to keep forever. With no financial help other than scholarships, I had realized my dream. I believed in Betty and Lyman and they believed in me.

Lyman and Betty Dunn open their home to the "Chicago Family." Top (L to R): Willard Payne, Ethel Wood, Jay Payne, and Lyman Dunn. Bottom: Norma Dotson, Betty Dunn, and Adeline (Jo) Kulig, 1946

Betty Hinckle Dunn

Adeline (Jo) Kulig, as a Junior Prom Queen Candidate, University of Illinois (1949).

Adeline (Jo) Kulig, University of Illinois Senior Yearbook photo (1950).

CHAPTER 12

CAREER AND GRADUATE SCHOOL

THE demand for speech correctionists in 1950 was unbelievably high. I believe that the influence of one of my University of Illinois professors was a contributing factor. In the late 1940s, Samuel A Kirk, Ph.D., in the education department, traveled frequently to state and federal offices to bring attention to the educational needs of "exceptional children," and his lobbying efforts led to regulations requiring public schools to provide for the needs of those children with vision, hearing, speech, learning, and physical problems. His influence in the education department at the university gave public schools in Illinois a head start in funding. Superintendents all over the state were looking for qualified personnel in these special fields, especially since local districts were funded by the state for these programs. Twenty years before the passage of Public Law 91-230 in April 1970, public schools in Illinois were already providing for the educational needs of children with disabilities. Consequently, I had no need to look for a job. Jobs were looking for me. Midwestern universities with training programs in these special education areas had bulletin boards filled with available positions.

I accepted a position as speech correctionist for the public schools in Sterling, Illinois, a small city with a population of about 12,000. The five schools I would be serving were conveniently located around the city, but I would need a car to travel from school to school. Not only did I not have a car, I didn't know how to drive, and I had two months in which to solve this problem. I returned to Houghton-Mifflin for summer employment and saved enough money for a down payment on a car. In the meantime, Lyman and Betty would take me out of city traffic, usually on a weekend outing, to provide basic instructions in driving. About mid-summer, Lyman called a Ford dealer in Sterling, Illinois, and ordered a very "basic" 1950 black Ford. By basic, I mean engine, heater, frame, and wheels. No radio, no extras, period. Although automatic drive transmissions were just beginning to come on the market, with "Power-Glide" and "Fluid-Drive," Lyman thought the standard shift would be more reliable, and he turned out to be right. Besides, he thought anyone learning to drive should learn how to shift gears, which also was good advice.

When the time came for me to begin my new job, Betty and Lyman drove me to Sterling, about eighty miles west of Chicago, where my new car was waiting at the Ford dealership. It was a beautiful Sunday afternoon and I received my last driving lesson from Lyman on this drive. The dealership was not open on that Sunday and Betty and Lyman returned to Chicago. Meanwhile, I arranged to have my new landlord drive me to the dealership on Monday morning. After a stop at the local bank, where I arranged to finance my new Ford, we drove to the dealership. In the salesman's presence, I acted as if I had been driving all my life. My landlord knew better. He kindly offered to drive the new car to my rented quarters and arranged to give me driving lessons the next day. We took the fresh-smelling new Ford out of town on a quiet road where I could become comfortably acquainted with the biggest purchase I had ever made. The next day, I drove to work—without a drivers' license—and the superintendent arranged for the local sheriff to give me a driving test two days later. Only an employee very much in demand could get by with driving around a town with a population of 12,000 without a drivers' license, in all the school zones, of all places. That small-town generosity gave me an extra couple of days of driving practice before taking my driving test with the sheriff. Frankly, between the superintendent and sheriff, I think I would have passed the exam even if I had backed that Ford into the school trash dump. Speech correctionists were very much in demand.

On my first day as a speech correctionist, I attended joint meetings of faculties from all the schools in the city. At a large banquet I was introduced to all the teachers and members of the board of education. Everyone seemed friendly, sociable, and happy to have a speech correctionist on board. I remember giving a speech describing my work, what types of speech problems I would be dealing with, how I would plan to survey all first- and second-graders, and how I would take referrals from teachers in grades three through twelve. I answered many questions from the upper-level teachers since they would be identifying the various types of speech problems in their classes. After my talk, many came forward with questions and descriptions of specific problems. One teacher later told me, "Jo, you can take my whole class; I can't understand any of them." Her remark reminded me of an incident at Maule Coulee School, described by my older siblings. When Anton was in the first grade, the teacher, Doris Anderson, asked him to name some things rabbits eat. Anton responded enthusiastically with a long list garden vegetables—in Polish. Although I would not be working with foreign language cases, the faculty was enthusiastic and happy to finally have someone help them with the children who had speech and hearing impairments.

It was September 1950, and Adeline Kulig, now known as *Jo Kulig*, was earning $2800.00 per year and driving a basic Ford from school to school, with speech-testing equipment and an audiometer for hearing screenings. On my first day of testing and with the building principal's blessings, I began screening problems in the first two grades, with each teacher inviting me into her classroom and introducing me to her charges. In the first class I entered, the teacher explained the purpose for my presence: "This is Miss Kulig and she will be showing you some pictures. Won't you please tell her 'Good

Morning,'" after which the entire class responded, "Good morning, Mrs. Kool-Aid." These little darlings never missed an opportunity to say "Hi, Mrs. Kool-Aid" in the halls, on the playground, or even on the streets away from the school. They loved my name—rather, their version of it.

Professionally and financially, my life seemed to be going very well. The superintendent, teachers, and the parents of my subjects appreciated my work and didn't hesitate to express their feelings to me. Sterling, Illinois, was a small city, and my living expenses were quite reasonable. Also those teachers had unlimited ideas for enjoying life without declaring bankruptcy. So we got together often, played bridge, and went to movies. I was able to pay off the $1600 cost of the Ford before the end of the first school year. Although I enjoyed my job, I missed my college friends and the social life in Chicago. When an opportunity for a similar position came up in a Chicago suburb, I applied for it. Speech correctionists were still very much in demand. At least, that is why I thought the superintendent from that Chicago suburb drove all the way out to Sterling to interview me, or maybe he just wanted to get out of town to see the country. To the disappointment of the superintendent and teachers in Sterling, I resigned my position and accepted a position in Forest Park, Illinois, a suburb of Chicago, with four schools conveniently located in close proximity to each other. I sacrificed a salary increase in Sterling to be near the exciting social life in Chicago.

Not only was I happy to be back with my alumni friends in the Chicago area, but I was delighted to learn that my brother Ed had just graduated from Marquette University with a degree in business administration and that he also would be working in Chicago. We spent a lot of time with Betty and Lyman, and their spheres of influence continued to grow. Betty had become national president of Theta Sigma Phi, the national fraternity for women in journalism, and journalists from different parts of the world would be guests at their dinners. Lyman's expertise in food chemistry led to similar international contacts. As sales manager of a chemical company, Lyman also had his group of sales personnel who were regular visitors to the Dunn household. Ed and I were always invited to be part of these events and we enjoyed this social aspect of business and journalism. We were getting a real education in the ups and downs of big business and journalism.

My position in suburban Chicago was similar to my previous position in Sterling, and I had no difficulty getting off to a good start. I was giving speeches at Lions Clubs, Rotary Clubs, and any other group with which the superintendent had influence. Such organizations were interested in making donations to my speech program, enabling me to add supplies and equipment to my program without dipping into the school budget and providing my students with a variety of motivational materials and equipment. In return, my students tried to impress me with little poems and pictures made especially for me. I often recall the poem told by a little first-grade girl: "Little Miss Muffet, sat on a tuffet, eating her *curves* away." To this day, I think of that child every time I overindulge. How I wish I had kept a diary of all the clever sayings from the mouths of those babes.

I tried to stay professionally active by attending association meetings at the state and national levels. As an early member of the American Speech, Language, and Hearing Association, I made contacts in high places while the membership was still small. Having my Illinois professors in top positions in the association made such contact-building easy. With a membership numbering little more than 3,000, we got to know each other as professionals, a nice change from the student-professor relationship we had had earlier. I looked forward to national conventions with the American Speech and Hearing Association (ASHA) as a way to see my professional friends and make important contacts. With many ASHA conventions held in the Midwest and the Chicago area, I had a pretty good feel for what was happening at the national level. By observing the attention given to my former professors at these national gatherings, I considered myself fortunate to have attended the University of Illinois—the professors' sessions were filled, often with standing room only.

I lived with Betty and Lyman between 1951 and 1953 while I worked in the Forest Park School system and continued to enjoy the stimulating environment they provided. It was during this time that Lyman's experiments were beginning to pay off. He had patented a number of food products, including the soft-serve formula he developed—the frozen custard that became popular around the country. It wasn't long before he found a market for his products outside the United States. He made contacts in Cuba, and his business took off. When Fidel Castro nationalized businesses there, Lyman helped his clients, who lost their businesses in Cuba, to become established in Mexico, Central America, and South America.

By working with the public schools, I had summers off for study and travel. In 1953, I was accepted into a graduate program in the Department of Communicative Disorders at Northwestern University. It was also the year I changed to a better position in a new school district south of Chicago, at Park Forest, Illinois. The new position made it necessary for me to move out of Betty and Lyman's flat to a location near Park Forest, where I shared an apartment with Katy White, a friend I knew while we were students at the University of Illinois. When I began my summer classes at Northwestern, I moved into a dorm on campus because my graduate program was too demanding in time and energy to allow time for commuting.

Although summers at Northwestern were busy, pursuing a masters degree in my special field was inspiring. My professors, along with visiting professors, were well known in their areas of specialization. I believed I was getting great reinforcements to my strong undergraduate training. Furthermore, I was meeting many of the directors of university clinics from around the country who were participating in these summer programs. The summer sessions ended with my being overstimulated and in need of a good rest. It was fortunate that Eleanore and her husband had a beautiful farm, where I could enjoy peace and quiet before returning to my job with the schools in the fall.

Eleanore, her husband, and two young daughters

were a popular, socializing family. Anyone who dropped in at mealtime joined them at the table. Eleanore was always prepared for that. The assistant pastor of our large church near town was always welcome at their farm. On one of his visits, I could see he was a regular caller. When Eleanore invited him to stay for dinner, he went to the kitchen stove, checked what she was cooking, and said, "Hmm, I think I will."

Family reunions often were held at Eleanore's home. Their large lawn was ideal for potluck picnics, and the mowed grassy lower yard was perfect for adults and children to pitch horseshoes, play softball, and enjoy many other active games. The new cars parked in one area were symbolic of the success my siblings and I were enjoying in our jobs or local businesses, and I felt proud of all of us. But I was touched most as I watched my brother Cliff limping around the yard. Three years earlier, he had come home from Milwaukee to have a hernia operation and soon after he became severely afflicted with rheumatoid arthritis. I later learned that while he was recuperating at home from surgery and fighting the debilitating effects of arthritis, Julia abused him and refused to cook and feed him. Cliff was the last brother to remain working the farm, but Julia made life so miserable for him that he moved first to Mrs. Maule's farm and later to Mrs. Louis Kulig's home. His painful arthritic condition did not stand in the way of his becoming a success. He acquired a position as a salesman for a midwestern company that sold household and farm supplies and animal feeds. He served his clients well and became a top salesman in the state. During our visit he told me of his plans to build his own home in Whitehall.

Eleanore always invited my father and Julia to these gatherings. Although my sisters welcomed Julia, she seemed to feel awkward at our reunions. After making life at home miserable for us, she now watched as we enjoyed success and each other. It was my father who was the tragic figure. Drawing him into a conversation was difficult. He just seemed satisfied to sit back and watch his successful family enjoy one another. If there was anything pleasant for him to contemplate during these visits, it must have been a feeling of redemption, a feeling that the mortgages on our lives were finally redeemed.

I was at a loss in trying to converse with my father. In fact, it was a painful experience that I really couldn't explain. I noticed this in all my brothers and sisters, but Eleanore made the greatest efforts to draw him out. My brothers-in-law would talk to him at length, especially my bilingual brother-in-law. They would humor him, but he rarely smiled. When we would talk to him, Julia would often sarcastically answer for him. It was as if she was afraid he would say something she didn't want us to hear. She always had that "cat-that-ate-the-canary" look about her, and her sarcastic remarks were always followed by inappropriate giggles. Whether this was intentional or not, communicating with her was stressful. Considering my early experiences with her, it was easier for me to just ignore her by staying occupied with my brothers and sisters.

My trips alone back to Chicago did not depress

me as I thought they would. I had state and ASHA conventions to attend, many friends in Chicago to enjoy, and the upbeat life with the Dunns to keep me focused. I had also just parted with my basic Ford. As a Ford salesman my brother Clarence had arranged to sell it and get me a classy 1955 model. I became the proud owner of a new Ford with an automatic shift and all the extras. My basic model served me very well through my first five years. I drove it everywhere in Chicago traffic, a feat that should make any car famous. My basic Ford rightfully shared this honor with the best and most elegant of cars.

In 1955, I was halfway through my graduate program at Northwestern University when I began to feel restless. After working four years in the Chicago area, I began to yearn for a change to a different climate and a different locale. Mary Farquhar, one of my colleagues at Northwestern, was moving to Palo Alto, California, to teach at Stanford University. She invited me to visit. I took the summer off and flew out to see her. While she was teaching, I went sightseeing in the northern part of California and into Oregon. Before I left she told me about a "speech therapy" position available in Monterey, California. During the past year or two, speech correctionists became known as *speech therapists*, due likely to the number of speech and hearing clinics being established around the country. I expressed my interest in the Monterey position, and while I was traveling in northern California and Oregon, she arranged an interview and made the necessary hotel reservation for me in Monterey. I followed up with the interview and took the job. A house belonging to a University of Chicago professor, which he used only during his summer vacations in Monterey, was available for rent to teachers who would vacate when he and his family returned. I made arrangements to lease it and to find a teacher to share it with me.

Before returning to Chicago to arrange my move, I went to Los Angeles to see a long-time friend of the Dunns, Dorothy Gunning. Betty and Lyman nicknamed her "Lady Vere de Vere," because she traveled with such a cumbersome and extensive, although elegant, wardrobe. In fact, I didn't know her real name for many years. She was the lady who gave me cashmere sweaters from I. Magnin's when I was a senior at the University of Illinois. Her work with a prominent Los Angeles attorney put her in touch with some well-known people, such as Howard Hughes and many of the movie stars under contract with Twentieth Century Fox and Paramount Studios. When she heard I was coming to L.A., she arranged for me to meet some of her acquaintances. When we visited the Paramount set that was filming *The Ten Commandments*, the guards at the entrance gate seemed to know her, so they just smiled and waved her through. After parking in what appeared to be a restricted area, we walked in on the set. There the not-so-friendly guards eyed me curiously as I watched Cecil B. DeMille direct the scene with Jethro's daughters at the well. Shepherds were herding dozens and dozens of exotic sheep, which DeMille had imported from Europe for that scene, back and forth across the set as Jethro's daughters enthusiastically repeated their lines. I don't know how many times the scene was shot, but after each take, the girls looked up to DeMille, who was directing from a boom high above them, and waited for his approval. Finally, as they all looked up for his final OK, he smiled and told them, "The sheep were fine."

Not long after we arrived on the set, Vere de Vere quickly left the scene to take a call from Europe. Suddenly I found myself surrounded by those suspicious guards. Apparently, no visitors were to be on the set. Although Vere de Vere was an excellent legal secretary, outside of her office she was not known for her strict adherence to any rules. I felt uncomfortable until she reappeared, very excited. Her boss had called from Ireland to tell her that he had purchased another racehorse, and he was going to name it "Gunning," after her. How appropriate. Meanwhile, DeMille came off the lowered boom and, as he walked toward us, greeting us cheerfully, the guards quickly dispersed and I finally felt at ease. Vere de Vere introduced us as the sheep were herded off the set. While DeMille and Vere de Vere chatted about the new horse, I watched Yvonne de Carlo and Charlton Heston rehearse some sort of sparring scene with long poles. Neither of them looked as if they wanted to fight. Heston kept looking at me as if he knew me from somewhere. He didn't. He and Patricia Neal were long gone from the Northwestern drama department before I enrolled in the related department of communicative disorders. Anyway, he was not made up as Moses, and I think that scene was cut from the movie. I didn't dare tell DeMille or "Moses" about my early experience with the Ten Commandments—that in the third grade I had confessed to "committing adultery" and "coveting thy neighbor's wife."

After leaving the Paramount set, Vere de Vere

and I drove to the Brown Derby where someone had already arranged for our dinner. Our host remains a mystery. We sat down and Vere de Vere enjoyed several rounds of drinks before our dinners arrived. She was thrilled that I would be working in Monterey, and when the waiter asked about another round of drinks, she said that my new job was a legitimate cause for celebration. I was beginning to think I would end up being the driver and declined a second cocktail. During dinner, the maitre d' and several waiters kept checking on our services, while Vere de Vere discussed plans for my Christmas visit. DeMille always gave her a turkey for Christmas, and I would have to drive down to share it with her and her friends. DeMille didn't know she couldn't cook, and every year she got an uncooked turkey from him. Just as I was wondering how she would manage the uncooked turkey, she began talking about taking me to a place near the CBS television studios. I suggested we make that on another day. After a fabulous meal, with more introductions to her friends at the Derby, we left. I still don't know who hosted the evening, but I suspect it was her boss, all the way from Ireland. Oh well, this was Hollywood, I thought. Anything can happen here.

The next day, Vere de Vere left her office early so we could catch the cocktail hour at a restaurant near the CBS television studios. It was a crowded and noisy place, but Vere de Vere had friends who invited us to join them. Soon Bob Crosby and a host of engineers from his and other shows joined us. They arranged for tickets so I could join them at several shows they were working. From the restaurant we went to a party that was going strong. We walked in, and everyone was kissing and hugging everyone, including me. I wasn't used to this and didn't much like it. But the tickets for the next day's shows were arranged for me and I had to be cordial and appreciative. After a long evening, Vere de Vere and I left. The next day, she went to her office, while I found my way to the CBS studios where my tickets were waiting. One of the engineers I met the night before was operating a camera on the *Art Linkletter Show*. He zoomed in on me as he panned the audience and later told me that I looked like a zombie in the crowd. He thought that was funny. I looked at him and said, "Next summer I'm going back to Northwestern University."

I flew back to Chicago to arrange for my move to Monterey. I loaded all my belongings and therapy materials into my brand new 1955 Ford with all the trappings and left Chicago for a short visit with my family in Wisconsin. Betty and Lyman and all my Chicago friends wished me well, and I assured them I would be back the next summer to continue graduate school at Northwestern. I had to borrow money from my brother Adolph to pay for my return trip to California. My family didn't like my leaving alone on the long drive to California, but I had lived through scarier things before, such as my walk through the rain, barefooted, to escape Julia's wrath and my first trip alone to Chicago in 1945. It was a long, lonely drive, with only one stop to visit friends in Denver before continuing to my new home in Monterey. My summer off from school and work was interesting and exciting, and in many ways confirmed my need to complete my masters degree in speech pathology.

My work in Monterey was quite different from my work in the Midwest. I had been educated in the heart of the Big Ten college conference, and like their football teams, their university speech and hearing programs were very competitive. I didn't realize the value of this professional environment until I found I was the only speech pathologist clinically certified with the American Speech and Hearing Association working in Monterey County. This situation resulted in my getting referrals for private cases, usually adults, requesting speech and hearing services after school and on weekends. Feeling swamped with 8 schools and 240 elementary school cases needing help as a result of my survey, I was not interested in a private practice on the side. Enjoying the beautiful weather and the scenic area was more important. Cold winters were a thing of the past. I felt sorry for my brothers and sisters and for their children going to school in the snow, while the schools in Monterey had open hallways and outdoor playground activities year round.

Christmas came all too soon, and before I had a chance to enjoy the scenic beauty of Monterey and Carmel, it was time to join Vere de Vere in Los Angeles for Christmas. She had farmed out DeMille's uncooked turkey to a lovely young couple—gourmet cooks—and we would be joining them for Christmas dinner. The husband was the set designer for the Pasadena Playhouse, and his wife was a talented costume designer for several major televisions shows. I regret not remembering their names; however, I do remember they had a large black poodle named "George." George also had a well-established reputation. One night before a major performance, his master took him along for a ride to the Pasadena Playhouse. As final details and finishing touches were being made on the set, George became overpowered by emotion over the sight of the beautiful set. In a moment of ecstasy, he took a flying leap into his master's artwork, and before George could be controlled, a major portion of the set came down on top of him. As he gleefully scrambled out of the mass of drapery, lumber, broken lamps and lampshades heaped on the stage, he panted happily for his master, who was standing in shock at the corner of the stage where he had taken refuge from the falling debris. George was immediately enrolled in a reform school for dogs. It must have been one of the best in the country, because he returned as an angel. He obeyed every command his master gave. In fact, he made us all feel guilty. When George was given his dinner just before we sat down to ours, he was not to eat it until he was commanded to do so. In the middle of our feast of DeMille's turkey, truffles, dressing, and exotic fruits, our host shouted, "Oh my God. I forgot about George." We all jumped up from the table and rushed to the porch where George was looking sadly at the dinner set before him, waiting for the "okay" command from his master. I'll always remember George's expression as we found him waiting.

It wasn't long after I returned to Monterey that my friends from Monterey, Carmel, and Pebble Beach planned the annual social event in conjunction with the Bing Crosby Pebble Beach Golf Tournament. (Bing Crosby supported Boys Clubs of America, which enjoyed generous contributions from these tournaments.) We followed the professionals and their celebrity partners around the course. It was serious golf, followed by serious socializing. We trekked around the various courses, rain or shine, made many friends and received many invitations to visit Beverly Hills and Hollywood. I usually visited Vere de Vere instead.

During the first two years that I worked with the Monterey city schools, I vacated the professor's house each summer and returned to Northwestern to continue working toward my master's degree while he came back to Monterey each summer to write. Meanwhile, Lyman was successfully expanding his company, and Betty was chaperoning and playing tour guide to college students in journalism on trips to Europe. I remember her role as tour guide for our many weekends together visiting museums and zoos around Chicago. After one of our outings to the Lincoln Park Zoo, she came home to tell Lyman she was certain the monkeys remembered her because they waved when they saw her coming. At the Theta Sigma Phi National Convention in 1957, Betty was awarded the Distinguished Service Award for her outstanding contributions to this journalism fraternity.

The summer of 1957, my final quarter at Northwestern University, was busy with attending seminars, researching and writing seminar papers and term papers, and preparing for the dreaded comprehensive exam, all of which I had to complete before the end of July. My clerical background helped immensely in completing the course work during all four summer quarters. Term papers, required for every course, had to be typed, so students who couldn't do their own typing had to hire someone to do it. My knowledge of Chicago also helped, especially when researching the special areas related to my field. The medical libraries were immensely important for resource materials, especially in speech and language problems relating to aphasia, laryngectomy, voice disorders, cleft lip and palate, cerebral palsy, hearing impairments, and others. I spent as much time at off-campus libraries around Chicago, as I did on campus. Much of our clinical practice also was conducted at hospital clinics off campus. In this respect, graduate school was very different from undergraduate work.

The comprehensive examination toward the end of this last quarter raised every master's degree candidate's anxiety level to its highest peak. Students began preparing for the exam long before it was actually scheduled. In my case, course work was spread over five years, and I would have to recall and organize it all in one evening in July 1957, the night of the exam. I didn't wait for that day to review my work. On weekends in the spring of 1957, I would pack my notes and head for the private area of a public beach in Pacific Grove, California. Settled against a rock where the pounding surf would drown out the noise of beach revelers, I would systematically go over the notes I had taken during the past five years. When my day of reckoning arrived the following July, I was nervous; but I was counting on my past performance to carry me through the evening. I had arranged to take my typewriter to the examining area, where four of us were given a private room for putting our knowledge to print. Three students began typing before I had my typewriter out of its case. I looked at the test questions and spent the first fifteen or twenty minutes outlining and documenting my responses. Then I began typing. Four hours later I closed my typewriter and handed in the results. About eleven students gathered after the exam, but no one discussed the questions and how they felt about them. Relieved and exhausted, we followed through on our plans to drive to Howard Street where we could meet for cocktails. Over our "nightcaps" we began fatalistically discussing our performances on the exam. As the discussions progressed, I began to feel pretty good that it was over. Later that week, when it was announced that exam results would be posted in envelopes on the bulletin board outside the department chairman's office, I didn't bother to join the anxious group in line. I stayed in my room where I was deeply involved in a final project for my speech therapy session that afternoon. Word soon filtered back to me that several students had failed. This news should have alerted me to rush over to that bulletin board and snatch my sealed envelope. It didn't, and I didn't. I somehow knew I wasn't one of the disappointed ones, and I continued working on the assignment. On my way to the speech therapy session, I stopped at the department chairman's office to pick up the lone brown envelope with my name on the bulletin board. I was alone in the hall when I opened it and breathed a big sigh of relief. I had done it. I felt as though I had conquered my world.

We completed the last week of classes without the stress of comprehensives hanging over our heads. I was told that some of the students who failed would be given a second chance by taking oral exams from a committee of professors. I hoped they would do well, because many of them sacrificed so much by traveling a great distance each summer to study under various professors.

I received a congratulatory letter announcing the date and time of commencement exercises and a notice from the department chairman to pick up our final papers and reports from the secretary in his office. On the appointed day, I stopped in as suggested, gave my name to the secretary and expected my reports, after which I would return to the dorm to start packing to leave campus. Instead, I mentally changed my plans as I heard the secretary say that the chairman of the department wished to speak to me. Could it be bad news, some mix-up, some mistake? The sudden panic left as quickly as it came. The chairman of the department of communicative disorders met me in his office to discuss my research in the various specialties I had covered. I was flattered that he remembered my research papers over past summer sessions, and I was surprised at his interest in what I intended to do with my career. Professors like to hear that their students have great plans to become famous and change the world. When I told him I planned to continue my work as a clinician, he seemed a bit disappointed. I didn't want to insult him by telling him I felt administrative work was not stimulating for me, so I elaborated a bit about my opportunities for a private practice. I accepted his compliments graciously and walked out of his office knowing full well that my work as a clinician would always be my first choice.

I walked back to the dorm where I had spent my

last summer session, looked at the letter about the coming commencement exercises, and began packing. I skipped commencement exercises and the receptions following them, which enabled me to spend more time with my Chicago friends, Betty and Lyman, and my brothers and sisters in Wisconsin. Before leaving Chicago for Wisconsin, a friend took me to two places I remembered nostalgically—the Edgewater Beach Hotel, where I enjoyed my first elegant brunch with Betty and Lyman, and the Pump Room of the Ambassador East Hotel, less than a block from the apartment where I spent my first frightening and lonely night in Chicago.

CHAPTER 13

MARRIAGE, FAMILY, AND CAREER

After several parties in the Chicago area to celebrate my completing graduate school successfully, I headed to my sisters' farms in Wisconsin, where all my siblings were enjoying success with their jobs and businesses. Each year when I visited them, I saw the many improvements in their lives and enjoyed hearing about their travels around the country. They were independent and competitive, yet very much the caring siblings I always knew as a child. When I arrived for my postgraduate rest, we all gathered for our family reunion on Eleanore's farm. Only this time, I was going to be the hostess.

Among the many invited guests were Mrs. John Maule and Mrs. Louie Kulig, the two ladies who made it possible for me to escape Julia's tyranny exactly sixteen years earlier. Both were widowed now, and it was obvious they were self-sufficient. Mrs. Louie was doubly proud. She had not only encouraged me as a youngster, but also had been surrogate mother to my younger brother Ed. Because he lived with the Louie Kulig family since he was one-and-a-half years old, he identified closely with that family. He also considered himself lucky and made no secret of it. We didn't celebrate his graduation from Marquette University in 1951, and it seemed like a good idea to celebrate it now, especially since we both worked our way through college. The two "surviving puppies" no one seemed to want after our mother died were now a source of pride to those who had cared enough to help us. It was only fitting that Mrs. John Maule and Mrs. Louie Kulig should celebrate with us.

As my sisters and sisters-in-law tried to out-do each other with potluck dishes and desserts, I decided to provide the beverage. I asked Adolph to pick up a "pony" of beer (one-eighth of a barrel) and deliver it to the farm. In addition to celebrating our graduations, I was going to celebrate my thirtieth birthday. I was happy and excited to see everyone and decided I would be the one to put the spigot in the pony, but instead I came very close to spraying the lawn and all the guests with beer.

My family never indulged much in drinking, and it was obvious that a pony of beer was far too much for that crowd. I tried to give some away, but I had no takers. I thought I was going to have to dump it, when Mrs. Maule, who had lived through Prohibition, told me it "would keep" if I emptied the pony into large fruit jars and put a teaspoon of sugar in each one. That turned out to be an excellent idea. Eleanore's refrigerator was soon filled with the best beer I had ever tasted. How did Mrs. Maule know about that?

After the combined celebration—our college degrees and my thirtieth birthday—I flew back to Monterey in late August 1957 to resume my position as speech therapist for the Monterey city schools. I was enjoying an increase in salary, a new freedom from the pressures of graduate study, and more time and money for weekend trips to scenic areas around Monterey and the San Francisco area. My life was happy and carefree when, in December of that same year, I received word of the tragic death of Julia's daughter-in-law. Julia's son, born before her marriage to my father, ended an episode of domestic violence by fatally shooting his wife in the presence of their four-year-old daughter. He followed up this shooting by searching the countryside for other victims, but was apprehended in another county where he surrendered to police before more shootings could take place. After a trial of revelations about his childhood and marriage, he was sentenced to several years in the state penitentiary. The irony of it all was that Julia was given custody of the four-year-old child, who went to live with my father and Julia. There was considerable doubt about Julia's suitability for her new role as custodian. We were well aware of her temper. By now she had run out of victims in my family and was known to abuse her own sisters who often stayed with her.

My life in Monterey was far removed from both the Chicago and Wisconsin scenes. Ever since meeting the Dunns in 1945, I had divided my life and loyalties between two families. After I moved to California, Betty's journalistic skills kept me informed about the activities of the Chicago family I had become so close to. Now the members of that family were married and scattered from New York to Missouri and from Texas to California. We kept in touch, thanks to Betty, who kept all of us informed about each other and Lyman's business ventures. I missed the inspiring people around the dinner table, but I was too involved in my own career to dwell on that. Eleanore and Verna wrote regularly and kept me informed about family activities in Wisconsin. They rarely mentioned anything about our dad and his life with Julia and their five children on our farm in Maule Coulee. I would have to wait until I saw them during the next summer break from my job with the Monterey schools.

With the summer graduate school frenzy well behind me, I had time to contemplate less demanding, and certainly more pleasurable, activities. The luggage Betty gave me for my birthday several years before was luring me to travel and have fun. Before long I began seriously planning a long overdue trip. I decided I was going to spend the next summer in Europe. I cancelled all bids to pursue a Ph.D. in my field and spent the next school year reading and learning how I might "travel Europe on a shoestring." Betty had always encouraged me to travel, and now I was finally free to do so.

I attended a meeting about traveling with the American Youth Hostel (AYH) organization, conducted by a well-traveled teacher from Carmel,

California. She discussed a two-month trip, one month with the AYH and another on our own, with the first month's accommodations made by the AYH. We would be traveling and staying with European youth. It was recommended that our baggage be limited to 25 pounds, including a sleeping bag and rucksack, which sounded rather skimpy to me, until I realized we would be carrying our own baggage. I bought the recommended travel paraphernalia and met a group of eight students in Quebec, Canada, where we boarded a Greek liner for Europe. We were having such a great time in our second-class accommodations, the young travelers in first-class chose to join us whenever they could. After we disembarked in Europe, our on-a-shoestring accommodations varied widely—from sleeping outdoors in sleeping bags in Switzerland, to sleeping in comfort in Italy at the elegant home once owned by Mussolini's mistress.

We spent an exciting week at the 1958 World's Fair in Brussels, enjoying all the free exhibits. The United States and Russia tried to outdo each other in the size of their buildings, but several travelers in our group believed the U.S. building was more popular because it had free toilets. We went on to enjoy operas in Amsterdam and Rome. We bargained for our food in languages we had never heard before. I remember how we took turns shopping for food, usually in pairs, with one of us trying to speak the local language while the other gestured and pantomimed. In fact, we tried to outdo one another in bringing back food for our picnics in the countrysides of Germany, Switzerland, and Austria—all on a shoestring budget, of course. When I returned to my public school job in Monterey and described my experiences, my friends invariably said, "I can't believe you did this," especially sleeping out in the pastures of Switzerland, with cow bells ringing all around us. When I thought about my terrifying experiences with cows at age four, I also couldn't believe I did it.

In all, we traveled to ten different countries, and I thought life in Monterey and Carmel would be a letdown after that, but it wasn't. While I was gone, the Monterey City Teachers Association voted me to be their social chairman for the coming school year, which meant organizing committees, hiring a band, and arranging for a hotel ballroom to accommodate about 300 party people at our annual dance. I organized committees that helped assemble meetings. To provide dancing partners for the single teachers, I had the much-welcomed cooperation of the bachelor officers attending the U.S. Navy Postgraduate School in Monterey, who not only helped with invitations but also made our planning meetings a lot of fun. We decided to have a dollar-dance, charging the dollar admission to pay for the band, with attendees buying their own cocktails. Our first dollar-dance in October 1958 was a whopping success. It was at this party that I met Joe Puccini, a lieutenant commander and naval aviator attending the post-graduate school. My life was about to take another different course.

During the next year-and-a-half, Joe invited me to all of his social functions at the Navy Postgraduate School and to all the parties given for his class in private homes or local restaurants. If there wasn't a social function associated with the postgraduate school, he would invite me to dinner at one of the many excellent restaurants in the Monterey and Carmel areas. On Sunday afternoons, we often drove around the scenic areas of Monterey—Pacific Grove, Carmel, Carmel Highlands, Point Lobos, San Simeon, Carmel Valley, Corral de Tierra, and Salinas. After his graduation from the Navy Postgraduate School, Joe invited me to meet his parents and visit his relatives and friends in Texas, where I was introduced to Texas style entertaining—horse shows, Mexican meals, and dinners at the country club. I returned to Monterey and planned to visit my family later that summer. Joe was assigned to Air Group 15 and had to report to Moffet Field near Mountain View, California, about sixty-five miles north of Monterey. We were engaged the following spring.

Joe and I decided on a date immediately following the end of the school year in June 1960, when my contract with the Monterey city schools expired. It was not a good time for my family to leave their farms during the spring planting, or the dairy business for which there is never a good time to leave. So Joe and I planned a simple ceremony and reception to be held at the Navy Postgraduate School chapel for our friends in Monterey and Moffet Field. I had less than eight weeks to order my wedding gown, send invitations and announcements, and to complete the reports necessary to close the school year and resign. In addition to the frenzy of planning the wedding and attending showers, I worked until two days before the wedding and had neither the time nor the energy to entertain my family had they made the trip. They would have seen me fleetingly for two days and then left on their own while Joe and I left for our honeymoon. Frankly, I felt a relaxing visit after the wedding would be more enjoyable.

Navy protocol pretty much determined the etiquette for our military wedding. Lyman, Betty, and Vere de Vere flew in for the occasion, and Lyman gave me away. Joe's retired father and stepmother surprised us when they decided to come from Texas. Several Air Group 15 officers from the aircraft carrier U.S.S. *Coral Sea* served as ushers and formed the Navy arch-of-swords after the ceremony. Everything went off without a hitch—well, almost. Just before we were about to leave for the rehearsal and dinner the night before the ceremony, we received a call from the flight surgeon for the air group. He told us that the *Coral Sea*, and most of the squadron pilots, was headed out to sea to search for a missing weather balloon. This sounded very much like a Navy joke to me. Most of our wedding ushers flying around the Pacific looking for a weather balloon? Very funny! Except that it wasn't funny, and it wasn't a joke. If Joe hadn't taken leave the week before, he might have missed the wedding. Fortunately, there was only a fifteen-minute delay in the ceremony. After a fruitless search, the commanding officer, squadron commanders, and several others in the air group boarded their aircraft and were launched from the carrier, somewhere out in the Pacific, and flew directly into the Naval Air Station in Monterey. They arrived at the chapel on schedule for the ceremony. So why the fifteen-minute delay? Their wives, who were expecting to ride with their husbands to the wedding ceremony, had to drive alone to Monterey and got lost.

This experience was a very appropriate introduction to my new life as a Navy wife. From that point on, control of my life would go up and down like the carriers at sea. I would have to be prepared to deal with the unexpected. We had no sooner settled into an apartment near Palo Alto than we learned that the *Coral Sea* would be called two months earlier than scheduled. Problems in Southeast Asia were heating up. The pilots were immediately sent to Nevada for more training, followed by carrier exercises. Friends who were concerned about my early separation from my husband had no need to be alarmed. My life had always been filled with separations, and I had no problem adjusting. Besides, Navy wives are a very self-sufficient group. They know how to manage without husbands, and I knew I would appreciate that in my new soul mates. I had been professionally established for ten years before my marriage. My husband had had ten successful years as a Naval aviator. We were both independent and self-sufficient.

Our plans to meet in Hawaii, where the *Coral Sea* was supposed to have been in port over Thanksgiving, were immediately cancelled. I arranged to take part-time work with the schools in the area, joined the wives' activities, and made the most of the carrier's nine-month cruise. In the midst of all the adjustments, I learned I was expecting a baby. When I attended the ASHA convention in Los Angeles that November, I was too excited about the coming baby to fully appreciate the sessions I attended. It was more social than professional; everyone was happy for me. And when was this baby due? The week the *Coral Sea* was due back from a nine-month tour.

While the husbands were gone, I became a kind of surrogate husband and father. There were about five wives, including myself, who were expecting babies during the cruise. We took turns driving expectant mothers to the hospital to deliver their babies and sending messages via the Red Cross to the fathers on board the ship. Some of the overly anxious doctors were concerned about the missing husbands and would require the expectant mothers to arrive earlier than was necessary, which meant a longer wait for us surrogates. By the time my turn came, I was so well versed in the procedures that I told the group I wouldn't call on anyone. I would drive myself to the hospital. My doctor took a dim view of this idea. He told the hospital to tell me that I was not allowed to leave my car in their parking lot unattended while I went in to have my baby.

One evening about two weeks before the end of the cruise, I was invited to a bridge party with a group of friends from our apartment building. They surprised me with a baby shower with several lovely gifts. We had a wonderful time. I arrived back at my apartment about 11:30 p.m. to hear the phone ringing. Since it was a late call, I assumed it was someone from the party calling to tell me I had forgotten something. I got the surprise of my life when I heard Joe's voice at the other end of the line. He was at Travis Air Force Base and expected to be home in about an hour. Why hadn't somebody warned me? I forgot I was a Navy wife and should have been prepared for the unexpected. I looked around the apartment and realized I had dishes to wash, floors to vacuum, bed linens to change, furniture to move, and most of all, closets to rearrange since I had taken over his share while he was gone. I rushed through this list of chores and finished just in time to shower and answer the door. I was still out of breath when I opened the door to see the husband I saw so little of after our marriage. When he asked how I was doing, I said, "I'm fine, except I have this terrible backache." I had a million questions about this sudden surprise. It seems that the air group would be coming home in two weeks, and at the last minute, chose him to make the arrangements at Moffett Field, near Mountain View. As we talked, my backache didn't improve, but I refused to call the doctor at that hour. We finally decided to call the hospital and they suggested we come immediately. Our daughter, Nancy Ann, was born the next day, May 12, 1961—two weeks early—weighing in at six pounds, 11 ounces. My husband would never surprise me again.

Suddenly, I found myself readjusting again from my single lifestyle to living with two relatively new family members. Three of us were now occupying a one-bedroom apartment. Then there was the exciting return of the naval aviators in Air Group 15. The *Coral Sea* had been operating near Japan for nine months and was returning to Alameda, near San Francisco. Since the air group would be operating out of Moffett Field, the planes were launched while the ship was in the Pacific from where they flew in formation, squadron after squadron, and landed at Moffett Field. The excitement of the returning pilots was memorable. They greeted their wives and met their new offspring for the first time. Equally memorable was the sadness over the missing wingmen in the formation, the missing pilots who would never return. One of them would never see his son, who was born the day before our daughter in the same hospital.

There was no time for rest and relaxation after the air group's return to Moffett Field. There were parties, dinners out, and change-of-command ceremonies. Joe was involved in all of it, but still found time to become acquainted with his tiny daughter. Nancy was only six weeks old when we were about to move to Maxwell Air Force Base in Montgomery, Alabama. We loaded the car with baby formula, sterilizer, baby bottles, and disposable diapers and took off for Wisconsin to see my family. They had never met Joe, but they had learned all about him during our year-and-a-half courtship. My nieces were very excited over their new little cousin and spent her every waking moment playing with her. My father looked happy when he met Joe and his new granddaughter, but he said very little, so unlike Joe's father and stepmother who were very outgoing and enjoyed conversation.

Julia had nothing to say to Joe. Her conversation with the rest of the family consisted of meaningless remarks followed by meaningless giggles. Perhaps she was preoccupied with the changes in her life—my father put the farm up for sale and bought a large house in town earlier that year. Two of their daughters were already married, a third daughter was working in Milwaukee, and their two sons stayed on the farm, leaving only the child in Julia's custody—now about 8 years old—to live with them in town. My brother Anton was interested in purchasing the farm and made a deposit on the property. Exactly twenty years had passed since my escape from Julia in July 1941, and I was pleased to know that with Anton and his wife Doris as the new owners, I would finally feel welcome back to my home.

Leaving Wisconsin to continue our trip to Maxwell Air Force Base was sad. We reloaded the car, tearfully said our good-byes, and drove south to visit Joe's relatives in Oklahoma and Texas before continuing our trip to Alabama. Again we were entertained with parties and receptions given by relatives and friends. Leaving Joe's parents in Texas was not as sad as leaving Wisconsin because by then we were looking forward to making new friends in Alabama. Furthermore, we would be seeing his family at Christmas that year.

Our wardrobes, wedding gifts, and meager belongings were shipped earlier from California and were waiting for us in Montgomery. We stayed in a motel until we found a house from the list of available rentals posted at the Air Force Command and Staff College where Joe would be a student. Before we could move into the house, we had to furnish it. We didn't even have a baby bed for Nancy. In California, she slept in a borrowed bassinet while we lived in a furnished apartment. Furnishing an empty house was exciting because we were in an area where furniture factories and stores flourished. We purchased living room, dining room, and bedroom furniture and within a week, the three of us were settled in our house. Nancy was three months old and had traveled over six thousand miles before she had her own bed. Joe invited Navy pilots he had known earlier and we began our usual socializing. We were settled down comfortably—for ten whole months.

During the ten-month tour of duty in Alabama, Verna and her husband drove down from Wisconsin for a visit. I was very excited to see them and we had a wonderful visit, marred only by some disappointing news about our farm in Maule Coulee. We never learned whose idea it was to sell the farm, but it would not surprise me if coercion by Julia hadn't played a big part in the process. She always needed to spend time in town, so why wouldn't she want to live there? After making the required deposit, Anton waited for purchasing arrangements to be made. When Julia's second son, our half-brother, learned of Anton's plans to buy the farm, he threatened to shoot him and destroy the property. In a fit of rage, he went into the house and put his fist through the wall. With Julia's first son in the penitentiary, who would be fool enough to challenge her second son, who boasted with pride about handling his affairs with a shotgun? Anton wisely withdrew. A few months later, my father sadly told Anton how he had "given the farm away." Julia's son "acquired" the property and it was widely suspected that Julia was involved in some way. My father's plight was no secret. Within two years, the new owner of the farm got married. My father had to borrow money from a businessman in town to buy the bride and groom a wedding gift.

I was sorry to learn of this unfortunate turn of events. I realized immediately that I would never be invited to see the inside of my childhood home again. The home where my mother sang happily to my brothers, sisters, and me was gone from my life forever. For my father, this must have been the final blow. The property deeded to him by his parents was ruthlessly taken from him. The Kuligs are kind and gentle people. My father was never prepared to cope with the behavior of the new blood devouring him in his second marriage.

Joe was in his eighth month of classes at the Command and Staff College and Nancy was eleven months old when we were getting ready to attend church on Easter Sunday morning, April 22, 1962. The phone rang, and when I heard Eleanore's voice at the other end of the line, I knew immediately that she had bad news. Julia's third son, another half-brother, was killed in an automobile accident the night before. He was prone to have earlier accidents with motorbikes and other curious ventures, one of which involved a minor explosion resulting in severe burns. Ironically, he was one of four male occupants of a car that went out of control and killed three of them, all nineteen or twenty years of age. According to the one survivor, speed was a factor, and Julia's son was not the driver. Eleanore was deeply saddened by this loss of three young lives. This half-brother was born after I left the farm and Eleanore was the primary caregiver when he was an infant.

After graduation from the Command and Staff program at Maxwell Air Force Base, it was back to Navy duty at Norfolk, Virginia. Since Joe would be at sea a good deal of the time, we moved into a house in Virginia Beach, near Norfolk. He would be sailing out of Norfolk on the aircraft carrier U.S.S. *Forrestal,* for a seven-month cruise to the Mediterranean. The day before he was to sail, a heavy rainstorm flooded the yard and driveway of our new home. A month later, while he was deployed in the Mediterranean, and before I had been able to unpack the cartons left in our double garage by the movers, hurricane rains had flooded everything. I remember the six inches of water in the garage and the water gurgling in the heat and air conditioning ducts of the house. On top of all that, news of our ships confronting Khrushchev's fleet near Cuba was alarming the entire country, especially on the East Coast. The thought of a nuclear confrontation there could have sent a tidal wave up the coast that would have obliterated Virginia Beach. Families packed their cars and were leaving the area. I talked to the neighbors, and they were all worried. I waded back to our flooded house, looked at our sixteen-month-old daughter asleep in her crib, and thought, "My God, you have seen me through many a trial; please spare me one more time!" The next morning we awoke to the news that Khrushchev had backed off, and the water around our house had subsided. I spent the next few months canceling the loan on our new home, renting a house on higher ground, and moving for the third time in less than a year-and-a-half. Joe knew we had moved, but when he returned from his seven-month Mediterranean cruise, he had no idea where we were living. There's an old saying among Navy wives: "Everything bad happens when husbands are gone."

During this Mediterranean cruise, Nancy was going through interesting developmental stages, and I was sorry Joe missed so many of them. I mailed many photographs, documenting her progress. Because of my specialized training, I was naturally interested in her language development. Her transition from simple words to conceptualization was especially exciting to follow. I didn't have this kind of opportunity during my graduate training; but if I hadn't had the training, I might not have been aware of her developmental changes. One morning she asked me, "Do we have two faucets, an *each* and an *each?*" The concept "each" is not easy for a two-year-old. Her question gave me more insight into the difficulties children have when they are making transitions from one level of language development to another.

I tried to help her remember her father during his absence and gave her a special picture of him, which she would bring to me when I asked her about her daddy. Unfortunately, she also associated the photo with anyone in uniform. On one occasion at the Little Creek Base near Norfolk, while I was having the gasoline tank filled at the filling station, she put her head out the window and yelled, "Hi Daddy!" to a group of naval officers passing by. They looked surprised. They were probably bachelors.

My experience with "daddy teaching" wasn't working much better at home. After Joe returned from the long Mediterranean cruise and came home every night, I would ask her, "Where is Daddy"? She would run to get his picture and give it to me. Then she would look at him, run for the fly swatter in the pantry, and swat him repeatedly. At first, she thought he was an intruder, but it wasn't long before she realized who he was, and they became very close.

The *Forrestal* was in and out of the Naval Operating Base in Norfolk for the next year and a half. I can't recall if it was in more than out, or out more than in. During one of the outs, my neighbor Jane Arnold, also a Navy wife, asked me to give her a recommendation for a teaching position she was interested in. I happily obliged, and she took my recommendation along with her application for the interview. She stopped by after the interview to tell me that she wasn't sure about accepting the position. Then she added enthusiastically, "but I got a job for you!" I was stunned. I wasn't looking for work. Then I thought about how much Nancy enjoyed the children's nurseries, and how I might do part-time work while she was enjoying the "Happy Days" playschool. I looked at my neighbor and told her I would consider it. I got directions to the private school where she had applied and decided to give it a try. A meeting with the head mistress turned out to be very successful. The private school would provide a workroom, clerical services, and case referrals that would pay privately—a perfect set-up, because Nancy enjoyed her time at Happy Days, twice a week for four hours, while I worked.

My return to speech and language pathology services made it important for me to renew my contacts with members in the American Speech and Hearing Association. Although I continued to pay my dues and keep up with the latest techniques by reading the professional journals, I had lost contact with many of my colleagues, except for Mary Farquhar, who had earned her doctorate in speech and language pathology and was a professor at Boston University. In November 1963, Nancy and I flew to Wisconsin, where I left her on the farm with Eleanore and arranged to meet Mary during the

ASHA convention in Chicago. Mary was always an asset to me. She willingly gave her time and energy to write character references for me and made important suggestions for me to use in job interviews. She even recommended me to the University of Wisconsin speech and language clinic as her replacement when she decided to leave to pursue her doctorate in the field, but I declined graciously because of my marriage plans. Mary was strong professionally and was presenting a paper at the convention in Chicago. It was wonderful for me to be back with her and her friends and to include Nancy, Joe, and our Navy life in our discussions.

While attending this ASHA convention, I spent some time visiting the Dunns. Betty had just returned from Los Angeles where she had been in charge of settling the estate of Vere de Vere, who had died suddenly of cardiac failure. We lost a dear, interesting friend, and I was saddened to know that I would never be seeing her again. Because she looked so well and so chic at our wedding in 1960, I thought I would have many more happy times with her. I remembered how we enjoyed our visit to Paramount Studios during the filming of *The Ten Commandments*. She had shown me an eight-by-ten photo of Charlton Heston made up as Moses. It was one of her prize possessions. We don't know what happened to the photo. I wish I had it to remind me of our wonderful times together.

After being inspired at the ASHA convention in Chicago, I began reading my professional materials in earnest. My private practice was doing well, Nancy enjoyed her friends at playschool, and Joe was on the *Forrestal* going in and out of the naval operating base at Norfolk. We knew that he was due for orders and waited to hear about his new assignment. After he was assigned to Quonset Point, Rhode Island, and while he was looking for housing at our next location, I closed my practice in Virginia Beach. Nancy and I flew to Wisconsin to spend some time on the farm with my sisters and enjoy the company of my brothers, nieces, and nephews. Clifford visited us often and we were excited to hear about the new home he had built in Whitehall. When I visited him in his new home, I was impressed with its oversized double garage, floor plan, spaciousness, huge bedrooms, and numerous large closets. I wished Joe could have been there to see it before he looked for housing in Rhode Island. And I wondered how Julia felt about Cliff's new home—larger and more attractive than the one she lived in with my father. Did she think about the times she refused to feed him and forced him to leave during the onset of his painful rheumatoid arthritis?

We were enjoying family and friends on Eleanore's farm when we learned that my father was stricken with a heart attack. He had been in and out of the hospital before, but he seemed to rally each time. We were not prepared for the seriousness of this last episode, so I decided to extend our visit. My family took turns visiting him in the hospital, with someone always keeping a night vigil. On the last night I stayed with him, I had a lot of time to think. He was resting comfortably and didn't seem to be aware of my presence when, in his semiconscious state he sat up in bed for several seconds and spoke the following words: "You shouldn't force someone to (pause) . . . you shouldn't force them to . . ." and before completing his sentence, he fell back into his semiconscious state. Those were the last words I heard him say. He died before I was able to hear him speak again. I have often tried to put meaning to this unfinished sentence. Perhaps time will provide the answers.

Julia's family and the local funeral director made funeral arrangements quickly and efficiently. Julia played the pious and bereaved wife during our time of mourning, but I saw no sign of any tears. On the day of the funeral my brothers and sisters, along with Julia's three daughters, waited in the funeral chapel while Julia and her son, the new owner of the farm, stood before the open casket. She made a noble effort to show some sign of grief, but all I could observe were a couple of child-like whimpers, after which she turned to leave the chapel. She looked straight ahead, avoiding our eyes, as she and our half-brother followed the casket to the hearse for the drive up the hill to the church. She had that all-too-familiar look about her—that cat-that-ate-the-canary look. She knew that my brother Ben was the executor of my father's will and that he would find the lock box empty. All records pertaining to the life insurance taken out after my mother's death, the deeds to all the properties, and the records pertaining to the sale of the farm and purchase of the large home in town would never be found.

I felt guilty about not being able to shed any tears during the funeral service or at the reception following it, until I saw that my brothers and sisters had that look of immense relief about them. Instead of grieving, we enjoyed a sumptuous buffet, followed by visiting with relatives and friends who came from all parts of the state. It was as if we knew our father was finally enjoying the peace he had been denied for the past thirty-four years—since our mother's death. It was a merciful end to that vow of "permanency" he made so piously thirty-one years earlier when he married Julia. While I was busily becoming reacquainted with relatives and friends I hadn't seen for many years, I noticed Julia sitting with her daughters pretty much alone. It never occurred to me to offer her my condolences as she sat there. It reminded me of all the times she sat and watched my emancipated brothers and sisters enjoy one another other after we became successful in spite of her.

Toward the end of the reception I noticed my brother Anton leaving. He told me he was going out to the cemetery. My brother Ed and I decided we would join him. We followed him out to my father's grave, freshly covered with sod, where we noted the triple tombstone marking the plot for the half-brother killed two years previously, my father, and Julia. Since there was no graveside ceremony, this was my first opportunity to see the triple marker. Without saying a word, Anton walked several yards down to our mother's grave. Ed and I followed to find him down on one knee, sobbing uncontrollably. The plot next to hers was vacant. I could see Ed was struggling to maintain his composure and he did, but I was unable to hold back my tears. The three of us were now grieving for what we had been denied the past thirty-four years. Time had not healed what we had repressed.

After the funeral Nancy and I left Wisconsin, to join Joe in Rhode Island. He had arranged for us to live in a small two-bedroom motel apartment while we looked and waited for housing. December was approaching and we still hadn't found a place to live. We never had military housing before this tour of duty, and it wasn't likely that we would get it at Quonset Point. We had packed our suitcases at Virginia Beach in August, and it was now snowing in Rhode Island. With everything in storage, I decided to drive my husband to work and then stop to shop for some warm clothes. The store clerks looked strangely at Nancy and me as we shopped around in our summer clothes, which prompted me to head for the first dressing room where we both changed into our new purchases.

We drove back to the motel, appropriately dressed, where I found the mail forwarded to me. Included in the stack of letters was the will made out by my father in 1947. My bequest was fair and generous. Unfortunately, the property was no longer available. Julia had it all signed over to her before any of us could intervene. She made sure she got it all, including the life insurance my father purchased to protect us after my mother's death. The tragedy was not that she had taken everything from my brothers, sisters, and me. We were all doing fine. The tragedy all along had been Julia's demeaning treatment of my father. She had stripped him of every vestige of dignity a man could have—his money, his property, and his family. Fortunately, she was unable to strip him of his honesty and good name.

We finally found a rental house in East

Greenwich, Rhode Island, and moved in with our furniture and belongings on December 1, 1964. It seemed like the coldest day I could remember in years. As soon as we settled in our home, we began returning parties for all those people who felt sorry for us during our two months in the motel. We made wonderful new friends, some of whom we still see and hear from today. It turned out to be our first opportunity to forget sea duty and enjoy family socializing and Friday Happy Hours. It was a three-year tour of duty and Nancy was approaching preschool age. I enrolled her in an excellent day program where she received French lessons and ballet training.

I didn't realize that the suggestion from Jane Arnold, my neighbor back in Virginia Beach, would launch me on reestablishing myself professionally. Speech pathology positions were available everywhere we moved. Unfortunately, with each move it would be necessary to start over salary-wise, since credit for earlier years' experience was not always transferable. A most unfortunate case scenario occurred during one of our "displacements." During the two months Nancy and I spent in Wisconsin, I had no official address other than the *Forrestal*, so my annual dues notices from the American Speech and Hearing Association were forwarded to the ship, and then returned to the national office. After several months in our new residence I realized I hadn't received my annual notice to pay my ASHA membership dues. I decided to mail my dues and inquire about my notice. They regretfully returned my check, stating that I would have to requalify for my national certification by taking the national exam.

Since the certificate of clinical competence from ASHA was not required for public school speech and hearing programs in 1965, I decided to accept a position with the East Greenwich School District, with an office just two blocks from Nancy's preschool.

I enjoyed a successful year with the East Greenwich School District in Rhode Island—three elementary schools, one junior high school, and one senior high school. It was the right size program for me, and the teachers were cooperative and interested in my work. Nancy was taking ballet and learning French, and when she helped me put the candles on Joe's birthday cake that year I was surprised to hear her count the first ten of them in French. We enjoyed the Christmas, Easter, and graduation programs at her school, especially the children singing songs in French.

Because Rhode Island is a small state, it was not unusual for the three of us to go sightseeing, driving through three states in one day—Rhode Island, Connecticut, and Massachusetts. New England had much to offer, from Newport mansions to Boston, Cape Cod, the beautiful Atlantic coast, and the scenic mountains. We took advantage of every weekend for traveling. During our summer visits to Wisconsin, we would continue our family tradition of reunions on Eleanore's farm. Julia and her son and daughters were always welcomed. For reasons obvious to all, however, her son usually declined. Shotgun diplomacy was not acceptable in our family. Nothing was ever mentioned about the farm sale or the will. It was as if we never expected anything from my father's estate, so we all just forgot about it. We moved on to enjoy peace and plenty for many years.

These were good, normal times, and we enjoyed them. We often visited Joe's elderly father and stepmother in Texas and enjoyed meeting his friends and relatives. Joe was an only child and his visits were important. While Nancy and I were visiting relatives in Wisconsin in the summer of 1966, Joe's father died after a long and serious illness and Joe was called home. I left Nancy with Eleanore and her family and flew down for the funeral. After that our visits to Texas would never be the same.

After three years in Rhode Island, Joe received orders to return to the Navy Postgraduate School in Monterey, California, to pursue a master's degree in computer sciences and management. I was delighted to know I would be returning to old friends and teachers in Monterey and to the postgraduate school where we were married. I resigned my position with the East Greenwich schools, Nancy graduated from preschool, and we made plans to drive across the country from the Atlantic to the Pacific. It was the first time we traveled with two cars. We followed each other from Rhode Island to Expo 67, the Montreal World's Fair, and drove west across Canada to Detroit, stopped to call on Betty and Lyman in Chicago, then headed northwest to Eleanore's farm in Wisconsin. Nancy was six years old and believed it was important to share her time as passenger with each of us. We had a nice, long visit with family and friends and Nancy was challenged as she tried to remember the names of her many cousins. After leaving Wisconsin, Joe headed south to Texas and then continued west to California along the southern route. Nancy and I were more adventurous—we took the northern route to California via the Badlands and Black Hills of South Dakota, Yellowstone Park, the Teton Mountains, Salt Lake City and Salt Lake Dessert, across the Sierra Mountains, including Lake Tahoe, and on to Monterey. Before leaving Wisconsin, Joe and I arranged to have Eleanore as our point of contact and each night I would call her to report where Nancy and I settled for the night. We failed to make contact only once during our trip—during our stopover in the Teton Mountains. Because there was no phone in our rustic cabin, I skipped the call to my sister. She and Joe both became alarmed and thought we were lost. Nonsense. We knew exactly where we were. We were riding horseback on the mountain trails near the Grand Teton, and having a ball. The scenic area was enough to forget all about the mundane, including phone calls.

Joe and I arrived in Monterey about the same time. We found a beautiful five-bedroom, three-bath rental house in the area known as John Steinbeck's "pastures of heaven" and enrolled Nancy in the first grade at San Benancio School. As soon as we were unpacked, I was employed by the Washington Union School District in Salinas, California, as the speech pathologist for two junior high and three senior high schools. Again, we were back to postgraduate school parties and formal affairs. During Joe's class breaks, which coincided with Nancy's and my school breaks, we would take weekend trips to Yosemite and another of our favorite places, the Alisal Ranch near Solvang, California. Growing up on a ranch in Texas, Joe became an excellent rider, and Nancy took to horses like bees take to honey; but I had to work at it. Remembering so many frightening experiences from my childhood on the farm added to my fear of horses, but I was determined to take those trail rides up the beautiful Santa Ynez Mountains with them. Those rides in the fresh mountain air were wonderful and our appetites were always ready for the sumptuous meals served each day.

Joe received his master's degree before Christmas and had to report for duty with the Naval Air Systems Command in Washington, D.C., in January 1969. I had a contract with the Salinas schools that did not expire until the following June, so we decided that Nancy and I would complete the school year in California before moving to the Washington, D.C., area. Joe left alone in January, taking the southern route, visiting relatives and friends in Oklahoma and Texas, and heading for Washington, D.C.

Our move that year went in stages. Joe made a shipment of clothing, flight equipment, and other paraphernalia before he left. Before the second stage of that move, I arranged to have the packers put everything in cartons ready for shipment. Then, Nancy and I and her newly acquired dachshund, Gretchen, flew to Wisconsin, where I left her and the dog, and flew on to Washington, D.C., to meet Joe and to begin our hunt for housing. After buying a house in Virginia, I flew back to California to arrange for the third stage of this move—loading the van with our furniture. After the moving van left, I spent the night with friends in Pebble Beach. The next day I got into my 1965 white Ford Mustang and started back east alone, stopping in Reno to spend the night. After dinner, I decided to try my luck in the hotel casino where I was staying. Good idea. In two hours, I made enough money to pay for gasoline, food, and lodging for the trip all the way to Wisconsin.

I had made that trip alone several times during my summers in graduate school. By now my family had taken my solo drives for granted. I had also learned to enjoy these opportunities to reflect, think, and plan future activities with three different families—the Chicago family, my brothers and sisters, and daughter and husband. On this solitary drive through the plains of Nebraska, I was deep in thought about the excitement of living in the nation's capital, when I heard the lonely sound of a train whistle. It came from the engineer of a freight train traveling on the tracks that paralleled the highway I had been driving for the past several miles. We waved to each other, as if pleased to be reunited with civilization. He passed me as I continued on. Miles later after the train made its quick stop at a grain elevator, I heard the same train whistle as it passed me for the second time. Again, we exchanged greetings. When, after another elevator stop, he passed me for the third time, I remembered an old superstition: When anyone passes you three times, on foot, horseback, bicycle, or in a car, you are to make a wish. This wish would more than likely come true. On that quiet Sunday morning, with no other car, pedestrian, horse, or bicycle in sight, I made a wish to be settled somewhere for a while. I picked up Nancy and Gretchen in Wisconsin, drove on to the Washington, D.C., area, and arrived at our new home on July 19, 1969.

To say that our years in the D.C. area were stimulating would be an understatement. The social and political climate in our nation's capital was unmatched by any earlier Navy assignments. Besides being reunited with friends we hadn't seen for many years, we were meeting top-level leaders in all branches of military service. Embassy receptions, Navy luncheons, and welcome, farewell, and retirement parties made socializing a real pleasure. One of the most memorable affairs was a luncheon to welcome a former POW, Rear Admiral Jeremiah A. Denton and his wife; I was so inspired by their remarks and their lives. Nothing I experienced as a child could compare to life as a prisoner of war with a wife and family worrying at home.

While I was juggling roles as mother and Navy wife, my "pot-luck" career took a back seat. After all, I had three brothers who served in the Army, the Navy, and the Marines. I also had a nephew serving in Viet Nam. My career would always be there. Furthermore, the demand for speech pathologists was not what it once was, and jobs were not looking for me as they had in the past. Almost two years went by before I learned about a position available with the Virginia State Department of Health. During my interview, I learned that my employer knew several of my graduate school professors. They were his consultants during his tenure with the Veterans Administration (now the Department of Veterans Affairs) and he seemed pleased to welcome me to the health department. On November 7, 1972, the day I was to begin my new position, Joe was suddenly hospitalized and I had to cancel my first day on the job. I reported the following day, but Joe was off from work for two months.

Joe's illness was a sobering experience. It made me realize that perhaps I should become stronger in my profession by requalifying for ASHA certification and by taking the national exam. It had been sixteen years since I took my comprehensive exams at Northwestern University, and I wasn't sure I was up to the task. I had heard horror stories about the test and they were coming back to haunt me, but I was determined to go for it. While working part time for the Virginia State Department of Health, I read and reviewed the books and papers dealing with the ten areas covered by the test. In July 1973, I appeared at George Washington University at the appointed time to take the examination for the certificate of clinical competence in speech and language pathology, prepared by the board of examiners of the American Speech and Hearing Association. The test covered all areas of speech and language pathology with a good choice of questions dealing with hearing impairments. I remember the feeling of relief I felt on my drive back home, but I had no idea how I had done.

After the exam, Nancy and I flew to Wisconsin and were having our usual good time visiting and resting, when Joe called to say the results of my exam had arrived. Before calling me, he contacted my friend Dr. Mary Farquhar and asked her to interpret the results. She told him I scored higher than any of her graduate students—recent graduates, no less. It was my forty-sixth birthday and I was definitely in the mood to celebrate with my family.

When Nancy and I returned to our home in Virginia, I immediately called Mary. We discussed the ASHA exam, our professors at Northwestern, and how fortunate we were to be their students. She told me about the last ASHA convention, where a special committee chose a "panel of the experts," or members who contributed most to special areas in speech pathology and audiology. Six of my former professors were seated on the panel of seven.

I returned to work feeling rejuvenated. My work with the State Department of Health was every bit as interesting as any position I had held in the past. My caseload consisted primarily of stroke patients, people with head injuries, and young children with developmental speech and language problems. Working with such a wide range of patients required my being proficient in administering the latest tests in those fields. My caseload was limited, which enabled me to complete thorough evaluations. Instead of handling a large number of similar problems, I was dealing with special cases, each of which was decidedly different. Medicare and private insurers required complete evaluations with treatment plans that were specifically designed and appropriate, or coverage would not be approved. Because I maintained my professional contacts over the years, I also was receiving private referrals. During this time, I was fortunate to be accepted early in the American Academy of Private Practitioners in Speech Pathology and Audiology—so early, in fact, that I was one of the only two members accepted in Virginia. The Academy was an excellent group for getting things accomplished through Medicare and private insurance. I found myself on committees working directly with senators involved with Medicare, an experience that helped in my quest to get my own provider number from major insurance and Medicare providers.

While I was moving forward with my speech pathology career, Nancy's earlier interest in horses was revitalized. We lived not far from a riding stable, with an ancillary kind of pony barn within walking distance from our home. She was spending a lot of time with her friends there. It wasn't long before she acquired a horse of her own and became a "pony club" member. Joe and I became pony club parents and spent many weekends working with this worthwhile organization. Weekends during her high school years were now spent with pony club activities and a whole new group of people. We volunteered our services for judging competitions, building cross-country jumps, and participating in all pony club activities in general. It was a time for observing young teenagers growing into busy, responsible young adults. Watching a young child take charge of a young pony, whose ideas about cooperation leave much to be desired, can be a real learning experience, for parent and child. Parents are not permitted to assist. Every pony-clubber knows that his horse is his responsibility and that school grades set the criteria for continued membership in pony club functions. Pony club levels were graded from D-1 through A, involving written testing and a practicum for each level. As a working parent, I was never concerned about our daughter's extra-curricular activities. Her horse took care of that. Pony-clubbers were responsible associates. They were all dreaming about passing that challenging national A-level test and competing with members of the U.S. Equestrian Olympic Team.

Life was going well for Nancy, academically and in pony club. She was enjoying the camaraderie of club members, riding lessons, and equestrian events. For Joe and me, things were not going as well. He was up for a prestigious command in 1972 when he was hospitalized, and missing that opportunity was disappointing for him. After that, his return to duty in another position left him disenchanted and he retired from the Navy in 1975, after thirty years of service. We both would have to make a major adjustment, and I don't know which of us was having more difficulty with the changes in our lives. Counseling proved to be ineffective in resolving our differences. After a couple of years of indecisiveness, I felt a separation would be beneficial for both of us and arranged to move out.

The day after our separation, still reeling from the sudden changes in my life, I was getting dressed for work when the phone rang. It was Joe calling to tell me about the death of Ed's wife, Arlene, my sister-in-law. I knew she was battling cancer, but I didn't know her condition was that critical. I was too involved with my own problems to realize she was that close to losing her battle with the dreaded disease. I sent Nancy, a sophomore in high school, to spend the time with her father while I would be away for the funeral. I packed my bag and left for the airport. On the flight to Wisconsin, I could only wonder why this beautiful young woman had to leave my brother and two young children, ages eight and five. Ed was only a year old when our mother left us, and my father had to give us away. Our mother was only thirty-one years old when she died. Ed's wife was only thirty-nine. Whoever said, "Lightening never strikes the same place twice," was wrong. Dead wrong.

My sister Eleanore and her husband met me at the airport and we drove the fifty miles to Independence and went directly to the funeral home where visitors were already arriving. We were met at the door by Ed's son, five-year-old Willie, all dressed up in a suit and tie. Willie directed us to the chapel, bravely saying, "My dad's inside." I was completely shaken, but tried to keep my composure for the scene to follow. Ed was visibly upset, as he stood greeting friends and relatives in the room with the open casket. Behind Ed and the crowd gathered around him sat a distraught eight-year-old Amy. The handkerchief she was holding was too wet to absorb any more tears, so she spread it in her lap as if to dry it enough to absorb even more. Her third-grade teacher was sitting next to her with her arm around Amy's shoulders. In front of the two of them was the open casket where a beautiful young mother rested in peace. On the edge of the open portion of the casket was a tiny plant, one similar to all the others in Amy's third grade class. It was April 15th. In three more weeks Amy's tiny plant would have grown large enough to be her special gift for Mother's Day. The scenario broke my heart.

Ed and Arlene were active members of the community. He served as board member of various organizations, while she served on many committees at their church. They were both popular and often were called upon to organize and solicit help in local affairs. Therefore, it wasn't surprising that seven priests turned out to officiate the funeral service. It was especially appropriate that the church was still completely decorated with Easter lilies from the Sunday before and that the choir sang with voices more attuned to a resurrection service than a funeral. Even the eulogies were uplifting. When the time came for Ed and his two youngsters to follow the casket down the long aisle out of the church, however, there was not a dry eye in the congregation. It was the first time that the choir was known to break down and stop singing in the middle of a hymn. When the organist realized no one was singing, she abruptly stopped playing.

It was difficult for me to feel sociable at the reception following the service and I was glad when others took the initiative to speak to us. It helped a lot, but it also hurt when they asked about Joe. Only my sister Eleanore and her husband knew about my separation. I had told them about it during our drive from the airport the day before. The rest of the family would learn about it at a private gathering later that afternoon. Both Ed and I were about to be launched into single parenthood, but my circumstances were much less trying than his. My daughter was at the age where she was considered emancipated. She would be off to college in a couple years. More importantly, she still had two parents. Ed would have to bring up two young children alone, with the help of a housekeeper.

I flew back to Virginia and picked up Nancy, but I could not bring myself to describe the funeral scene to her that evening. The next morning I left for work as soon as she boarded the school bus. I was fortunate to have a stack of paperwork to clear off my desk, to keep my mind off the tragic changes in my life. And I felt some comfort in knowing that Nancy had her horse, her equestrian friends and activities, and her school work to keep her focused on things other than her separated parents. We were conditioned by Navy life to be strong and independent, and I knew we would both come to terms with the changes in our lives.

Betty flew out from Chicago to be with me for Mother's Day that year, but I found it difficult to make it a happy occasion. We had champagne with our dinners out, hoping to lighten up the gloom that settled over me. Betty, as always, could be very objective in her appraisal of my situation, and before she returned to Chicago, I had learned to think objectively and to avoid letting my emotions cloud my course of action. And most important of all, I had her support and knew how important it was to follow her advice.

I managed well on my own with a job as good as could be expected during that stage of my pot-luck career, and I was beginning to improve my professional competence by attending more meetings, seminars, short courses, and ASHA conventions. I continued volunteer work with Nancy's pony club and enjoyed the equestrian events she entered. It was obvious that Nancy had a special relationship with horses. When it was time for her to go to college, she sold her horse and bought another—to take to college. As I watched her load her pick-up truck and horse trailer for the six-hour drive to Virginia Tech in southwestern Virginia, I recalled how thirty-two years earlier, Ethel and I had tossed our clothes and suitcases—virtually all our belongings—in the trunk of Betty's car and had driven off. Times certainly had changed. Now it was college clothes, riding apparel, saddles, bridles, boots, and all the horse paraphernalia. To say nothing of the horse itself, wearing his shipping cap and boots, following her into the trailer as he was being loaded. And who was driving this rig? Nancy, with Joe as copilot. As I watched them drive off, I knew I would miss her and all the pony club activities of the past four years. So I went down to the nearest stable and signed up for riding lessons.

Times had changed for me also. Those days as a little girl on the farm, when riding horses was not considered to be a "girl thing," were definitely a thing of the past. I began enjoying my riding lessons and looked forward to them. A year later, after I felt brave enough to be responsible for a horse of my own, I purchased a half-thoroughbred, half-quarter horse. Like many of my earlier adventures, driving across the country alone and traveling in Europe with a rucksack and sleeping bag, my friends were again telling me, "I can't believe you did this." My horse, Beowulf, turned out to be a good friend in the days to come. While Nancy was attending college and involved in equestrian competitions on weekends, I was riding and competing with young pony club members at home. I was a novice rider; but I had a smart horse, so we did well.

In August 1980, I was surprised to learn belatedly that Julia had been hospitalized and died. I had seen her and her daughters, my-half sisters, earlier that year at Easter time when I visited. We always had a wholesome relationship with our half-sisters because they did not remember our problems with Julia when we were young. Furthermore, they were always included in our family reunions and felt free to visit my sisters at any time. We never felt they should be held responsible for Julia's earlier behavior, although I had difficulty forgetting how Eleanore and I were punished when *they* cried or misbehaved. Time had forgiven Julia for that, but forgetting was another matter.

When no one called to tell me about Julia's death, I wasn't surprised. Eleanore, who usually called me in such matters, no longer lived in Independence. She and her husband had sold their farm and moved to Arizona, and if she knew about Julia, she probably assumed that someone else in the family had already called me. Yet somehow, I felt left out. Perhaps it was because of an incident that happened twelve years earlier when Nancy was a flower girl at her cousin's wedding. I was sitting next to Julia at the wedding reception when Nancy decided to go up on the stage and do a solo dance. I noticed Julia watching her so intently that I became curious and asked her if Nancy reminded her of me at that age. She looked at me wistfully and nodded so slowly, I wondered what she was thinking. It was a side of Julia I had never seen before and I will always remember that look. Julia was buried next to my father and the twenty-year-old son killed in 1962, in the plot with the triple marker.

Nancy was away at college and I was getting ready

to go to work on Friday morning, April 12, 1982, when I was startled by an early phone call. It was Norma, from my Chicago family, calling with sad news. She said simply, "We lost Betty this morning." I couldn't believe what I was hearing. Betty had not been ill and I had just recently been thinking about what I might do for her for Mother's Day coming up in three weeks. The shock of this news, my mentor gone forever, was difficult to absorb and I drove to work in a daze. From my office I immediately called Lyman to tell him I would be out to help him with funeral arrangements. I could tell he was shocked by what had happened earlier that day. He told me that two days earlier he was at the kitchen counter, working on their income taxes and joking about paying Uncle Sam, when he heard a sudden thump behind him. Betty had fallen on the floor, fatally stricken with a heart attack. The rescue squad was unable to revive her. She died two days later at Northwestern University Hospital just two blocks from their hi-rise apartment. I assured Lyman that his foster family would be out to support him and I made reservations to fly out to Chicago at once.

Betty and Lyman were intelligent and efficient people, and as expected, they had their funeral plans made in advance, with papers completely in order. Betty had her father's legal mind and knew exactly how things should be done. A couple of Betty's friends from Chicago joined Lyman, and I drove them in Lyman's car down to Bloomington, Illinois, where Norma, her husband Willard, and many more friends, relatives, and business associates attended the memorial service and graveside ceremony. After the funeral, Lyman rode down to Missouri to spend some time with Norma and Willard, the two foster family members who had married each other. I drove Lyman's car back to Chicago and dropped off the two family friends at their homes. After turning the car over to the parking attendant in the garage, I took the elevator up to the forty-third floor of the hi-rise apartment building on Michigan Avenue where Betty and Lyman spent their last days together.

The view from their apartment was magnificent. It overlooked the entire north and northwest side of Chicago, including a large portion of Lake Michigan to the east. Down below about two blocks away I could see Northwestern University Hospital where Betty spent her final hours, the same hospital where I spent many hours during my years of clinical practice when I was a graduate student. As I stood there thinking about the many years Betty spent taking me around the city, visiting parks and museums, enjoying symphonies, theater, and ballet, I hoped she realized how much I appreciated her as a role model. I thought about the many students she guided through college, how she never tired of listening to their concerns. As I pondered over what I should do in appreciation, I remembered how she always said, "If you are going to give me flowers, do it while I'm still alive." I turned away from the beautiful view of city lights that went on for miles and miles, of automobile lights moving up Lake Shore Drive along Lake Michigan, and walked to the telephone. I called my friend Cissie, whose earlier invitation I had declined, and told her I had reconsidered. The thought of spending the night alone in that apartment was too much to bear. While I waited for Cissie to drive down from the northwest side, I began to make plans for a memorial for Betty, a contribution to a scholarship fund in the Department of Journalism at the University of Illinois. I looked at the empty vase that used to hold the flowers we would bring to her on weekends and special occasions and remembered how delighted she was while she arranged them. Today, the vase stands empty on my buffet, but the scholarship fund thrives.

When Cissie picked me up that evening, we drove north on Lake Shore Drive along Lake Michigan, the drive I had looked down on from the apartment an hour earlier. I had made this drive so many times with Betty and Lyman, to work with the vice president of Houghton-Mifflin Publishers, and finally alone in my basic black Ford. For some strange reason, the drive this night seemed especially bright and beautiful. It was as if Betty had lit up the city especially for me. And even stranger, I found I was suddenly rising out of the depression that had set in the morning of the day I received that shocking call. We drove past the Drake Hotel, the Oak Street Beach where I saw my first "breakers" in Lake Michigan thirty-seven years earlier, and past the little apartment area where I spent my first lonely night in Chicago. The following day Cissie took me to O'Hare Airport from where I returned to my job with the Virginia State Department of Health.

If I were to make a list of helpful healers, I would have to put my work, helping the less fortunate, near the top of my list of choices. I have always found my work as a clinician a source of gratification. For years I had watched Betty and Lyman help others. Their joy in helping others was obvious; in fact, I believe they had their happiest years when they were helping and guiding those of us who were fortunate enough to be their protégés. They deserved to take pleasure in watching us test our wings and to fly off into various careers. At the time of Betty's death, I was well into thirty-two years of my career as a speech and language pathologist. I was healing fast and I hoped Lyman was also. It was times like this that I felt fortunate to have my horse, Beowulf, and my friends at the riding stable to lighten up the serious nature of my work. As I became more proficient in my riding, I would ride the trails in the park near the stable and practice my jumping skills at the hunt club nearby. Yes, Beowulf was helping me to fill the void in my life.

Meanwhile, in Chicago, Lyman was receiving hundreds of letters and phone calls from friends and journalists who had learned of Betty's death. He decided to acknowledge their letters by writing a long tribute to Betty (see Appendix A) and sharing the messages on the sympathy notes with it. It was an opportunity to see Betty, as Lyman said, "through the eyes and hearts of her many friends." On my copy of this long letter, Lyman added the following postscript: "Betty loved you very much—thanks for being so helpful to me."

Attached to his long tribute to Betty, Lyman sent information about the memorial fund he was establishing in her name. He had made an initial donation of $60,000 and named it "The Betty Hinckle Dunn Memorial Fund." Included with information about the fund was this personal note from Lyman: "During the 1928 school year at the U. of I., I ran out of funds completely and couldn't get help anywhere.

As a last resort, I went to the office of the Dean of Men and explained my plight. He arranged a loan of $600.00 for me from a scholarship fund administered by the university, which saved my college career. In appreciation of this act and for a memorial to my darling Betty, I have already made an initial contribution of $60,000 to the BHD Fund to get it started. I am delighted, in a way, to return 100-fold the funds 'cast upon the waters' so long ago by a generous and thoughtful citizen."

On the bottom of the last page of the BHD Memorial Fund document dated 10-30-82 was a short hand-written note to me from Lyman. It reads, "Here it is Honey–Thanks for starting the idea."

Following one of my contributions, the Department of Journalism at the University of Illinois sent me this letter:

> *Dear Ms Puccini:*
>
> *On behalf of the journalism students and faculty at the University of Illinois, I want to thank you for your generous gift to The Betty Hinckle Dunn Fund. We are very excited about the ways in which the fund honoring Mrs. Dunn's memory will help journalism students and enrich our program.*
>
> *Sincerely,*
>
> */Signed/ Thomas B. Littlewood, Head Department of Journalism*

In Virginia I was busy with my job and enjoying pleasure riding and equestrian competition while back in Chicago Lyman was reorganizing the BHD Memorial Fund and forming a Charitable Remainder Trust with the Illini Foundation at the University of Illinois. He had sold his company and was in the process of establishing another. Nancy was away at Virginia Tech, competing in equestrian events on weekends. When she came home for the summer we often rode together because we boarded our horses at the same stable.

Lyman was making changes in his life. He married my friend Cissie, who had been a business associate with his company for many years, and they would be living on the northwest side of Chicago, not far from the new business Lyman had started with another partner. Lyman was working with the trust relations officers at the University of Illinois and the BHD Memorial Fund was enlarged and renamed the Betty and Lyman Dunn Charitable Remainder Trust. The trust was moving forward with provisions for scholarships, fellowships, and guest speakers.

Nancy was in her junior year in college when she called to tell me about an equestrian event about to take place not far from where I was living. I said, "Fine, I'll watch the competition." She said, "No Mom, I think you should *enter* the competition." She knew my horse could handle the course and the level of competition described in her equestrian literature, because she had used the same horse for lessons in preparation for her A-Level test the previous month. Her riding instructor said Beowulf was "well-schooled." I dismissed the fact that I was 55 years old, was a novice rider, and had never competed in a combined training event. With my daughter's blessings, I mailed the entry fee and arranged to have the horse trailored to the event.

We arrived at the competition, hoping we were prepared to take a dressage test, gallop a mile-and-a-half cross-country course over fourteen obstacles, and complete the event with the stadium phase, jumping twelve more fences, oxers, and barrels. All three phases of the event were to be completed in less than one day. I walked the cross-country course and became jittery when I saw all the obstacles flagged and numbered. Coops, hay bales, ditches, redwood benches, and stone walls were set up at various intervals on the course. Then I looked at the young athletic riders walking the course and asked myself, "What in Heaven's name am I doing here with all these young athletes?" At the same time, Beowulf decided he was missing his stablemates, none of which were at the event, and exercised his vocal chords in calling for his mates. He called and called and was making me very nervous. I was hoping he would see another horse he liked and quiet down. No such luck. He was upset and made sure everyone knew it. I tried to keep him busy by feeding him hay, which was merely rewarding him for the wrong behavior. Now we were both upset. The time came for our dressage test, exactly at 12:03 p.m. I knew I was not a quitter, and decided neither was my horse. We walked over to the dressage ring and waited for the judge's whistle. At that signal I tried to head Beowulf in a straight line to the center of the ring where he was to halt foursquare, but Beowulf decided it was more important to look around the event area for familiar horses and neighs, instead of concentrating on what I was asking him to do. He jigged at the halt, and reduced the 20-meter circles by a few meters. Fortunately, he was very accurate at changing gaits and picking up the right leads or we may have ended up at the bottom of the list. I walked him out of the ring very disappointed in his performance, knowing he was capable of so much more. We looked up to see his stablemate and rider waiting for him, too late for the test; but I was extremely grateful for their presence. Back at our trailer, the horses calmly enjoyed each other and some more hay. I decided to forget the test and enjoy a ham and cheese sandwich and a soda, before warming up for the cross-country gallop.

Having Beowulf's stablemate on the event grounds proved to be a real stabilizer. Beowulf immediately stopped looking around, and I started concentrating on our warm-up exercises for the cross-country course. We were doing fine, but I was beginning to feel the jitters again. I hoped he wouldn't sense my nervousness, which might make him hesitant in approaching the jumps. The result could be a strong canter followed by a refusal at the jump that would catapult me over his head and onto the ground.

Our cross-country time was rapidly approaching, so Beowulf and I headed for the starting box. In the starting box I heard the starter counting down, "10, 9, 8, are you ready?" I wondered, "Has anyone ever said "no" in this situation?" Should I make history by withdrawing now? No, I am not a quitter. The starter continued, 7, 6, 5, 4, 3, 2, 1, GO!" And we were off. I could see by the way Beowulf jumped the first obstacle, boldly and with great impulsion, that he was up to taking this course in stride. We had never jumped a coffin ditch before, however, and I didn't know what he might do. If he refused very strongly, I could be propelled onto the ground ahead, or even worse, could fall into the coffin ditch. A coffin ditch looks just like it sounds—a rectangular hole, large enough to accommodate a human body, horizontally. After walking the course the day before the event, I called Nancy to express my concerns about it. She suggested that I "go real fast and maybe Beowulf won't see it."

Nancy knows horses, I thought, as I continued on course. I'll just have to take her advice. We cleared fences number 2 and 3, the combination 4A and B, fence number 5, the Helsinki at 6, the tall brush at 7, a coop with hay bales at 8, another coop and over a fence followed by a sharp left turn to fence 9. Oops! A quick stop and popover, then on to fences 10 and 11, after which I was to "go real fast and maybe Beowulf won't see the coffin ditch," number 12. Hah! We went "real fast," but *he saw it*, took a flying leap, and galloped off as if chased by predators from the hole. His impulsion forced me back into my saddle, from which I had to regain my jump position for jump number 13, a giant redwood picnic bench at the top of the hill. He jumped the bench with such enthusiasm I could hardly make him turn into the 14th jump, a stone wall. As we cleared the final obstacle, I heard a crowd cheering and waving their arms out in the field to my right. My friend, a group of young pony-clubbers, and their parents were happy to see a "pony-club mother" in the competition. They were impressed with Beowulf's performance, especially since so many horses were eliminated because of refusals. It was the longest ride and jumping exercise I had ever completed. I was thrilled, but exhausted. Beowulf had redeemed himself. I knew he would do well on the final phase, stadium jumping, and he did. He went clean, and I was happy we placed eighth out of twenty competitors in our division, with a total of eighty entries in the entire competition.

When Nancy called that evening to see how Beowulf and I scored in our first event, all I could say was, "Where do you get the energy and strength to do this?" I also realized why she had spent so little time hanging out with her peers in high school. Pony club and academics were much more important to her. There was enough socializing in pony club and at the pony barn to satisfy her. I went to work the next day and told my staff what I had done the day before. Again each of them told me, "I can't believe you did this!" Two days later day I showed them the photographs of the event, photos of my galloping cross-country and over the jumps. From then on, they never questioned any of my adventures.

After the equestrian event I felt I had reached another goal. I had overcome my fear of horses and enjoyed my riding more than ever. My riding provided me with a sense of accomplishment that I was never able to feel as a child growing up on the farm in Wisconsin. I felt a sense of achievement similar to that of graduating from high school, college, and even graduate school. But somehow something was still missing. I remembered how our search for housing during our Navy moves turned out to be an adventure, and so did our adjustments to those houses we eventually occupied, those houses obviously designed for someone else. Kitchens were often inadequate for the type of entertaining we did. Garages were often at the wrong end of the house, so that groceries and party supplies had to be carried through several rooms before reaching the kitchen. One house we rented was especially weird. The garage was appropriately attached to the house, but there was no door for access to the inside. This made it necessary to walk out the back door of the garage, into the back yard, and then reverse course to re-enter the house through the back door of the kitchen. With arms full of groceries, two sets of doors plus storm doors, this could be a chore in good weather. In rain, snow, and sleet, it was dreadful. In the back of my mind, I found myself redesigning every house we lived in.

In 1983, I decided it was time for me to design a house that was suitable for my lifestyle. I spent several weeks in the library studying passive solar houses and waited impatiently for each new issue of magazines dealing with the subject. After ruling out undesirable features, I sat down with graph paper, ruler, pencil and calculator; allotted the appropriate portions for heat source, heat sink, and thermal mass; and presented my design to three builders. In 1984, I was enjoying the experience of watching my design rise from the ground, reach for the sun, and become a beautiful energy-efficient home. I finally had a house suitable for the lifestyle of this speech and language pathologist with two horses.

The house was situated on land I had purchased

several years earlier in Middleburg, Virginia, a beautiful twenty-one acre parcel with lovely hayfields and woods. I would need shelter for my horses along with paddocks, pastures, and a riding arena. I designed a stable to match a scaled-down version of the main portion of the house and added floodlights and jumps for the riding arena. I felt I had now gone full circle back to the farm, with my brothers and brother-in-law offering good advice regarding the farming end of this experience. I was a speech pathologist-turned-farmer involved with liming, fertilizing, and harvesting a hay crop and an active member of various farm agencies.

My early childhood experiences on the farm, followed by life as a Navy wife, contributed to my self-sufficient ways, which were proving to be immensely helpful with my farming experience. Like my brothers, I believed I could do anything. When it came time for the hay to be baled and stored in my barn, I hired and supervised the help. On one of these harvests we found ourselves short a driver for one of the tractors, so I drove the huge, tall tractor and pulled the hay wagon around the fields while three men picked up the hay and stacked it on the wagon. I felt the excitement I remembered as a child when I watched the threshing crew come down Maule Coulee Road to start loading the shocks of grain from our farm fields. I was proudly driving along when, above the noise of the tractor, I heard the men yelling, "Slow down! Slow down!" I looked at the instruments on the tractor and realized I had no idea about what to do to control the big, powerful, unwieldy vehicle I was driving. I quickly responded to their panic-like yelling by shouting as loud as I could, "I can't, I don't know how! You'll just have to keep running until I run out of gas!" With that, one of the men jumped up on the side of the tractor and made some sensible adjustments. We backtracked and picked up the bales they missed earlier when I went speeding by. After the hay was safely in the barn before the rain threatened to ruin the crop, I brought out the beer and sloppy-joes and joined my hired help for a picnic on the hay wagon.

While I was busy working full time as a speech pathologist, managing a small farmette, and caring for and riding two horses, Nancy completed her undergraduate work at Virginia Tech and was granted a graduate assistantship in the labor and industrial relations department at the University of Illinois. At the same time she was in graduate school, Lyman had finalized his trust agreement with the university and plans for graduate assistantships, undergraduate scholarships, and guest speakers were complete. On April 10, 1984, Lyman received the following letter from the department of journalism at the university:

> *Dear Mr. Dunn:*
>
> *The first Betty Hinckle Dunn lecture will be at 8 p.m., Thursday, April 26, in Room 112 (Auditorium) of Gregory Hall on the campus. The speaker will be Van Gordon Sauter, the president of CBS News, who will talk on television and the presidential election. We're expecting a big turn-out and hope you can join us for the evening. After his talk, there will be a reception in the Library Room of the Levis Faculty Center beginning about 9 p.m.*

> *Please try to be with us for the first in what we fully expect to be a distinguished series of Betty Hinckle Dunn lectures.*
>
> *Sincerely,*
>
> */Signed/ Thomas B. Littlewood, Head
> Department of Journalism*

I was unable to attend the lecture so I asked Nancy to represent me. Since she was already a graduate student on campus, she joined Lyman for Mr. Sauter's speech and reception and found it to be an interesting and enjoyable evening.

When I made my first donation to this department of journalism after Betty's death two years previously, I never dreamed it would lead to such important speakers being invited to address journalism students. I merely hoped that my donation would, in some small way, help a worthy student through college. With Nancy in graduate school, our family was becoming heavily degreed: Joe had three degrees, I had two, Nancy was getting her second, and her horse, Lincoln, had an "honorary bachelor's degree" for his four years at Virginia Tech. Not only was I pleased with the Illini Foundation's work with journalism students, I felt doubly blessed with Nancy's acceptance and financial assistance. Lyman told me that it took almost two years to finalize this charitable trust and I'm sure he felt it was worth the effort. His college career was saved in 1928, I was awarded a four-year tuition scholarship in 1946, another cash scholarship in 1949, and Nancy was given a graduate assistantship in 1983. As if that was not enough, I would later become a beneficiary of the charitable remainder trust.

    I was feeling grateful and happy with the course my life had taken when reality set in. I remembered Lyman's long, lovely tribute to Betty, dated October 30, 1982; the endowment agreement signed and sealed on October 28, 1985; when on the morning of October 30, 1986, at precisely 7:50 a.m., Cissie called me at my office to tell me that Lyman had died of a massive heart attack at 2:30 that morning. I didn't tell anyone on the staff at the health department where I worked but went on to see all the clients I had scheduled for that day. During my lunch break while everyone was out of the office, I made plane reservations to leave as soon as possible. Cissie, Lyman's widow, who had picked me up that evening after Betty's funeral, met me at O'Hare Airport. Just as I had four years earlier, I shared the ride down to Bloomington, Illinois, where we attended the memorial service and a graveside ceremony. The service was almost identical to Betty's. In fact, many of the same people were in attendance. The only new participants, whom I met for the first time, were the representatives from the trust relations department of the University of Illinois Foundation. We all left the cemetery located in the central part of the state and went our separate ways: east, south, west, and north. Lyman had already left to join his "darling Betty," exactly four years to the day that he wrote his loving tribute to her, dated October 30, 1982.

    A short obituary written by Norma Payne, my foster sister, was published after Lyman's death and mailed to his many friends and business associates (see Appendix A). There was no need to embellish or expand a tribute to him. We were all well aware of his brilliance and his accomplishments.

Lyman's most successful enterprise was probably the Marlan Company that he founded and of which he was chairman and president. His products included adhesives and sealants, office machines, automatic merchandising machines, and ice cream and frozen desserts. The standard industrial classification numbers for these products were listed in *Standard and Poors*. It was the company he sold to set up the charitable remainder trust with the University of Illinois Foundation. He had plans in progress, however, for a new company on the near north side of Chicago when he was stricken with his fatal heart attack. Lyman was not about to retire—ever.

I was seventeen years old when I met this happy, loving couple and fifty-nine years old when they left me for their lasting peace. They treated me as one of their own. I will always have the wonderful memories of our times together. They taught me to appreciate the simple and the elegant, from picnics and free concerts in the parks to box seats at the theaters and symphonies. Betty would often take me with her when she arranged her national conventions. One of the most memorable of these times occurred soon after I had met her. She was making arrangements for a national convention of journalists and one of our stops was at an office in the Wrigley Building in Chicago. At a concession booth in the lobby I bought the first pack of Wrigley's

Spearmint Gum available after World War II. We had a wonderful time, bumming around Chicago and chewing gum for the first time since World War II had imposed its rationing restrictions.

Lyman was always available to help any of us, together or privately, and we all admired his brilliance. He and Betty had given us so much of themselves. They both were extremely talented and they shared their gifts with everyone they knew. I consider myself one of the luckiest people in the world to have known them. My goal has been to pass along what they had given me and I hope I have given as much of myself in the forty years I spent in my career helping the less fortunate.

After bidding farewell to Lyman, I continued riding with equestrian friends, enjoying both the physical exercise and social activities related to equestrian events. I must, however, give credit due to Nancy and her pony club for my interest in horses. Without my exposure to her activities with that group I may have never overcome my fear of horses. By watching those tenacious youngsters in pony club and at the pony barn, I was able to learn from them and overcome my fears, and by observing those youngsters, I learned a great deal about the management of horses. Stories of events that took place at the pony barn often were humorous. In one incident a young pony stabled at the pony barn grew an especially heavy winter coat and was slow in shedding it in the springtime. To keep it from becoming over-heated during warm spring riding, its young owner decided to clip its fur coat. The pony rebelled at the sound of the electric clippers and refused to cooperate. No problem. The little girl gave it a tranquilizing shot. Still, it would not cooperate. So she gave it a second shot, which worked all too well. The pony lay down and couldn't be aroused. Two little girls quickly clipped the exposed half of its fur coat. Knowing they would have to finish the job before it regained its full spunkiness they solicited help from fellow riders. While several of them raised and held the pony upright the young owner was able to clip the other half. No proud pony rider was about to have anyone see her half-clipped pony in the paddock or on the trail.

Beowulf and I went on to trail-riding and hunter-jumping class competitions. His honesty and willingness to jump were real assets. These traits helped us win reserve champion ribbons in hunter classes. Meanwhile, Nancy received her masters degree from the University of Illinois. When she became established professionally in the field of labor and industrial relations, she purchased another horse, a new trailer, and continued her equestrian competition. Now she was competing successfully with Olympic team members and other international riders. My heart leaped to my throat at times, as I watched her master those cross-country and stadium obstacles. She was competing with professional riders, while holding a responsible position in the corporate world. I often thought about those high school days when we worked with pony club. How she trained an obstinate mare to become a first-class pony club event horse; how she progressed from the D level to capture that coveted A-level rating. I remember when she was invited to hunt with a group of women in a prestigious Virginia hunt. When she returned I asked her if there were any older women, like me, in the hunt. She replied, "Mom, they were not only old like you; they were jumping five-foot fences." I wondered if any of their horses went to college for four years and earned honorary bachelors degrees.

Horses became a large part of our lives. My daughter and I each added horses to our stables and rode together when she happened to be working in the area. Ordinarily, when companies transfer employees, they move furniture and household effects. In Nancy's case, they transported a horse and her pick-up truck. It seemed she was always on the road, pulling a trailer with a horse or two. Whereas she continued to be a serious competitor, I was satisfied with riding for pleasure. I would ride with all ages. Youngsters especially liked to ride with Beowulf. Quite often we would come upon a group of young riders struggling with ponies that refused to cross a bridge or a stream along the trails. No problem. They would wait for Beowulf to come along. He would lead them across and they would all follow. And I was finally learning what it was like to have a childhood.

Adeline (Jo) Kulig and Lieutenant Commander Joe Puccini leave the Wedding Chapel at the United States Navy Postgraduate School, Monterey, California, on June 18, 1960.

Adeline (Jo), Nancy, and Joe Puccini on Nancy's first birthday, May 12, 1962.

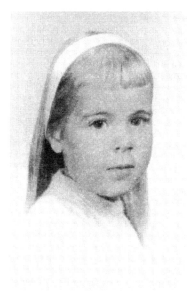

Nancy Puccini at age four.

Jo and Beowulf "on course" during the cross-country phase of a 1982 equestrian event.

Below: Jo and Beowulf compete in the stadium-jumping phase of the event (1982).

Below: Jo and Beowulf relax after a day of show-jumping (1984).

Nancy Puccini and Party Time on course (cross-country) in Las Cruces, New Mexico (1986).

Below: Nancy Puccini and Party Time taking a Dressage Test in Phoenix, Arizona (1987).

CHAPTER 14

PIETY REVISITED

COMBINING my career with farming, landscaping, lawn mowing, horseback riding, and caring for my horses was a busy life indeed. After a day at work, I would join my neighbors for a trail ride, feed the horses, build a fire in the fireplace, take a shower, eat a quickly prepared dinner, sit down before a warm fire with the newspaper, and before I finished the first page I would fall asleep in my chair. I would stagger off to the bedroom, set the alarm for an early wake-up in order to feed the horses before starting to work. I remember times in winter when it was dark I would go to the stable to find the horses still asleep. After feeding them, I would leave for work in the dark to meet my carpool in Middleburg for the twenty-five mile drive through the Virginia countryside to congested Fairfax to work. It was a demanding life, but I thrived and remained very healthy.

Not long after I took up farming, my brother Adolph retired from a job he had held for thirty-three years in La Crosse, Wisconsin. Adolph never married. The years of abuse from Julia, along with her demeaning treatment of my father could very likely have influenced him in his decision to remain single. It was not surprising that he should find marriage a frightening venture. He was generous with his time, money, and energy and he had the kindest, most pleasant disposition I have ever known. His concern for others was evident in everything he did. From that day in 1945 when he left me in Milwaukee and watched me ride the train alone on my first trip to Chicago, I could see he was a man who would always be concerned about others.

I tried not to abuse his generosity, but the farm venture turned out to be expensive for me. More than once I turned to him for financial help. He had helped me so many times earlier when I was making career moves, and now he was again ready to lend me whatever I needed. His retirement made it possible for him to visit me at any time. He made several trips out to my farm and seemed to enjoy helping me by splitting, stacking, and hauling wood. We would take driving trips together and visit cities on the east coast. His time in the Navy gave him a lasting love for travel and a need to move about the country freely. In his retirement years, he bought a home and was living comfortably near our hometown. Eleanore, Verna and her husband, and Ed also visited me at the farm. I was looking forward to my retirement when I would have more time to spend with them.

Before I retired from my position with the Virginia State Department of Health, I had already made plans to share my professional experience and materials with the education department in San Jose, Costa Rica; and through the Wisconsin-Nicaragua Partnership, I made contacts in Managua and Bluefields, Nicaragua. I retired from my position with the health department on December 31, 1989, forty years after my first therapy session at the speech and hearing clinic at the University of Illinois. Through my visits to Central America, I remained interested in sharing my professional experiences.

Meanwhile, after ten years on the farm, friends were openly expressing concern about my being alone in the country. I had private guest quarters on my property that I rented out, but my tenant was just as independent as I was and I rarely saw her. I finally came to terms with the fact that farming and maintaining the property was too much work and responsibility for one person. I sold my younger horse, and gave my long-time friend Beowulf to a girl as a wedding gift. She used him to teach youngsters how to ride and was so pleased with his performance that she decided to use him in her country wedding. The occasion was special for him. He enjoyed the attention he was given by photographers and guests as he walked down a country lane carrying the bridesmaid and flower girl. After the ceremony, he was rewarded with more than his share of carrots, which guests loaded on plates at the refreshment tables and vied for opportunities to feed him in his paddock. Following the reception, he willingly walked around the paddock for all the youngsters waiting their turns to ride him. I was pleased to see that he had a good home before I put my dream home and property up for sale. It sold quickly, and I moved to a retirement community in August 1996, where I would have no responsibilities and would be free to travel.

A family reunion coincided with the time I was moving and I was unable to make the trip home. The shakedown process of my new residence was taking longer than I had expected, and my unpacking was being delayed. I was in the middle of trying to decide which cartons to open first when the phone rang. It was my brother Ed. Three of my brothers, including Ed, were planning to pick up Adolph before they drove to the reunion near Minneapolis, but when they reached his home, he didn't answer the door. They called Cliff for the extra key, opened the door, saw the light on in the bathroom, and found Adolph lying on the bathroom floor. He was getting ready for the reunion when he collapsed and died suddenly. In a letter written to me earlier that year he stated that his doctor told him he needed a new heart. Adolph had said that he didn't want a new heart. He wanted to keep his own. I shared his feelings and most sincerely agree with his decision because no heart could possibly replace the one he had.

I left my partially unpacked cartons and made arrangements to fly home immediately. We were all saddened by Adolph's passing. It seemed that a master clock had started to tick down for all of us.

Adolph had my father's cardiac symptoms, yet he outlived him by seven years. A military funeral service was beautifully and efficiently carried out. I was impressed. I had gone to many Navy burial services, aboard aircraft carriers and in Arlington Cemetery, but the one for Adolph was special. He was laid to rest next to those who had fallen during World War II, many of them during my high school years. His will was opened before I returned to Virginia. Adolph left a sizable estate to all of us, including our half-sisters and the half-brother on the farm. He also generously rewarded his many charities. Again I felt that no heart could have replaced the one he took with him to his grave.

Adolph had lived a good life and many will long remember his generosity. He died two days before he planned to leave on a vacation, and we were thankful he was home near family at the time of his death. We all knew that he was a model citizen and believed he would be well rewarded in the hereafter for his good deeds in life. Such positive feelings on our part made grieving appropriately short. Furthermore, we learned early in life that protracted grieving is counter-productive; therefore, we all made the necessary adjustments and went on with our lives. I returned to my new residence, finished unpacking, and settled down for what I hoped would be my last move.

After completing my unpacking, I began making plans for more traveling. A trip to Spain and Portugal was followed by a cruise of the Eastern Mediterranean, Greece, the Greek Isles, Turkey, and the Black Sea with stops at Odessa and Yalta in Russia, and Constanta in Rumania. Each year I planned a major trip, including Eastern Europe, Canada and the Northwest National Parks, and finally, a cruise to Alaska and the Far East, including Japan, Korea, Vladivostok in Russia, and Shanghai and Hong Kong in China. In between these major trips, I made regular trips home to Wisconsin and, also Arizona, where I visited nieces and their families.

Not long after Eleanore and her husband moved to Arizona, he died after a severe stroke and heart attack. Although Eleanore lived near a daughter in Arizona, she was encouraged to return to Independence to live in a senior retirement apartment near her brothers and sister. She moved back to Independence into a retirement home near town, where driving was less demanding, and spent the cold winters with her daughter in Arizona. I made it a point to visit her and my niece's family in Arizona each year, and that wonderful relaxed feeling I remembered from my times spent on their farm would inevitably return. My last visit with them in Arizona was especially memorable, but unfortunately it would turn out to be the last visit for Eleanore. Two weeks after her return to Wisconsin, Verna made her daily phone call one morning and received no answer. She called Eleanore's neighbor across the hall and asked her to check on Eleanore. The neighbor returned to the phone with bad news. Eleanore was found on the floor near the refrigerator with the door open, holding an unopened container of orange juice.

The day of Eleanore's funeral was cold, combined with the kind of blizzard that I remembered from my childhood days on the farm. Fortunately, her family was able to fly in from Arizona before the airports were closed and before flights were diverted or delayed. The weather did not prevent family and friends from attending the funeral. Wisconsinites know how to cope with bad weather, and relatives and friends came from near and far. In spite of Eleanore's grieving family, I was able to keep my composure throughout the entire service. As the congregation left their pews, we followed the casket up to a point near the vestibule and turned left just short of the exit, to a stairway leading down to the social hall in the lower level of the church. I stopped in front of the heavy glass door of the side entrance to the church, and as the crowd filed past behind me, I stood and watched the pallbearers place the casket into the hearse for the drive to the mausoleum. The storm was raging furiously and my tears flowed unchecked as I bade my final farewell to a loving sister who stood by me during my troubled childhood with Julia. She sustained brutality like a martyr and never complained to anyone. I couldn't seem to move, so I just stood there. The frightening memories of Julia gashing Eleanore's skull for no better reason other than having dressed Julia's daughter in the wrong dress, or making a hot dish Julia didn't like, or going to a dance with her cousins, all flashed before me. All those bloody noses and blows to the head for so many years were suddenly frozen in time and I couldn't bring myself to leave that glass door. As tears flowed, the sadness I felt turned to anger. Why couldn't someone have helped us? She had sacrificed her own safety to protect us. I could only hope that her years of martyrdom were not in vain. Although Eleanore felt she was rewarded in her lifetime, I believe she deserved much more. I dried my tears and walked down to the social hall feeling a sad void in my life. Just as I was beginning to think I was never going to get over this loss, I saw my sister Verna waving to me to join her at the buffet. Verna was stoicism personified, and I wasn't going to disappoint her by not appreciating the crowd of mourners who came to remember Eleanore.

During the reception and buffet following the funeral service, I thought about all the things I would miss about Eleanore. She had been widowed for almost nineteen years but she remained socially very active. Before she and her husband sold the farm where so many family reunions had been held, it was home to Nancy and me when we were in-between military moves. My daughter spent many summers with Eleanore and her husband and developed a keen interest in animals, an interest she still expresses through her equestrian activities. After her return from Arizona, Eleanore continued her social activities at the senior housing facility where she lived. During my visits to her apartment, I could see she was a real asset to her neighbors. Her ability to take the initiative in creating activities for other residents would be missed by all who were fortunate to know her. Without her upbeat and positive attitude, my visits to Wisconsin and that senior facility would never be the same.

After friends and relatives left the reception, I decided to go back up to the sanctuary to see the large stained glass windows, memorials offered by Kulig relatives many years earlier. The raging blizzard outdoors, hiding all traces of sunlight, did not lessen their beauty. I moved up the long center isle to the front of the church. The large confessionals at the front were symbolic of our need to renew our promises to make amends for past failures in our less-than-perfect lives. These huge oak structures with their ornately carved Gothic designs were worthy of the piety they enclosed. If privacy was the objective of the architects who designed them, it was almost always achieved. The priest, as confessor, entered these confessionals and discreetly closed the door with the velvet drape behind him. Parishioners waiting to be absolved of their misdeeds entered through a side door and knelt before a little window opening. Privacy was never breached, except in cases where the little window through which one piously confessed was wrongly positioned; that is, too high for short people and too low for tall people. This inevitably resulted in the hard-of-hearing confessor to ask his parishioner to "speak up!" whereupon those within earshot waiting their turns assumed that the poor confessant had done something either terribly wrong or very exciting.

I recall several occasions when I watched my father as he emerged from the confessional and walked piously back to his pew. Each time I would ask myself, "What could this quiet, devout, and kind man possibly have to confess?" He never lost his temper and he never raised his voice to anyone in the family. "Martyrdom surely is no sin," I thought. On the other hand, this time of confession would have been a good opportunity for him to tell the elderly monsignor about what was happening to us in our home. But there is no commandment saying, "Thou shalt protect thy children." Furthermore, my father probably was not aware of Julia's behavior during our earlier years. As we grew older and the abuse got worse, he seemed helpless to protect us. Perhaps he was silently hoping that we would fight back, but our piety kept us from doing that. Merely thinking about fighting her made us feel that we would have to confess another transgression against that fourth commandment—Honor thy father and thy mother. As far as my father's marriage to Julia was concerned, we all felt trapped by that marriage vow and its precept called "permanency." Julia, on the other hand, was protected by it. She knew she was firmly entrenched and any thought of getting rid of her would never be followed up with action. Our piety overruled any consideration of that and presented a frustrating dilemma about fighting back and protecting ourselves.

When it came to judging piety in our family, we would probably agree that Adolph was the big winner. We often joked about it. We could always count on him to be the most charitable contributor to any fundraising affair. All who knew him admired his good citizenship, but shortly before he retired he was unfortunate enough to get a traffic ticket for speeding and we were surprised beyond belief. The news spread quickly in the family and we could hardly wait to hear his side of the story. When we did, we all laughed so heartily that he decided it was going to be his claim to fame. And the more he had to say about the incident, the harder we laughed. I wonder if his piety made him feel that this episode was a transgression serious enough to be mentioned during his next visit to the confessional. Why not? Like my father, what else could Adolph possibly have to confess?

Then of course, almost neck-to-neck with Adolph in the piety contest, was Eleanore. Actually, the two of them differed only in type of religious fervor. Adolph was seriously pious while Eleanore embraced such a light-hearted sense in her piety that I often wished I could be more like her. She could be serious in a most light-hearted kind of way; or, light-hearted in a serious way. This may sound contradictory, but quite frankly it is difficult to describe her deep religious fervor without acknowledging her gift for having fun and making others happy. I believe she could even make going to confession a fun experience. Listening to one of her confessions must have been a refreshing change for her confessor. I somehow got the feeling that there was not much variety in the transgressions by that long line of pious folks waiting their turns for confession. I'm sure Eleanore provided a welcome change indeed. She had her own interpretation of what constituted a transgression of any kind, including the Ten Commandments. Between Adolph and Eleanore, it would be difficult to choose the better model for piety. They both suffered unwarranted abuse by Julia and deserved lasting rewards in the hereafter.

With our parochial training, it would seem that there would have been more discussion among my siblings regarding our religious beliefs. Surely nine different personalities could have nine different interpretations of the scriptures we were taught. It was obvious to us that Julia had her own interpretation of Christian rules of conduct. Her doctrine of Christianity was heavily laced with opportunism. It seems that we all silently agreed and never questioned the piety pranks she used to dominate us. If we thought she was wrong in using her questionable piety to condone her behavior, we never discussed any measures to put an end to her abuse. We had many opportunities to arrange a coup, whereby she would have been intimidated and have retreated. The Maule boys had a few suggestions, like putting her into an outside oven and "smoking her out!" They were free to make jokes about getting rid of her; she was not their stepmother, and they didn't have to confess any such transgressions. At any rate, amusing us with their suggestions was great sport and gave us badly needed psychological relief. It did wonders to rid us of the guilty feelings Julia unjustly laid on us. We all knew deep down in our souls that if we made any attempt to intimidate her, she would turn on my father—and we were always afraid of that. In fact, we turned out to be exactly right in our concerns, because after Ben, my sisters, and I were gone from home, she did attack my father. It was one of these episodes that triggered his plan to initiate divorce proceedings, but Julia already knew that she could stop him.

Again, our hopes for my father had been dashed. We became reconciled to the fact that he was destined to continue his life of martyrdom, and if we couldn't save him, we would do our best to save ourselves. My sisters were happily married and had families, and one by one my brothers left the farm. I was secure with my exciting family in Chicago, and had long since given up on rescuing my father. Anton had tried to purchase the farm but was met with the shotgun diplomacy of Julia's oldest son living on the farm. Our only choice was to accept the situation and follow the pious precepts we had been taught, each in our own way. We had done all that we could to help him. Confessions continued to be a source of spiritual renewal for all of us, and we felt blessed in our own lives.

On my flight back to Virginia after Eleanore's funeral, I realized that almost thirty-five years had passed since my father's death, and I found I was again pondering the dilemma my father had faced. He, Adolph, and Eleanore had found their lasting peace, yet I still could not accept the circumstances under which we had grown up. We were all denied a normal childhood but managed to move on successfully and become productive members of society. None of my siblings expressed any malice or vindictiveness toward Julia. For this I will be eternally grateful and proud. We all wish we could have done some things differently; however, no one in my family will ever have to regret any act of ill will or revenge. How Julia reconciled her behavior with her piety was not for us to judge. Yet, repressed childhood experiences have a way of motivating one to ponder and reflect. Perhaps it was the emergence of these repressed feelings that made me recall a parish meeting I had attended sixteen years earlier, where a priest from the Diocese of Arlington, Virginia, addressed the subject of annulments in the Catholic Church. When I arrived home after the flight, before unpacking my bags, I decided to check my files for any notes regarding that meeting. What I found, written on the back of an old envelope, was the following information.

"Grounds for Annulment:"

1. Every person has a right to a valid marriage.

2. A marriage is made by consent between partners.

3. Criteria for a valid marriage:

    a. Exclusivity—faithfulness to each other.

    b. Permanency.

    c. Openness to children.

A long-forgotten childhood experience came vividly to mind as I recalled that day when I was about five years and eight months old, when Julia's mother came to visit. I remembered Julia's argument with her mother before I quietly went outdoors and waited near the milk house where my father was working. Then I remembered how Julia's mother stormed out of the house to find my father near where I waited quietly. In her strident, exasperating voice, she pleaded with my father. At first I thought she wanted him to take Julia's out-of-wedlock child, who was about four months old, but my father was firm. He had no need for more children. Julia's mother persevered and went on pleading and stating her case. I was bilingual at the time of this confrontation but this knowledge was hardly necessary. My father's demeanor clearly showed he was not interested in her proposal. Julia's mother raced back to the house for further confrontation with Julia while her oldest brother waited in his car.

So why was there a wedding within two months? Did Julia's mother coerce her and my father to go to our parish priest to finalize the marriage arrangements? From what I witnessed that day, this agreement clearly was not a "marriage made by consent between partners." And, "openness to children" was highly questionable. "Permanency" prevailed, much to our consternation, but the out-of-wedlock child never became part of our family.

The entire episode between Julia's mother and my father on that warm spring day in 1933 had taken place while my brothers and sisters were in school. After they came home from school, it didn't occur to me to tell any of them what had transpired that day. My heart breaks when I think of all those years we suffered through that marriage between Julia and my father—a marriage of questionable validity. The irony of it all is the fact that the piety that trapped us could have saved us in the end. Grounds for annulment certainly existed from the very beginning.

I looked at my suitcases and had no desire to unpack them. My unopened mail lay where I tossed it—on the desk in my den. I am usually anxious to open my mail, but that day I just slumped into the nearest comfortable chair. All I could think of right then, was why it had taken all these painful years to find the solution to my family's dilemma. Now that it was too late I just sat and stared out the window, thinking about that beautiful warm spring day back on the farm when I waited by the milk house and listened while my father remained essentially speechless, as his entire future was being reshaped and destroyed.

The sun had gone down and the sunset was beautiful, but I could not bring myself to get out of that chair. My mind was overflowing with memories of our unhappy childhood. I tried to find solace in the success my brothers and sisters had achieved, but my thoughts kept going back to my father's troubled life. After all, he was the real victim during those years of protracted conflict. My den grew dark, but I didn't feel like getting up and turning on a light. I continued to look out at the beautiful sunset and watched the sun disappear through the tall oaks and over the horizon when I suddenly recalled the last words I heard my father speak: "You shouldn't force someone to (pause) . . . you shouldn't force them to . . ." It was all finally beginning to make sense. Coercion was implicit in every decision he had made since that day when I was five years old as I watched and listened by the milk house.

CHAPTER 15

REFLECTIONS

THE question, "What's in a name?" has inspired many people to study and research, to spend years looking for their roots. Some day I hope to find the time to join this group of ambitious genealogists and search more deeply for my roots. In the meantime, I am satisfied with what others have found for me. In a research paper written by the late Professor Edmund Zawicki of the University of Wisconsin, he discusses the life of immigrants from Poland who settled in Wisconsin, their reasons for leaving their homeland, and the nature of their settlements in this country. As far back as 1588, the name *Kulig* showed up prominently in tax records of the provinces where they lived. News of available land on this side of the Atlantic was exciting and luring to Kulig families in Poland. Although they were living comfortably in their homeland, word of great opportunities in America prompted them to sell their properties in Poland and immigrate to America. It was not surprising that my grandfather's greatest ambition was to acquire land in his new homeland, and in this effort he was highly successful. An outdoor museum called a *Skansen,* located near the Odra River in southwestern Poland, a popular attraction to visitors, included a Kulig exhibit from the original Kulig property near Opole. Unfortunately, a major flood that devastated the area in 1996, washed away the museum, including the Kulig exhibit.

The name *Kulig* is mentioned again in the book *Madame Curie, Daughter of Poland* by Robert Woznicki, Ph.D. His research portrays the life of this brilliant lady who grew up in Warsaw, Poland, as Maria Sklodowska, the daughter of a school principal and teacher, before she went to Paris to continue her graduate studies at the Sorbonne and where she later married her scientist husband, Pierre Curie. In his book, Woznicki relates Madame Curie's description of her life in Poland as a young girl. The following special event from the book evokes images of my childhood and gives some insight into the fun-loving nature of young people of Polish descent, especially the sleigh rides, the dances, the Halloween and Christmas pranks, and the memorable wedding "shivaree" with all its mock features and surprises.

"Life was carefree and peaceful—There was often a winter-joust sport called a Kulig. Maria's first Kulig was a tremendous experience that she was to recall many times in her life. The night was dark. But it was lit by strange northern snow-light. Maria and her three cousins, wrapped in thick rugs, masked and dressed as Polish peasants, took their places in the sledges. Their comrades were boys in rustic costumes who lit the darkness with large torches. Through the dark forest they caught glimpses of other torches approaching. The cold night was filled with music—the traveling musicians were bringing with them four young Jewish musicians who for two nights and two whole days, were to play heart-stirring music on their violins. They played waltzes and mazurkas and all would sing the refrains in chorus, making the night tuneful and noisy.

"As the musicians played, other sledges joined them out of the darkness, three, five, ten sledges. In spite of hair-raising bends and glassy slopes, the musicians never missed a note as they led the fantastic troop under the frosty stars. At the first farmhouse, the sledges stopped with jingling bells—all the company laughing and shouting as they knocked loudly on the door, arousing the residents who were only pretending to be asleep. In a few moments the musicians were hoisted onto a table and the ball began in a room lit by torches. Presently supper was brought and after a signal, the whole house emptied. A large procession (of horses and sledges) was formed to make its way through the forest to another farm. Bells would ring out as they went their merry way. On the second night the vast train of sledges stopped with snorting horses and jingling bells before the biggest homestead for the real ball.

"The fiddlers played louder. The guests took their places for the famous figure dances. The best dancer a boy, handsome and dashing in his embroidered white costume, advanced to lead out the best female dancer. He chose Maria. She was radiant. She was dressed as a mountain maiden with a velvet jacket, puffed linen sleeves, and a star-like crown decked with long, brightly colored streamers. They danced through the night. They danced a mazurka until eight in the morning. Maria (Madame Curie) said that never in her young life had she enjoyed herself so much."

Such was the life in the area of Poland left by my grandfather, his brother, and two sisters. And we carried on with some of the traditions. I remember a shivaree at Verna's farm after her wedding. It was not the surprise it was supposed to be because Verna and her husband were tipped off and they were prepared for the large crowd about to surprise them with food, beverages, and music. Verna's husband moved the furniture aside, the musicians set up their instruments in one corner of her large living room, and the dancing went on till midnight. After that, food was served and the crowd left because farm chores were waiting the following morning. My older brothers and sisters had enjoyed some of these events in spite of Julia; but unfortunately, I left the community before I was old enough to take part.

I often wished I could have heard, first hand, about their happy experiences in Poland. Unfortunately, our need to become proficient in the English language often made it difficult to communicate with the older immigrants. There was never a doubt, however, about passing on those happy Kulig spin-offs—reunions, weddings, shivarees,

Halloween and Christmas fooling, and of course, love of horses.

Although my father enjoyed automobiles and always sported the latest models during his younger years, he was a Kulig in the true sense when it came to horses. His patience was his greatest asset when it came to training them. And his patience, kindness, consistency, and tenacity were matched only by Ben's, and we already knew that Ben could do anything. In my mind and heart, I believe the following quotations speak of my father and Ben:

"(Of the horse) The noblest conquest man has ever made." George Louis Leclerc de Buffon.

"Genius is nothing but a greater aptitude for patience." George Louis Leclerc de Buffon.

"Genius is an intuitive talent for labor." Johannes Waleus.

"Patience is a necessary ingredient of genius." Disraeli.

"Genius is capacity for taking trouble." Leslie Stephen.

The dying words of my father, "You shouldn't force someone to . . ."even as an incomplete quote, fit appropriately with those of the learned men mentioned above. For him, patience and a capacity for taking trouble were paramount; coercion, never. It was always obvious that coercion was never an appropriate way for my father to solve problems. It just wasn't a part of his nature.

Yet, coercion may have indirectly played a role in my early childhood. I have always wondered if paternal grandparents or other relatives may have played a role in my early move to Uncle Bert's. Although I was accepted as part of that family, I doubt that Mrs. Bert ever felt that I would be a replacement for the infant daughter she lost. Would she have sent her young daughter into the fields to tend cows in the hot sun at age four-and-a-half? Or into the big bedroom upstairs alone at age three? Or out on the highway alone to walk over half a mile for a spool of thread at age three? I would never do that to a child, especially after knowing how frightening these experiences could be. Even at those early ages, I was able to sense a feeling of rejection.

Many questions remain about the rationale for Julia's violent behavior. Did her father mistreat her? Did the father of her out-of-wedlock son reject her? Was she coerced into marrying my father? Was she unwilling to give up her freedom after her son was born? Did the responsibility of caring for someone else's children while unable to keep and care for her own illegitimate son drive her to violence? I always felt she resented having her single life cut short and she showed her resentment during my sisters' dating years. In fact, when my brothers and sisters went out for an evening of socializing, they were invariably met with violence when they returned home. It is astonishing to see how innocent victims pay the price for the bad choices and mistakes made by adults, especially parents.

Julia, no doubt, would have liked her role as mother to eight motherless children to be publicly recognized. Her letter to Ben while he was in service, where she asked him to write a "nice" letter which she could "put in the paper" may have been an attempt for her to accomplish this. What makes this seem so absurd is the fact that she was spending the Army paychecks he was sending home to my father. It was irony enough that there were people in the community who believed she was the noble parent, people who couldn't see through the pious charade at church every Sunday; but publicizing her charade in the local paper was beyond being absurd. It would have been ludicrous. But of one thing I can be sure: the hypocrisy of Julia's pious walks up the church aisle every Sunday was exposed by my barefoot walk down the creek to the Maule farm on that fateful day in the summer of 1941.

Julia could have been lauded for her role in our family had she actually fulfilled the role as most people thought. I had many opportunities to write to the editor of our local paper and would have been delighted to acknowledge Julia's good deeds in a letter for publication. But she destroyed her chances for an honorable recognition, over and over and over again. As Clarence mentioned in his four-page letter citing her abuses, "This doesn't even make a dent in the total amount of abuse" we lived through. For that matter, neither does this story.

When Nancy was about five years old, we spent a long weekend with the Trapp Family in a "Music on the Mountain" weekend in Vermont. We met the delightful Maria Von Trapp and several members of that famous musical family. Like the movie *The Sound of Music*, that weekend made me think back to my childhood. We were like the Trapp family in many ways—exuberant, happy, secure, innovative, and pious. All that changed when Julia arrived. She was definitely not a Maria Von Trapp. She didn't even come close. She didn't allow music in the house. If someone turned on the radio, she picked it up and threw it on the floor. I was the only one who sang, and that was to keep her children from crying. Now I feel that, like Maya Angelou, I also know *Why The Caged Bird Sings*.

Conversations with my oldest sister Verna this past year have been very enlightening. She described my father's personality during her early childhood. He was happy and enjoyed the children. He and my mother loved to play records on the Victrola. He loved to entertain the family by playing his harmonica, and to take them to the Roadhouse for ice cream. "He loved us," she would say. I listened as she went on describing him as she remembered him during the years my mother was alive, and I was very surprised at what she was telling me. She was describing a man I never knew. What happened? Did he have a silent breakdown over Mother's death? Did he feel guilty? I never understood him and unfortunately, couldn't bring myself to discuss his feelings with him. It may be that each of us had already drawn our own conclusions or perhaps drawn our own curtains to shut out the light. And I wonder now if he felt guilty because of what his decisions did to all of us. I only wish that I had had the opportunity to tell him I understood the dilemma he faced as the father of ten motherless children during the Depression; that it was not his fault that we didn't tell him about Julia's behavior before he married her. Perhaps then he might have found it easier to speak to us.

As I reflect on past experiences, I cannot ignore the remarkable ability of my family to face adversity, make adjustments, and move on. Our sense of humor has no doubt contributed much to our survival. It helped us avoid dwelling on hardships and unfairness; and of more importance, it made vindictiveness seem like a waste of time. Humor overshadowed any need for us to feel vengeful over Julia's embezzling property that rightfully belonged to us. There has always been a special kind of wit associated with my family's outlook on life. Ben's example of comparing his experiences during World War II with life on the farm with Julia was one example. On my last visit the year before he died, in failing health, Ben told me jokingly, "I may be losing ground, but one of these days I'll be getting six feet of it back!"

If I were gifted with special memory skills, I could probably write a book of anecdotes from conversations with my brothers and sisters. In recent years, I have become more interested in the nature of various types of memory because my brother Anton is obviously gifted when it comes to recalling special times and events. He continues to amaze people with his ability to recall recent and past events accurately and in detail. Until recently I was unable to identify with his rare skills.

When I first began writing this memoir I called Anton to see if he remembered certain incidents from our childhood in the 1930s. He not only remembered them, he could run through an entire day, almost hour by hour, and relate what had happened and who was involved. If family members happened to miss the incident he described, he could tell me where they were and why. When he was able to tell me where *I* was and what *I* did on a certain day in 1937, I was amazed. I decided to have his information corroborated by others, and I learned that he was exactly right. We referred to him as our "walking encyclopedia" and never hesitated to use his immense store of information. If one of us couldn't answer a question in our family discussions, we inevitably would say, "I don't know; ask Anton." And when I decided to go ahead with writing this story, I knew there would be many occasions where I would ask Anton for corroboration of dates and events.

Anton is quiet and reserved, a thinker with a special kind of wit about him. He could see humor in situations that might be unnerving to most people. We were sitting around the dining room table after a dinner party at his new home when the time seemed to be right for reflecting on earlier experiences. I decided to ask Anton about his military experience, his three-year tour of duty in the Marines. He started to tell us about his boot camp experience, and before he was finished, I was doubled over with laughter. From the time he took the bus to the nearest recruiting station to the day he left boot camp, he was in a winner-take-all frame of mind. At the recruiting station he was joined by a group of recruits for the trip to Milwaukee where they had their physicals. From there they boarded a train for boot camp at Parris Island, South Carolina.

He told about the Marine sergeants who talked about the hardships they would have to endure in their upcoming training. The first sergeant who spoke warned them that boot camp would be difficult and that "now" was the time for them to change their minds and return home. Anton watched as several recruits got off the train at the next stop and went back home. The next sergeant he met on the train was obviously intent on weeding out recruits that might be too tenderhearted for what lay ahead. This sergeant approached each recruit with "in-your-face" shouting, after which another group of recruits decided to leave and go back home. Anton looked at the dwindling group and decided there was no way he would go back to life with Julia. In fact, it was Julia who had conditioned Anton for the kind of life he was about to experience. If the Marines threatened to kill him, so what? Julia had been doing that for years, and he had survived. He decided that boot camp couldn't possibly be worse than life at home. And apparently it wasn't.

On the day he successfully completed training at boot camp, the Marines had a big party for all the "graduates" before they left for their next duty station. Unfortunately, the food served at the celebration was either spoiled or contaminated and the entire group became deathly ill—except Anton. He said, "I not only ate my food, but the guy next to me didn't like what was on his plate, so I ate his too!" Only Anton and another Marine, who probably skipped the meal, were on the train the next day headed for Camp Pendleton in California. The rest were left behind, all very ill at Parris Island. From what my brothers said about Julia's cooking after my sisters left home, she had prepared Anton for everything at boot camp, including spoiled food.

As I look back on my childhood, I realize how it has affected my self-image. An abusive environment left me with a stigma I found difficult to remove. All those years I was trying to be like my peers, who were enjoying movies, parties, and dances, and who felt comfortable inviting friends into their homes, left me feeling less than adequate. I made up for it, in part, by being a good student, but there was always something missing. Time after time I wished I had been more assertive. In my college classes, I sat back while some students monopolized class discussions. On the other hand, it was an opportunity for me to see how deficient they were in my area of specialization. I often recalled what my high school principal had to say: "Empty barrels make the most noise." I made sure my professors knew I was not an empty barrel.

I remember the day that three other students and I went on a field trip with the chairman of the department of communicative disorders at Northwestern University. We were driving from Evanston, Illinois, to Milwaukee, Wisconsin, to participate in a cerebral palsy clinic. As he drove, the professor stated that he had begun reading our research papers. He had read only three and remarked, "Two were not up to graduate standards, but one was very good." In the back seat of his car, I immediately decided that one of the "substandard" papers had to be mine and I avoided that professor all day. It was obvious to me that he didn't know our names, and I made sure he was *not* going to learn mine on that field trip. The following week when we lined up outside his office to pick up our papers, I went to the very end of the line. I didn't want anyone to know or hear anything about my "substandard" work. My place at the end of the line assured me that the line of students ahead of me would be gone when I picked up my work. As I waited nervously, I heard the students in front of me asking each other, "Who did the research on Convulsive Disorders?" Suddenly I became aware of the professor's remarks in the car on that field trip, and the relief that came over me felt wonderful. As I walked past the students in line to answer the professor's call, I felt as if my spirit had been redeemed, and that Betty and Lyman were right—I did worry too much. The professor's remarks and the students' compliments were gratifying. Some of them appeared puzzled, as if some stranger had suddenly entered the competition and walked off with the prize. My notes on the subject were never returned with my research paper. I expect they probably ended up in the professor's private files. Seventeen years later, this same professor was invited to be the headline speaker at the Virginia Speech and Hearing Association's annual meeting. I welcomed him to Virginia during the social hour before the meeting where I brought him up-to-date on my life since graduate school. The next day, as he addressed an audience of over a hundred association members, he told them he still couldn't remember my name, but he remembered my grades. The crowd roared, and I still don't know how they interpreted his remark. Oh well, what's in a name anyway?

Instead of dwelling on a poor self-image, I found

that thinking positively and moving on was a successful way of coping with the repressed feelings that contributed to it. By tenaciously pursuing my life's work with those who are truly handicapped, I believe I have not only succeeded in helping myself, but I have found that success in helping others is immensely rewarding. In many ways I believe that my repressed anger about things I couldn't change as a child was converted into a kind of tenacity that often is necessary for treating the less fortunate—those with challenging communication disorders brought on as a result of severe head injuries and strokes, or developmental language problems. This tenacity was often called upon while treating subjects of all ages. At one time, I was seeing children and adults ranging in age from eighteen months to eighty-eight years. This required a rapid adjustment in realistic expectations, not always optimistic, but I never recall being discouraged about my work. By nature I don't consider myself to be a very patient person; however, when it came to my responsibility for helping those depending on my services, my patience was never exhausted. At my retirement after forty years of work, I was still ready to share my professional experience with colleagues in Costa Rica and Nicaragua, Central America. That poor self-image I harbored for so long beyond childhood disappeared as my career as a professional grew to gratifying heights. Returning to society whatever gifts and skills one may have is the greatest reward of all. I can think of no better way to improve one's self-image.

Today I find I have a problem relating to children who deliberately choose to skip school. I realize that there may be legitimate reasons for poor attendance, but to make truancy a habit, is difficult for me to understand. I remember how we struggled to maintain good attendance, how we sneaked out of the house to get away before Julia forced us to stay home and work. I remember how I picked strawberries for one or two cents per quart and cucumbers for not much more. I used my earnings to pay my bus fare to high school. In our elementary grades we walked two-and-a-half miles in freezing weather. And as for time spent playing in the streets, our chores before and after school left no time for that. Although I envied those children at the time, I am grateful to have learned to be disciplined at an early age. In fact, I think child labor laws need to be reconsidered. Child labor to the point of abuse needs to be addressed. But if children want to work while maintaining appropriate attendance at school, they should not be denied the opportunity. I wonder about the crime rate among children who work as opposed to those who spend their time being truant or wandering the streets. When I was a child, one of my teaching nuns told my class, "An idle mind is a devil's workshop." I feel fortunate to have grown up with a strong work ethic.

My mentors, Betty and Lyman Dunn, had an interesting philosophy regarding helping young people become educated and responsible citizens. They believed in opening doors, but their young protégés had to walk through them on their own. I was reminded many times by Betty's comment: "We will open doors for you, but you must walk through them." They gave me exactly the right amount of help to make it on my own. They were always generous with verbal rewards for our accomplishments; they generously applied positive reinforcement, and I can recall no instance where they used negative reinforcement. I was especially fortunate that they were careful to avoid feeling sorry for me. Sympathy that is overdone can hinder progress. When I look at Betty's photographs with her signature hairstyle, the long braid encircling her hair, I think, "How appropriate!" She wore the same hairstyle her entire life, a braid that represented a halo she so well deserved. In 1957, at the national convention of Theta Sigma Phi, the national fraternity for women in journalism, Betty received the distinguished service award for her contribution to the fraternity. I keep this award with its golden matrix hanging on the wall in my den to remind me of all the things Betty had done for me. I can't recall if the nun in the third grade ever finished reading "Cinderella" to us. It doesn't really matter because after surviving the abuse of a violent stepmother, I met Betty, a real-life fairy godmother, an angel in my valley.

CHAPTER 16

RESOLVE

UNTIL Eleanore's passing on March 4, 1999, I had not given much thought to writing about my childhood because I thought my family, especially Eleanore and Adolph, would not be comfortable with the idea. Although I was concerned about reopening old wounds, I believed that it was time to end the cover-up. Our friends never really got a complete and accurate picture of the abuse we sustained in our early years. As siblings we had each other, but fear and shame prevented us from telling anyone else.

The day that I stood before the heavy glass door at the side entrance of the church and watched as the pallbearers placed Eleanore's casket into the hearse, some kind of overpowering sense of rage took hold of me. Tears poured down my cheeks as I tried to control my sobs. I was filled with anger over the abuse Julia had inflicted on Eleanore over the years. I saw again the images of the towels Eleanore used to wipe her tears and soak up the blood from her bleeding nose and scalp. I recalled how I watched helplessly so many times as anger dominated my emotions during these violent episodes. As the hearse drove off to the cemetery, I felt that the floodgates damming up these painful experiences were finally opened and my tears flowed unchecked. I vowed that Eleanore's painful secret would not be buried with her. It was time to reopen the old wounds that had been festering all these years and allow proper healing to take place. It was too late for Eleanore and for Adolph, who had been buried three years earlier; their worries and problems were mercifully over. And so it was that Eleanore's funeral on that cold, blizzard-like day was a turning point for me. From that day forward, I would pledge my soul to speak out on behalf of abused children. Never again would I stand by helplessly if I suspected an incident of child abuse.

We had grown up at a time when no services were available to protect abused children. To add to this problem, an unwritten code seemed to prevail in our community. Perhaps it was part of that piety syndrome, where one does not meddle in other people's affairs. It was up to the abused to speak out and be heard. This principle was self-defeating. We were too frightened and ashamed to tell anything to anyone about our abuse. I know now that by not speaking up and telling someone, we were actually rewarding Julia for her behavior. In fact, our silence played directly into her need to be violent, and it was inevitable that her abuse would escalate with time. As victims, we provided the "high" she needed to make it through the day. Our silence reinforced her violence so dramatically that neither her mother's warnings to stop abusing us, nor her trips to the confessional, could reverse her behavior. Silence may be the greatest obstacle to overcoming child abuse and domestic violence. To put an end to these dreadful domestic events, it is imperative that the stigma attached to child abuse, or to any other type of violence in the home, be removed.

Abused children react in different ways. Some may express themselves by outwardly releasing their frustrations. Fighting, temper tantrums, or other socially unacceptable behavior may be a way for them to cope. Others may cope by withdrawing into a world of daydreams. Sadly, most abused children suffer in silence. And, ironically, the more socially perceptive a child tends to be, the less likely it is that he will talk about his life with abuse. I know this type very well. I have lived it. I watched in terror as my brothers and sisters were being abused. Fear and shame kept me from telling anyone. Repeated threats such as, "If you tell, you will be next," or, "I will kill you if you tell," were the usual follow-up threats following physical abuse. In my case, shame and the stigma of living in an environment different from that of my peers, were definite contributors to cover-up. I will never forget that feeling. I wanted to be like everyone else with a safe and wholesome home environment. As I listened to my schoolmates tell about the movies they had seen and other activities they had shared with their parents, I felt a deep sense of shame. I daydreamed about how I would like my life to be.

And I covered up what now seems like many a life-threatening experience. So why am I finally speaking up? Eleanore's funeral somehow triggered an entirely new attitude in me. Painful experiences with abuse were suddenly coming back and filling me with such anger that only a determination and resolve to do something about this problem could ease the pain and dissolve that anger that welled up in me. I felt as if I were standing on a bridge overlooking a pond while the gates to the dam were being opened, the pond was being drained, and the debris that had been dammed up for years at the bottom of the pond was finally coming back into view.

It was too late for Adolph and Eleanore to realize that their lives growing up might have been different had we not been silent about Julia's behavior. They both felt it was easier to keep their problems buried and forgotten. I think of both of them as they used to walk past the large scenic pond that provides a lovely setting for our town. The big silver steel bridge was a popular place to stop and watch the water flow noisily over the dam. In winter, the ice froze so thickly that heavy equipment could be set up on the pond to saw large ice blocks for ice boxes in the homes and ice houses on the farms. Although refrigerators, freezers, and the local locker plant have made sawing ice from the pond obsolete, swimming and boating in the summer and ice-skating and ice fishing in the winter continue to provide interesting activities for our town. When it became necessary to dredge the pond, however, the scenario changed drastically. It was sad to see the water drain away as the gates to the dam were opened and the bottom of the pond was exposed. Instead of the beautiful reflections off the bridge, the view was changed to one of debris and silt. Water had hidden from view all the debris and reflected only the beauty of the surrounding homes, trees, and flowers. Yet, it was necessary to open the gates to the dam, expose the debris, and dredge the entire bottom of the pond before it could become clean and healthy. Yes, it is too late for Adolph and Eleanore; however, I hope other victims can make up for them by speaking out instead of remaining silent.

Because I was fortunate to be rescued, I was able to spend many years preparing for a meaningful and rewarding career. I recall the many hours I spent in the stacks of those well-stocked medical libraries in Chicago. My fascination with the complex functions of the human brain was, and still is, endless. Even as an undergraduate, I had access to many models of human brains from which we used to chart cerebral activity. Although our knowledge of functions of various centers of the brain seemed immense at the time, later use of techniques such as positron emission tomography (PET) provided extraordinary insight into brain activity by showing live pictures of the brain at work. This information should add to our concern over child abuse, especially when we consider that the skull is the area of the human body often targeted by the abuser.

Signs of child abuse can be very subtle and identifying them can be a real challenge. Julia and abusers like her seem to know where to strike to avoid visible scars and bruises. Unfortunately, the head often becomes the target area, because hair can cover up bumps and bruises. A child who sustains repeated blows to the head, however, could have contusions that could seriously affect his performance in school. The soft tissue of the brain is encased in the skull, which an abuser may think is tough and hard enough to protect the brain. Spaces (ventricles) in the soft tissue and between the soft tissue and the hard skull are filled with fluid, making it possible for soft tissue to move within the skull. The impact of a blow to the skull can cause the soft tissue to bounce away from the point of impact. In fact, a blow to one side of the head may cause a bruise, or contusion, to the opposite side as the soft tissue reacts to the impact. Bruises may heal, but repeated blows to the head may have devastating effects. Even mild contusions may contribute to learning problems, especially when accompanied by psychological problems associated with such abuse. My studies made me wonder if Julia's beatings may have left us with residual damage, but our performance in school seems to deny that.

Any sudden changes in a child's behavior should be observed and noted. Identifying child abuse victims may be challenging, and classroom teachers should not hesitate to discuss child behavior aberrations with school counselors and psychologists. It may be helpful to encourage suspected cases to express themselves by drawing pictures of their family constellations. The positioning of family members and the colors chosen may offer some clues to the possibility of violence. A child whose photos show a dominance of dark colors—for example, black characterized by rigid strokes—may be portraying a home environment that is less than ideal. This type of artistic expression can be corroborative to other problems, including child abuse. Special services in the schools, had they been available during my childhood and adolescent years, may have made a big difference in my life. But the question persists: "Would I have told these professionals about my abusive environment, or would I have chosen silence?" I believe I would have told them, not just about my problems, but also about the abuse of everyone in my family. I wonder what would have happened if I had taken Eleanore's bloodied towels and run all the way to the nun's residence and showed them this kind of evidence of what was happening in our home; or if I had gone even further, taken this evidence to the church rectory and showed it to the monsignor who married Julia and my father. I could have told him about our need for an Eleventh Commandment: "Thou shalt love, nurture, and protect thy children."

Before I was a sophomore in high school, I was determined that my earlier trauma and disappointments were not going to stand in the way of my future, and I was especially fortunate in that I had people who cared. They gave me just enough help so that I could make it on my own. Starting with the man on the cultivator and my sister Verna who saw (and heard) me tending cows at age four; Sister Leonitia, who encouraged and rewarded me in the fifth grade; Mrs. Maule, Mrs. Louie Kulig, and Aunt Anna George, who arranged to keep me away from Julia at age fourteen; and Betty and Lyman who encouraged me to continue my education at age seventeen. They all contributed to my becoming a productive member of society. The world would be a better place if we had more of these caring people. They made it possible for me to adjust, to move on, and to concentrate on the future and avoid dwelling on the past.

During my years as a protégé of Betty and Lyman Dunn, I made an interesting observation. I found that their friends all seemed to want to help also. It was as if they envied the role Betty and Lyman played in my life. In many ways I must have contributed something to Betty and Lyman's lives as well. Before I ever met them, I had already learned to set goals and strive to achieve them, and they were aware of this. Therefore, it is only natural that I pass along this advice: Never give up in spite of disappointments. Many wonderful people in the world are interested in helping the abused and downtrodden. But they can't be expected to help if the child or teenager doesn't want to be helped; or, if doors are opened for them and the incentive or desire to walk through them isn't there. Any child with the will to improve his status in life can do so if he chooses to and follows this up with right choices. Many times I could have taken the easy way out and dropped opportunities. Instead, I felt I owed it to those who rescued me to set realistic goals and do my best to achieve them.

To give up and accept unhealthy circumstances in the home is a sure way for the abuser to win and escalate his abusive behavior. It is not the victim's fault that he is abused. Therefore, he should not hesitate to tell someone. If a responsible adult is not available or approachable, he can tell a friend who may know someone. Child abuse is never supposed to be a family secret. The earlier the victim does tell someone, the more likely help will be forthcoming, and wounds may be prevented from becoming deeply imbedded.

Dredging the bottom of the pond can be a slow and tedious process. Picking up debris while it is still afloat, before it settles deep in the silt, is easier and healthier in the end.

I understand that a bad home environment contributes to criminal behavior, but I cannot accept that thesis as a blanket statement. If this statement is an acceptable premise, why did my family of nine survivors beat the odds? Why did they successfully out-perform their peers in their contributions to society? Other factors must come into play. It can't be just the help and encouragement given by the rescuers, because I was the only one in my family to be this fortunate. Furthermore, I do not believe that an abusive home environment should automatically license the victim to become a burden to society, or for that matter, to choose a life of crime. Choices are available.

To be successful in overcoming and rising above child abuse, the victim must learn that he also has a responsibility in the rescue process. First of all, he must be motivated to help himself. Open doors will be of little value if he has no incentive to walk through them. Wings to fly will be useless if he chooses to be grounded. He must sell himself and make others proud of his efforts to move on. Above all, the abused child must waste no time by being vindictive to those who hurt him. Such vengeance is counterproductive and will only cause him to buy back what he has sold and will slow down his progress in moving forward. The joy the child experiences by using the wings he is given is shared even more so by those rescuers who are watching him soar.

It is not always possible to return those favors one enjoys while growing up, getting educated, and becoming established in a career and family life. Yet everyone has something good in them to pass on to others, by word or deed. The greatest reward I could possibly receive was a compliment given to me by my niece, Amy, who lost her mother when she was eight years old. She was an excellent student who became a dedicated elementary school teacher, and when she told me this past year that I was a role model for her, I could not have been more proud. Of course, it should be understood that I was able to be a role model only because of those wonderful people who were role models for me.

During my flight back to Virginia after Eleanore's funeral, I began thinking about how I might follow up my vow to Eleanore, myself, and my family. I was never able to repay all those people who helped me on my way to independence and success. I can pass on my experience, however, to encourage, inspire, and give hope to others suffering abuse. On the day following my return to Virginia after the funeral, I called the social services departments in the two counties near my residence. Their directors arranged to have me address their family assistance and foster care workers. By speaking with and sharing my experience with these child abuse workers, I was able to encourage and inspire them in their work. By speaking to foster care workers and Court Appointed Special Advocates (CASA), an organization of volunteers who are trained to represent an abused or neglected child in court, I believe I am helping them to become aware of special problems unique to the abused. Through this kind of communication,

I can share my training in behavior modification with them. In addition to these goals, I am especially dedicated to making the public aware of the need for removing the stigma attached to child abuse. A child may eventually outgrow the fear of his abuser, but the stigma remains. Making the public aware of the need for removing this fear and shame will help a child to speak up before his abuse escalates. And most of all, I hope my story will increase awareness of the need for mentors, those angels who rescue these unfortunate victims.

In the past two years while I was involved in giving speeches about my experience with child abuse, the family farm in Maule Coulee, the farm my father lamented about "giving away" almost forty years earlier, went into foreclosure. The property had been in the Kulig family since the early 1870s. It was a happy, thriving family home for many years. My brothers and sisters managed, through hard work and sacrifice, to save the farm during the Depression. Julia and her son acquired it during the good years and managed to lose it. When the sheriff's auction was held on January 18, 2000, none of my brothers bothered to bid on it. Too many painful memories, perhaps; but some day I hope a Kulig descendent will recover it. My grandfather deserves this. Regardless, the original 160 acres acquired by my grandfather in the 1870s has increased to between 900 and 1000 acres in and around Maule Coulee, as the Kulig legacy continues to grow.

In May 2000, I began planning the trip I would make to Wisconsin in early June—a drive from Virginia to Wisconsin with stops in Champaign-

Urbana and Bloomington, Illinois. Ben had been in failing health for some time and I was looking forward to our visit. His sons now owned much of the land in the township and he enjoyed going out to their farms and assisting with the fieldwork. His life as a country squire, however, was marred by hospital admissions followed by recuperation periods at home. I called him on his eightieth birthday in March and could tell by his conversation that he was too distracted by his health problems to enjoy the special birthday card I had sent, with several military officers' signatures and well wishes. About a month later, the day before Easter, I received a shocking phone call from my brother Ed, telling me that Ben's wife Ruth had died suddenly. As his caretaker, she showed no signs of serious illness; her passing stunned everyone. I decided not to change my plans for my June trip home but kept in close contact with Ben and his family.

Less than a month later, Ben was rehospitalized, but this time he was not about to rally as he usually did. My brothers and Verna visited him regularly. A couple of days after visiting Ben in the hospital, Clifford was found dead in his home. Verna, my half-sister, and a niece found him sitting at the table with the local paper before him. His glasses and jacket were still on. It was May 20, 2000, and my June plans to drive to Wisconsin would suddenly change after Ed called me that evening with the sad news. I started packing for the drive home. In the middle of my packing on Sunday afternoon, I received another call from Ed. He stated simply, "I hate to be the bearer of sad news, but Ben died at 3:00 this afternoon." In less than a month, my family had grown smaller by three people.

I started driving before daylight on Monday morning and continued driving for 765 miles from Virginia to Bloomington, Illinois, from where I called Ed to advise him of my whereabouts. I arrived in Independence about 4:00 p.m. the following day, in time to shower and go to the wake services. Clifford was finally free of the fifty-one years of painful and crippling arthritis he had endured, after being stricken at age twenty-five. The evening after the prayer service was socially uplifting, as cousins from everywhere came to pay their respects. I was again reunited with relatives, and the evening was far from somber. My big surprise of that evening was the appearance of Doris Anderson Hanson, my first and second grade teacher from Maule Coulee School. I hadn't seen her since that picnic at the end of my second grade. She was as tall and statuesque as ever. I will always treasure the picture she gave me, taken when she was eighty-five years old.

Along with the sadness at Clifford's funeral the following day I was disappointed to know that questions I had planned to ask him would never be answered. From what he had told Ed a few weeks before he died, Cliff remembered the day Ed and I were taken away to live with relatives. He was five years old as he waved good-bye from the kitchen window. He must have been deeply disappointed when we were driven off without waving back. His living toys were being taken away, very likely with no explanation. The events preceding that traumatic parting will always remain unknown to me. I only know that it must have been just as traumatic for me as it was for him for I too remember it as the day I came alive by making that transition from precognition to cognition.

After Clifford's funeral reception and buffet, we gathered at Anton's home to write thank-you notes. Before we had time for any closure regarding Clifford's passing, we were getting ready for Ben's wake and prayer service that evening. Many of the same people were present, and we carried on where we left off at Clifford's reception that afternoon. Recalling the two events as separate gatherings became difficult, as people, places, and conversations blended together. I will always remember Ben's funeral the following day, however, as a time of tears and goose bumps. We entered the church to the sound of a man singing one of the Polish hymns I had learned at three years of age, while I was living with the Uncle Bert family. I hadn't heard those lyrics in seventy years. Yet I recalled them well enough to follow them sub-vocally as we followed Ben's casket up the long church aisle:

Serdeczna Matko, opiekunko ludzi. Niech Cię płacz sierót do litości wzbudzi. Wygnańcy E~ wy do Ciebie wołami. Zmiłuj się smiluj niech się nie tułamy.Do kogóż mamy, wzdychać nędzne dziatki Tylko do Ciebie ukochanej Matki. U której Serce otwarte każdemu. A osobliwie nędzą strapionemu.

It seemed strange to hear these lyrics at a military funeral. I doubt if that song was ever heard aboard a Navy aircraft carrier or at Arlington National Cemetery. After the funeral mass, we followed Ben's family and the American Legionnaires out of the church, while everyone sang "The Battle Hymn of the Republic." I could hear my cousins singing with the same patriotic spirit inspired by Doris Anderson at Maule Coulee School sixty-seven years before. I had goose bumps, but I'm sure Ben would have loved it. Military honors were bestowed at the cemetery, and thus ended the life and career of a man at age eighty, a man who said he never expected to come home alive from World War II.

The funerals of two brothers in two days left another void in my life, but I had to admit to feeling proud of their accomplishments, especially their rise above hardships they endured while growing up. On my drive back to Virginia alone, I thought of my siblings, and how each of them became successful. I thought of my father giving three of us away, as Ed mentioned earlier, "like three puppies in a basket." Yet Ed and I grew up to be survivors. As I drove, I recalled those "ponderings in the woodshed" when I was a child with dreams for a future filled with happiness and success. Those dreams became reality many times over. While driving through the scenic areas of western Wisconsin, my mind wandered back to those long drives, to and from work, through the Virginia countryside. One of those drives became especially meaningful. I was driving through the town of Middleburg, Virginia, and up the knoll where the Blue Ridge Mountains came into view, when I turned on my car radio and sat back to listen. What came over the airwaves at that most appropriate of times was the song, "I Have a Dream," by the Swedish Rock Group, ABBA. I had never heard the song before but was so impressed with the music and lyrics that I went out to buy the album at my very first opportunity.

I felt the lyrics so closely resembled my dreams that I couldn't have expressed them more accurately myself. Now as I drove on alone, I recalled the words: "I have a dream . . . to help me cope . . . I believe in angels . . . something good in everything I see . . . my destination . . . makes it worth the while . . . I believe in angels . . . ." And then I thought of all the angels in my life.

It has been a long time since my barefoot escape from Julia during that storm in 1941. Along with enjoying a rewarding career, I gave twenty years to the military as a Navy wife. My life has taken me from the dignitaries in Washington, D.C., to the moguls of Hollywood, California. Of one thing I am most certain; my forty years of work in the field of speech and language pathology have been the most stabilizing and rewarding experience of my life. An evening "on the town" several years ago seemed to confirm that for me.

A friend with whom I often rode horseback invited me and three others to be her guests on a flight to Atlantic City for the Frank Sinatra dinner show. She chartered an executive-type Beechcraft with two pilots and we left Dulles International Airport around 3:30 p.m. We were met in Atlantic City by two limousines that took us directly to the dinner show. It was an exciting evening of food, entertainment, and gambling, but what I found to be the most impressive part of that evening was the flight home. The pilot and copilot decided to fly over our nation's capital and show us Washington, D.C., at midnight. It was a beautiful, clear night, and the view of the lighted buildings and monuments was spectacular.

As we headed back to Dulles Airport, I thought of the Frank Sinatra show earlier that evening, and what I would tell my colleagues at work the next day. For some reason, all that moment could suggest was, "Yeah, Frank, I also did it my way." And I wouldn't have changed a thing; well, almost.

* * * * * *

Postscript: I have tried to be concise in my description of my family's experience with child abuse. If the documented portion of child abuse in this story seems too short or inadequate, feel free to multiply each episode by ten or twelve years. One might ask the question, however, "How many bleeding skulls and bloody noses should it take to make a point?" There should be no need to repeat episode after episode of physical and mental abuse in anyone's life. Once is already one too many.

BIBLIOGRAPHY

ABBA. "I Have a Dream." 1979.

American Speech-Language-Hearing Association, Rockville, Maryland. Telephone conversation, January 31, 2000.

Angelou, Maya. *I Know Why the Caged Bird Sings.* New York: Random House, 1969.

Arrington, Representative W. Russell. Letter, May 10, 1946.

Arrington, Representative W. Russell. Letter, July 12, 1946.

Arrington, Representative W. Russell. Letter, July 12, 1946.

Buffon, Georges Louis Leclerc de. *L'Histoire des Mammiferes. Le Cheval.* Paris, 1788.

Disraeli, Benjamin. *The Young Duke.* Bartletts Familiar Quotations. Boston: Little Brown and Company, 1992.

Halama, Verna. Telephone conversation, February 11, 1996.

Halama, Verna. Telephone conversation, September 19, 1997.

Halama, Verna. Telephone conversation, December 5, 1999.

Halama, Verna. Telephone conversation, December 12, 1999.

Halama, Verna. Telephone conversation, December 19, 1999.

Halama, Verna. Telephone conversation, January 9, 2000.

Hérault de Séchelles, Marie-Jean. *Voyage a Montbard.* Paris: Solvet, 1801.

Kirkpatrick, G. L. "Adeline Kulig Receives Honors at Illinois U," Independence News-Wave. Independence, Wisconsin, May 1947.

Kirkpatrick, G. L. "Interesting Letter Received From Miss Adeline Kulig," Independence News-Wave, Independence, Wisconsin, July 18, 1947.

Kirkpatrick, G. L. "Miss Adeline Kulig Wins Scholarship," Independence News-Wave. Independence, Wisconsin, July 2, 1949.

Kulig, Anton. Telephone conversation, June 26, 1999.

Kulig, Anton. Telephone conversation, July 3, 1999.

Kulig, Anton. Letter, August 4, 1999.

Kulig, Anton. Telephone conversation, August 7, 1999.

Kulig, Anton. Telephone conversation, September 11, 1999.

Kulig, Anton. Telephone conversation, December 19, 1999.

Kulig, Anton. Telephone conversation, December 25, 1999.

Kulig, Anton. Telephone conversation, January 8, 2000.

Kulig, Anton. Telephone conversation, March 3, 2000.

Kulig, Ben. Telephone conversation, June 26, 1999.

Kulig, Ben. Telephone conversation, September 19, 1999.

Kulig, Ben. Telephone conversation, December 26, 1999.

Kulig, Clarence. Letter, July 18, 1999.

Kulig, Clarence. Telephone conversation, August 22, 1999.

Kulig, Clarence. Telephone conversation, September 5, 1999.

Kulig, Clifford. Letter, July 23, 1999.

Kulig, Edward. Telephone conversation, February 6, 2000.

Payne, Norma. Telephone conversation, December 26, 1999.

Pope, Alexander. *An Essay on Man*. Cambridge: The Riverside Press, 1903.

St. Leo's Parish Meeting, Fairfax, Virginia, 1983.

Stephen, Leslie. *Bartletts Familiar Quotations*. Boston: Little Brown and Company, 1992.

Smieja, Theresa. Telephone conversation, January 8, 2000.

Walaeus, Johannes (Jan Van Wale). *Bartletts Familiar Quotations*. Boston: Little Brown and Company, 1992.

Woznicki, Robert, Ph.D. *Madame Curie—Daughter of Poland*. Miami: American Institute of Polish Culture, 1983.

Zawicki, Edmund. *Polish Immigration to Independence, Wisconsin*. (Unpublished).

APPENDIX A

A-1. LYMAN'S TRIBUTE TO BETTY

LYMAN D. DUNN
333 E. Ontario Street, Apt. 4307B
Chicago, Illinois 60611
October 30, 1982

Dear Friend of Betty Dunn:

What a fortunate man I am to have had a lifelong love affair with Betty. In our very eventful life we shared together the good, the bad and the beautiful for half a century and were closer to each other at the end of her life than ever before. She was the center around which my life rotated. Her beauty, love, wit, sparkle, companionship, and compassion still haunt me. I miss her enormously as I journey on down the road to my destiny, whatever it may be.

To the 200 letters I sent out announcing her departure,

I received 96 written replies and many comforting phone calls. They helped sustain me during the saddest period of my life and I thank you greatly and sincerely for your thoughtfulness. In fact, I wish I could, by some magic, stand by each of you so that I could put my arm around your shoulder and thank you personally for the role you played in Betty's brilliant life and for the wonderful support your letters and calls gave to me—they really touched my heart.

Betty had a lot of dreams as most of us do but almost all of hers came true. Toward the end of her life she felt that she had completed her mission and destiny and that she would not feel cheated when her days on earth were over. She was at peace with the world when the end came, but I just can't accept the fact that she won't be back.

Betty built many lasting friendships and it is fitting that the memory of such a wonderful gal be honored, and to that end I have set up a "Betty Hinckle Dunn Memorial Fund" for scholarships to journalism students at the University of Illinois, her Alma Mater. The memorial scholarship idea was first suggested to me by Adeline, one of our foster children, then one day later by two more of them, Norma and Willard, followed by requests from dozens of friends who wanted to share in whatever memorial to Betty that was decided upon. It is NOT a family affair but one for all of us to share who loved her. I will tell you more about this in detail later on in this letter.

Since this may be my last letter I may ever write to many or most of you I want to sort of talk to you and relate three things, namely:

1. A few more interesting and revealing aspects of Betty's life for your enjoyment which you may not have known.

2. *Excerpts from the many beautiful and informative letters and phone calls that I received.*

3. *Details of the Betty Hinckle Dunn Memorial Fund.*

#1. Betty was sentimental, as most of you know. Her favorite song was "Always" followed closely by "Love Song" from Dr. Zhivago and "Third Man Theme." My favorite is "You Are My Sunshine" which is the way I felt about her ever since the day we met so long ago. One of her favorite remarks was, "Everybody is lonely now and then but not at the same time or the same place." It was impossible to be lonely around Betty because of her vitality and spirit. She believed in the philosophy "you shouldn't worry because you won't get out of this life alive anyway." She said,"It's the living you should be concerned about and not the dead, their worries are over."

When Betty was a young girl, her mother told me she was stricken with polio. The treatment required years of exercise and special medication over an extended period of time. Betty stuck with it until all evidence of the disease was erased. Her determination and discipline were evident at this early age.

Betty could be tough when the occasion demanded it. Once I attended a convention in Chicago in which she was in charge. The pre-convention arrangements were not getting done by the management in time for convention to open, whereupon Betty asked the management to put her in charge of arrangements, which, surprisingly they did—and with her hand in a velvet glove holding a padded club she took charge, and the job was finished on time. The workers were so pleased at her charm and leadership they gathered around her and gave her a "toast". She had real leadership and a way of winning your support.

She was dependable. One of her friends remarked to me one day, "Betty is so dependable I would trust her with my sou."

Betty was programmed by the "Master Compute" for living in our time. She was a pleasure to live with—always clean, cheerful, orderly, adaptable, considerate, chatty, affectionate and seldom complained about anything. Her heroes were Hoover, Lindbergh and Tunney and her heroine was Bess Truman. Oh yes—her favorite food was peanut butter and milk her favorite drink.

Betty had a sense of humor which sometimes indicated her spontaneity and originality. One time at a football game between the Illini and Minnesota, when the huge looking Gophers trotted onto the field, Betty remarked, "Golly Moses, look at that Bevy of Bruties."

I always kidded her about her vast store of useless information and once when we were going to the theatre, out of a clear blue sky she said, "Did you know that Sarah Bernhardt had a wooden leg?" I asked, "'Which leg?" to show a little interest and she said, "the left." She said it so convincingly I never had the nerve to check it out. She knew the personal habits of about everyone in Royalty. In an attempt to be funny once I asked her, "Who did Henry the 8th sleep with on the night of August 10, 1526?" She thought a moment and replied, "He went to the bedroom of Anne Boleyn that night but she told him she had a bad headache and for him to go play with his armor." Maybe this is one of the reasons why she lost her headache along with her head later on.

Betty's mother told me of a time when Betty and a girl friend went sledding on one of the hills near Peoria, Illinois where she was born and when the sled was about half way down the hill the wooden runners hit an exposed rock and spilled the girls onto the snow. Betty told me of the spill and after the spill she said she "slid down the rest of the hill on her Lady Astor."

A friend once remarked to Betty in my presence, 'You're the most organized person I ever met,' to which Betty replied, "Yes, and sometimes it bores the hell out of me."

Betty told me that when she was young and her piano lessons were a failure because they got in the way of her reading, her mother gave her $50.00 and told her to go buy any musical instrument she wanted. She bought a typewriter instead and learned to play it like no one I have ever seen, which turned out to be the key to her contact with all of her friends far and near.

Many times when Betty and I went out to dinner in a crowded place she would tell me what was going on all around us. She had the outstanding ability to listen to two conversations at another table and not miss a word while carrying on a conversation with me. That takes a great mind.

Betty had the ability to invade your soul. She had no malice toward anyone and she loved everyone she met—until they proved unworthy. She was a born psychiatrist and was almost completely uninhibited—she could almost, but not quite, read your mind (for which I was occasionally grateful).

Betty had impeccable manners and great humility. She

never realized how unusual, how exceptional, and how great she really was, which is one of the many reasons she was loved so much by so many.

She had a magnetic personality—and like a magnet, wherever she went she seemed to attract people and events. Things seemed to happen when she was around. Perhaps it was her keen sense of observation or perhaps it was because she was many people (and I loved them all), journalist, hobbyist, conversationalist, traveler, historian, friend, companion, counselor and wife all wrapped up in one beautiful personality.

I thought you might be interested in seeing her through the eyes and hearts of her many friends as revealed in the excerpts from some of the many letters and phone calls I received. I'm glad to share these with you and regret space won't permit me to share all of them. Here they are:

#2 Colorado: Betty was a great spirit and many will remember her twinkling eyes, her beautiful sense of humor and her ability to give to others in words and action.

Georgia: Betty was a most unusual lady and a fun person to be with.

Indiana: I've admired the visionary leadership Betty exhibited through the years and have willingly followed her lead—I share your loss.

Texas: She was a great lady with sensitive intelligence and perceptive kindness. She touched all our lives and we will miss her.

Florida: She had such a bright outlook.

Florida: I felt more comfortable talking to her than anyone else anywhere. A world full of 'Bettys' would be a wonderful place in which to live.

Australia: Betty is still as alive to me as she ever was. She was such a distinctive person that she will never die.

Georgia: She was a super lady and I will remember her always.

California: I'm remembering all the nice and wonderful things about her and I know she will be with me always.

Australia: I still can't believe that she is gone. Your letter gave me insight into the many facets of the life of that wonderful character.

Ohio: She was the most unique person I ever met and was admired and loved by my whole family.

Texas: Betty would get a kick out of the fact that for once I am tongue-tied. I would not want her to be here and suffering. I have never felt closer to her in my life. Her bright spirit will be with us always.

Ohio: We know Betty now better than we ever did. Our sad memories will be swept away by our recollections of the fun and worthwhile episodes that Betty seemed to trigger.

Maryland: She was a great gal. I will remember her always. She had unique qualities and it was a privilege to have been her friend.

Illinois: She was the only one on earth who could watch the Rules of Order at a convention and make the whole routine funny. Whenever she was present there was an extra sparkle.

"Pennsylvania: Betty was a true and loyal friend, so kind and compassionate. I enjoyed her friendship and shall never forget her.

Hawaii: Betty's life was a blessing to all of us who knew her and were touched by it. We will miss her very much as she was a most wonderful person and I count myself fortunate to have had her friendship.

California: I always enjoyed being with Betty, for along with her beauty and ability she seemed to have an unfailing sense of humor. She always seemed so vibrant and beautiful. I thought she would outlive us all.

Massachusetts: When I lost a son-in-law, my oldest daughter, my mother and my husband in a space of three years, Betty's letters to me were immensely helpful. Your letter indicates a man who loved and understood his wife.

West Virginia: You have voiced with artful sincerity the feelings of many of us who were privileged to move in Betty's wide circle of friends.

Illinois: Betty was one of my precious friends. I loved her dearly and will miss her. What beautiful memories she left us.

Ohio: Betty must have been one of the Lord's pets, judging from the fact that all five things she wanted were granted. I knew Betty's depth of spirituality for we discussed it a number of times. I knew you and Betty loved all the Sisters of the Precious Blood—and we love both of you still.

Ohio: She was a beautiful woman in all ways. I loved her very much. A great loss but she can now help us more from Heaven which I'm sure you have felt these last few months.

Illinois: Betty was a rare individual—but please always remember that it takes two such special individuals to remain together for 55 years (many thanks).

Washington State: I noted in the IRAC Bulletin that Betty has passed away. Her activities in the fraternity world most certainly furthered their program. We are grateful for her energies and interest.

Illinois: You wrote a superb clinical report on what happened to your good wife. Your observation that we all should have the luck she had is so, so true. Frankly, I was flattered to be among those who were acquainted with this good and interesting lady.

Ohio: I met Betty in 1955 when she led a group of Theta Sigs and friends on a grand tour of Europe. She was all the nice things you said about her and I felt privileged to have known her.

Ohio: Thank you very much for your comprehensive letter. A beautiful tribute to a grand and lovely lady. I shall treasure it as a memorial to my very dear friend.

Utah: How fortunate you are to be "full of happy

memories." *When you have lived so that your thoughts of the past are beautiful, they bring strength and comfort and bless the whole length of your life.* Betty will forever be locked in your heart. Life is sometimes full of hearts and homes also, and sometimes rooms are empty and arms also except for memories.

Georgia: Thank you for your delightful tribute to my favorite Betty and for the lovely picture—wonderful that she accomplished the five wishes. How many of us do that?

California: Your concern for all of her friends was beautifully shown in your courageous letter. Thank you for taking the time to write to us about her.

Ohio: I shall never forget the day I met Betty. I was beaten in spirit but she befriended me and helped me to see things in an entirely different way.

Indiana: She always wrote an interesting letter filled with her acceptance of life—yet, humorous and reflective of her positive attitude. You can be proud that you had such a talented helpmate through the years.

Colorado: Your acute and loving perception so vividly captured the Betty I knew and loved that it made me feel she was standing there beside me when I read it. The memory of the time we shared will always remain with me and be a shining memory.

Ontario: Nothing you mentioned about Betty in your lovely letter surprised me. She was a charming person and a most unusual one. The Good Lord has recalled her home.

Michigan: I loved Betty's sense of humor and her originality and outspokenness. She was certainly unique and I enjoyed all my contacts with her.

Virginia: Thank you, oh so much, for the beautiful letter about our Betty. She was beautiful in appearance, in her life, and in her affection for me, which I have prized through the years since I first met her in 1928.

Hawaii: She had many friends throughout the whole country. She lived a wonderful, well-rounded life, and she will be missed by many people, but they will rejoice that she had such a long and happy life and a quick and painless ending.

California: My life was enriched by Betty in very special ways. She was unique and even though we were separated by many miles, I felt closeness. Whenever I received one of her delightful letters the years and miles just dissolved.

Florida: Betty was such a beautiful person and I always felt honored that she would add me to her long list of 'good friends'. Her letters were always such a joy to receive and, at the time of my great loss she, more than anyone else, helped me with her inspirational words and prayers.

Indiana: She was a truly wonderful friend. She took us under her wing and tried to console us for all our troubles and here all the while she was ill herself and didn't let on. She was beautiful.

Illinois: From the first, I was impressed with her warmth

and sparkle and felt she was a rare person and I felt privileged to know her.

Illinois: She was indeed a wonderful woman and I especially loved her sense of humor as well as her writing talent and gift of public speaking.

Wisconsin: What a lovely, lovely tribute to darling Betty. She was one terrific gal.

Florida: Just want you to know that this 'friend of Betty Dunn' feels extremely grateful for having known her and is appreciative of receiving this tribute and the marvelous picture of her.

Illinois: Your letter was beautiful and so very accurate concerning Betty's personality. You couldn't bluff with that gal. She could see through it in a minute who was genuine and who was not. She was such a sincere and kind person to those who had earned her friendship. I felt so very privileged to have been considered on her list of many, many friends. And that mind of hers was always going 'a mile a minute'. What a brilliant woman Betty was.

Ohio: I'll miss her long, witty and encouraging letters. I guess Betty has done all she could on earth and God has other things in store for her in Heaven. So now I'll communicate with her by praying to her and I know she'll surely help me if possible.

Texas: I miss Betty terribly but life must go on. I hope you are picking up the pieces and going on with your life, as all of us have to do.

New York: There would not be a HVWP (Hospitalized Veterans Writing Project) today if Betty Hinckle Dunn had not gotten the project accepted as a national service of Theta Sigma Phi when she was National President. As a little retreat during a busy day, I remember how Betty often sat alone in churches wherever she might be.

Australia: We all felt your summing up of Betty could not have been bettered as it was exactly as we knew her when first we met 30 years ago. Yes, and we shall miss her too and I can assure you each of us shed the proverbial silent tears.

Missouri: Once I attended a meeting of about 200 professional women where Betty was the chairman. She presided with such firmness, fairness, knowledge and justice that all of us were delighted. Her ability to call everyone at the meeting by her first name was astonishing. She had complete control of the meeting all the time. Some of us thought she should run for President. She was great and how I will miss that charming, smart and eloquent gal.

Illinois: When I read your beautiful letter I said, Oh God. No. And I couldn't stop crying for three days. She meant so very much to me. I realize her life had to end sometime, and I'm grateful for so many wonderful memories, but the hurt is still there.

California: I knew Betty back in the great depression days of the 30's. She gave a series of lectures to whoever could pay for them under the title, 'Blazing a Trail Through Literature'. Her beauty and mannerisms were so touching that people didn't pay as much attention to what she was saying as to her personality while she was blazing a trail to their hearts. I expected great things of her and was not disappointed. I have loved and admired her all my life and will miss her greatly.

Missouri: Judging by your letter you really knew and understood your wife. I don't know whether I would like that or not. I loved her and will miss her.

Texas: What a beautiful tribute to Betty your letter was. Each life leaves an afterglow but Betty's leaves a beacon light for all to follow. My life is richer because she was my friend.

Florida: The bible says 'To whom much is given, much is expected.' Betty was given among other things beauty, intelligence, affection, compassion, energy, frankness and a special 'way' with people and I'm sure the Lord is very pleased with the way she used those gifts.

Oklahoma: Betty lectured to young people on many campuses and 'got across' to them because she was interested in them and was open, frank, perceptive, knowledgeable and understanding and they knew it. I admired the way she handled them. I loved her professionalism. She was so approachable unaffected and great. We need more of her kind these days.

Illinois: Little bubbles of joy creep up through my soul as I reminisce on the pleasant hours I spent with Betty. I miss her dreadfully and am so glad for the happiness she brought into my life but Oh God, how I hate to give her up.

Ohio: At Kneipp Springs, her favorite Resort, Betty liked to go 'bumming' and I felt it a privilege to go with her.

As we drove along in her car she saw everything and missed nothing. When we got back, always before dark, we would go into the back yard and lean on a fence and 'put the sun to bed' as she called it and she would often remark, 'No matter who you are or how much money and power you have, you can't stop the sun from going down for which I am grateful.' She had a great love for people and nature. Kneipp Springs is gone and now she is too and the loss is hard to bear.

California: What amazed me about Betty was how she could mean so much to so many people and have time for her own life as well. She was organization and love personified and oh, how I loved, and will miss that beautiful and loquacious gal. I know how lost you must feel but rest assured you will be together again someday.

Texas: Betty has taken that Big Trip to the Sky and I just can't stop crying. She gave so much to me—my outlook on life, the love I feel in my heart for people and the enjoyment of life itself. She taught me to appreciate art and music, that winning in the game of life wasn't as important as playing it fairly, and don't try to sell something you wouldn't buy yourself were you in the other fellow's shoes. Her code of living was wonderful. While I am heartbroken now, when I take that Big Trip to the Sky, thanks to the Good Lord, I know she will be there to meet me and again my happiness will be complete.

Arkansas: A family record just didn't exist until Betty became one of us. She took pictures, interviewed old timers, searched graveyards and courthouse records, asked a lot of questions and came up with a written record of who we were, where we came from and who we are now. She did a monumental job. She was the 'angel' of our family and loved by every one of us. She was an inspiration to us all and thank God she came along.

Michigan: One thing in particular I liked about your letter was that you didn't go into details about all the Honors Betty received and all the important positions she held and all the important people she knew in her lifetime but you told us about Betty the woman—the darling I admired so much. She was so human, so understanding and so lovable. To have shared the friendship of such a truly great person is a wonderful experience. Life won't be the same for me without her.

Illinois: Betty made a difference in our lives for the better, she gave you her heart, but as your friend she expected the best of you. She loved you but she wanted you to be strong. She was so exciting and down to earth. She was unique. We are eternally grateful for her love and friendship and oh how we will miss her.

California: When we didn't know which way to go, we were loved, protected and guided by you and Betty. Her impact on our lives can't be expressed in words so I won't even try, but the legacy of help, love and understanding she left us will remain in our hearts forever.

Texas: I have heard Betty say, 'Never stay at the party too long'. Since Betty had such a full and rewarding life, the Good Lord ended the party for her without suffering and pain. I loved her dearly and will miss her greatly and pray that the Master won't let me 'stay at the party too long'.

Missouri: She had a storybook life and the sparkle of

her star fire personality will always glow in my heart. She was the complete lady and I, like each of her many friends, shared one of life's most precious gifts—her friendship.

Illinois: When I finished your letter I put it down and through my tears I said aloud, 'Goodbye Betty Dear and thanks for making my life meaningful. Heaven is welcome anytime now since I know you will be there to greet me.'"

Thanks again to each of you for your sincere, beautiful and revealing tribute to my darling Betty. I'm bursting with pride. And now may God Bless each of you and enfold you in His everlasting love would be Betty's closing wish, and Dear Friend, it is mine too.—Amen.

Cordially and affectionately,

_____

/Signed/ Lyman D. Dunn

A-2. Lyman DeWitt Dunn

1907-1986

Lyman DeWitt Dunn was born June 6, 1907, the son of William Sherell Dunn and Augusta Hicks Dunn in Cherry Valley, Arkansas. His father died in 1910 and his mother later married Sidney Payne. Augusta died two years after the birth of their daughter Ruby. Lyman's maternal grandmother took both Lyman and his brother to Illinois to live with her. As the boys grew up both realized the importance of an education. Lyman was fascinated with science and eventually entered the University of Illinois as a pre-med student. Those were lean times and he realized his dream was financially beyond his reach. It was then that he developed a new dream. He was determined to learn all he could about the chemistry of foods and nutrition. His active mind began to develop the idea of "Proving foods needed for healthy bodies must be chemically sound." Over the years he obtained more than twenty patents in the food field. He was still working on these health products at the time of his death.

Lyman married a Bloomington, Illinois native, Betty Hinckle. It was during this time that they took an interest in several youngsters. This group became a very close-knit foster family. Both Lyman and Betty gave each one much support and love and they have always remained loyal to each other as well as to the family. Betty Hinckle Dunn died in 1982. Lyman married Eleanor Feehan in September of 1985. She worked closely with him and supported his ideas and plans. Lyman felt he was very close to meeting the high standard he had set for his food research at the time of his death on October 30, 1986.

One must not forget the following goals Lyman had set for himself: (1). To produce a perfect nutritional food for the aged and the young which would be not only well balanced but palatable and reasonably priced. (2). Any dedicated youth must have an opportunity to carry on this research by means of grants, loans and scholarships. (3). His ready-made foster family would pass on to others the standards he set for himself.

Lyman has left a void in all the lives he touched. However, as one sees the many things he has left as his legacies, he did not pass this way in vain.

Lyman did not wear a badge to show everyone he was

a firm believer in Christ. Lyman DeWitt Dunn lived his faith.

Another, perhaps more precise, coverage of Lyman's career was published in the 1977-1978 edition of *Who's Who in Illinois and the Midwest*. (See Appendix A in which I translated the abbreviations in the article for easier reading.)

A-3. Lyman Dunn's Listing in *Who's Who in the Midwest*

Dunn, Lyman, *chemical engineer; born in Cherry Valley, Arkansas, June 6, 1907; son of William DeWitt and Augusta (Hicks) Dunn; student University of Illinois, 1926-1929, Illinois Institute of Technology, 1931-1932, married Elizabeth Hinckle, July 11, 1931. Chemist, Bowman Dairy Company, 1929-1938; head, alkali research at Detrex Corporation, Detroit, 1938-1942; Sales Engineer and Consulting Engineer for various firms, 1942-1952. Founder and Manager of Special Products Division, City Products Corporation, Chicago, 1952-1961. Founder and President of Marlan Company, Chicago, 1961-___; Director, Wittmore Manufacturing Company, Altoona, Pennsylvania, Marco Finance Company, Chicago, Tastee Freez of Arizona, Phoenix, Village Enterprises, Inc., St. Louis; Patron, Sisters of Precious Blood, Rome City, Indiana, 1964-___ Chicago Yacht Club. Patentee chemical, mechanical, and food industry fields. Home: 535 N. Michigan Avenue, Chicago, Illinois 60616. Office: 325 W. 25th Place, Chicago, Illinois 60616."*

APPENDIX B

B-1. LETTER FROM CLARENCE KULIG

July 18, 1999

Adeline:

It's raining in Whitehall today so I will try to get you a list of the abuses we lived with all the years that "Mother Dearest—Julia" was supposed to take care of the William Kulig family.

As you know, our Mom died February 11, 1930, at age 31, leaving behind ten children, the oldest of which was Verna, age 11. Can you imagine our Dad being left with ten children during the depression with the drought coming up? Also, the hot record temperatures we had in the thirties still stand today.

Clifford and I both started school the same year, in the fall of 1930. I was five years old and walked to school, one mile each way. We carried our lunch in old honey pails and most of the time we had only dry bread with lard. We couldn't eat butter because it was about 8—10 cents a pound, so we had to sell the cream for income. We went to school barefoot and I remember the teacher calling us aside to discuss why we were still coming to school barefoot when it was starting to snow in the fall.

Now getting back to Julia and some of the things she did to us:

When I was in the fourth grade I had appendicitis and needed emergency surgery. While I was in the hospital in Whitehall for two weeks, our Aunt Nellie, Mrs. Joe Kulig, brought me a toy—Popeye pushing a wheelbarrow. When you wound it up and put it on the floor, away he paddled! Well, I wasn't home from the hospital very long before my Popeye disappeared. I later found out she gave it to (her out-of-wedlock son).

I remember the time when she sent Dad to town in the morning to buy fruit jars for canning and that same afternoon she gave them to her "ma". She got us together and said she would kill us if we told our Dad.

I remember the many times she pounded Eleanore, where she lay on the kitchen floor, nose bleeding, lips bleeding, crying, scared to death and pleading for her life. Eleanore was beaten because she didn't dress (Julia's oldest daughter) in the right dress for the Sunday afternoon trip to (her parents). Many times she dumped our Sunday dinner on the kitchen floor; a whole devil's food cake with whipped cream was dumped into the kitchen sink while we sat around the table waiting to have some of it.

When Eleanore was in high school, in Home Ec she learned how to make some good hot dishes. One time Julia dumped a large roaster of Spanish Rice on the kitchen floor. We loved it, but she dumped it.

I also remember that we had some meat that spoiled (no refrigerators those days). Julia wouldn't let us throw it out. (My sisters were forced to cook it and serve it to the boys.) We had to eat it. The whole house smelled bad and I even (threw up) at the table.

On Saturday nights she (Julia) wanted to get to town early and park on Main Street so she could sit in the car and watch people walk by. One Saturday night we worked on the (neighbor's) farm until about 7:00 p.m. to get the dry hay in the barn. When we got home, after taking care of the horses, we wanted to eat. She had thrown our supper out in the yard because she didn't get to town early enough. After a hard day's work (putting up the hay on the neighbor's farm) none of us had anything to eat Things like that happened often. Anytime she got mad at one of us, she would stand in the doorway with a club (wood stick) and use it on us so we couldn't eat.

I suppose you remember the time she kicked Verna's bedroom door to pieces trying to beat Verna for not going out with (Julia's brother). The next day she put the pieces together with shoe nails.

When Bennie was 21 years old and worked at home for free, she would go into a fit if our Dad gave him 50 cents to spend on a night out with the neighbor boys. None of us ever got the car; we always had to bum a ride with neighbor boys.

We never had toys after Mom died and there were no Christmases for us for about five or six years, until Julia decided to have Christmas for her family at our house. Then, she would buy gifts for all of them and have a few things for us.

On Sundays, on the way home from church she would reach across the seat in the Chandler, swear at us and try to pound us—calling us "God damn boar pigs!"

She would break broom handles over our head and back because we used some warm water to wash up to go to church.

She would take a butcher knife and keep poking me in the chest, yelling "God damn you I'll jab you right through the heart.

On my 15th birthday at Sunday dinner she took a big China cup and came straight down on the top of my head, making a gash one and one-half inches long with blood running down my back. The next day in school (high school) everyone kept asking what happened to me. Boy, did I have to make up a story to cover that one up.

I'm the guy that ducked when she threw the fork that took a 4 to 5 inch sliver out of the wainscoting wood-work behind me.

I remember another time when she waited up for Verna to come home from a date one night. She was upstairs actually pounding Verna and trying to push her down the stairs. I got out of bed to help Verna and then I got beat up too.

Any time we were out at night she would not let us come

back in the house. She would stick knives in the woodwork (door frame) so the door would not open. We would have to come in through the basement and there she would be at the top of the stairs with her woodstick ready and waiting to pound the hell out of us.

One day when we came home from school all our clothes and the our beds were out in the yard. Cliff, Anton, and I had to take them to the old empty house on (the neighbor's) farm. We were supposed to sleep in a mouse-infested house that had been used for chickens and a granary. We had to walk almost a half mile to get to bed. That's when she got the poker hot and started to burn and kick us around—even broke a window out that night, kicking us around. When she kicked us we almost flew across the room.

When Bennie was in service during World War II (about 4 1/2 years) we wrote to each other. As you already know, he had seven battle stars, many other medals, and was wounded twice. Still he wrote to me and said, "When things really got tough, he thought of our life at home, and he figured he had it pretty good in the Army".

When Bennie was in the service, he sent money home to be put in the bank (about 7 or 8 hundred dollars). When he came home, got married and bought his farm, he asked for his money, but it was all spent. Julia felt it was theirs to spend. Bennie had to take them to court to get his money. Julia went into another one of her rages and accused Dad of "giving Bennie everything".

There were times when she would open two small cans of food, eat one can herself, and divide the other one among the rest of us. For example, if we had pork and beans, I would eat them one at a time to make them last longer.

You know, today at graduations or communions, if you don't give a $10.00 or $20.00 gift, the younger generation thinks you're a cheapskate. So for the record, I went to First Communion, Confirmation, graduated 8th grade, high school, and had seventeen birthdays in between. Putting all these together I did not even get enough money to buy a cone of ice cream—and it only cost a nickel (5 cents). Today, kids think they have it bad.

I left home in September of 1941. Adolph and I rode to Milwaukee with Edward Maule in a Model A Ford. Dad came to see us before he left to take Julia for her Sunday visit to her family. He wanted us to go to (a local businessman) to borrow some money because he had none to give us. He did feel quite bad. Edmund Skroch came over to see me; took out his billfold and gave me a $20.00 bill. Ed Maule got Adolph and me a job in Cudahy, and when I got my first check I hopped a bus and rode 30 miles and gave Ed Skroch his $20.00. So to this day I can honestly say I didn't get a dime from home since the day I left. When Dad died, he had a Will, but Julia had already arranged to get everything. He had nothing left for his family.

You know, the few things I wrote on these sheets wouldn't make a dent in the amount of abuse Julia caused us. But to this day I think the good Lord saw to it that we all did well in our lives, and especially in my case, gave me the most wonderful person I ever met, to be my wife. Theresa is just a super person. In other words, I am blessed and still in pretty good health. You know, I will be 75 on September 17, and married 53 years on September 9, 1999.

I also want you to know that while writing this letter I had to stop a few times to wipe a few tears because it did make me cry. The end!

God Bless,

*/s/ Brother Clarence Kulig
Whitehall, Wisconsin 54773*

PS I left out some of the things she (Julia) did because I'm ashamed to talk about them. Call me if you wish.

B-2 LETTER FROM CLIFFORD KULIG

July 23, 1999

Hi Adeline,

I am writing a week late for it was very hot here. You asked about the time we met with D. A. Kostner sometime in July, 1941. The four of us (Verna, Adolph, Cliff and Eleanore) told the D. A. (District Attorney) how she (Julia) acted. We told the D. A. what she would do during her temper tantrums. Even our Dad said some things about her. After we got through talking about her to the D. A., the D. A. told her, "You are the meanest woman in Trempealeau County."

I also saw her hit Eleanore after she (Julia) dumped the food on the floor, and also saw her pull her pants down and show her rear end to us.

The agent that handled Life Insurance for our Dad told me that the policy was for us kids, and she (Julia) made the Company put it in her name. The agent said that was very dirty of her.

If I played the radio at home she got mad and banged it on the floor. So when I put it on again she hit me with a steel poker, right on my back.

When I got sick in 1949, I was at home. She (Julia) wouldn't let me eat at home so I asked Mrs. John Maule if I could stay there.

This is all I know for now. I can't remember much more than you already know about her.

As ever,

/s/ Cliff

(Note: Referring to Julia as "she" was typical of my brothers. Also, it was surprising to the four brothers and sisters present at this meeting with the district attorney, that my father actually spoke out against Julia. It was the only instance where any member of my family could recall his speaking negatively about her. AKP)

B-3. EXCERPTS FROM ANTON KULIG'S LETTER

August 4, 1999

Here are some notes of things that Anton remembered:

It was Sunday morning. Eleanore prepared a large hot dish for dinner that morning which she had heating in the oven. When Julia came home from church she was angry about something. She opened the oven door, pulled out the hot dish and dumped it on the kitchen floor so the family wouldn't have anything to eat for dinner. She then proceeded to continually hit Eleanore.

On Clarence's 15th birthday Julia hit him on his head with a cup and the blood ran down both sides of his head.

While the family was sitting at the table, Julia threw a knife that went between the boys.

One night while having supper, in her anger she threw a dinner fork that again missed the boys who were sitting on the bench. The fork entered the wainscoting and took out a sliver an inch wide at the top and about five to six inches long. Dad was at the neighbor's threshing when this took place.

On July 4, 1942, Eleanore went to the milk-house to get some cream for the breakfast cereal. When she came back to the house with the cream, Julia was again angry about something so she hit Eleanore on the head so hard that she fell to her knees.

Julia always wanted Verna to go out with her brother, Johnny. One night Verna and Eleanore went out with the neighbors. When Verna came back, she saw how mad Julia was. Verna went upstairs and locked her bedroom door. Julia came upstairs after her and kicked the door so hard she broke the panel.

Do you remember the time when Julia burned Adolph with that hot poker?

Another thing: We had been haying late on a Saturday, which was the night that Julia had to be in town by 7 o'clock. When we came home for supper she was so mad she threw all the food out to the geese so that we had nothing to eat.

These are just a few of the things I remember. Maybe they are duplicates of what Clarence and Clifford wrote to you

/s/ Anton Kulig

APPENDIX C

FROM THE SCRAPBOOK

ADELINE KULIG PUCCINI

Adeline Elizabeth Kulig, daughter of William Kulig, Independence, and freshman at the University of Illinois, was one of the honor students at the 23rd annual "Honors" convocation May 2 at the university when public recognition was given to those students whose scholarship ranks them in the first ten per cent of their classes during the first two semesters immediately preceding the current semester with the exception of freshman honors which are based solely on records of the first semester's work. Miss Kulig, graduate of Independence High school in 1944, worked as a civil service employe in the Treasury department, Chicago, before receiving a scholarship to the university at Urbana. She is majoring in foreign languages.

Adeline Kulig Receives Honors at Illinois U

1947

"Honors Day", which was established in 1925 at the University of Illinois, Urbana, held the twenty-third annual convocation in the university auditorium May 2 at 10:15 a.m. The university takes occasion on that day to give public recognition to those students whose scholarship ranks them in the first ten percent of their class. Adeline Elizabeth Kulig, daughter of Wm. Kulig, this community, was one of the group to receive class honors that day.

Class honors are awarded students ranking in the upper ten percent of their respective classes during the first two semesters immediately preceding the current semester with the exception that freshman honors are based solely on records for the first semester's work.

Miss Kulig is a graduate of the Independence high school with the class of 1945. She later did Civil Service work with the treasury department, Chicago, before entering the university on a scholarship, where she now majors in foreign languages.

Letter to Mr. Kirkpatrick from Tabor Farm, 1947.

Interesting Letter Received From Miss Adeline Kulig

G. L. Kirkpatrick and daughter Eileen received the following interesting letter from Adeline Kulig, former Independence girl, and pass it on to readers of the News-Wave:

Tabor Farm
Sodus, Michigan
July 18, 1947

Dear Mr. Kirkpatrick and Eileen:

So much has happened in the last six months that I have lost all count of time since my last letter to you.

First of all—I completed my first year in college and have been working at this summer resort in Michigan since the first week in June. I was referred here by friends who have been guests here for years. This resort, unlike most resorts, is really a fruit farm. Though it has every advantage for a vacationer, it is known primarily for the food it puts out. Our dining room accomodates approximately 125 people who eat as much as they wish during the three regular meals, and spend most of the day picking fruits and berries, and if midnight still finds them hungry, they are welcome to raid the iceboxes of midnight snacks. A vacationer's paradise. I'd best describe it.

Now all is not play for, as I said before, I'm employed out here and must not be confused with the guests. My work as a waitress is a lot of fun, though a bit strenuous at times. However, any time off may be spent using any facilities of the resort and eating any of the fruit and berries. I do my share of both and find that working awhile and golfing, swimming, and playing tennis, etc. during my time off, makes up for an ideal summer out of school. And for anyone wanting to work in the summer, I can think of nothing better. Yes, this is the way I dreamed of spending my summers—but I will be glad to get back to school in the fall.

The University of Illinois is intending to enroll all it possibly can this fall. That will mean that a greater percentage will have to drop out as the competition gets keener, and housing facilities are overcrowded. At the pace it is now going, it is expected that all three divisions of the University (Chicago, Champaign and Galesburg, Ill.) will be filled to capacity. Thus, if I thought it was hard sharing a room with three other girls last year I will probably have to park in someone's garage and live out of a suitcase this fall. This may sound hectic, but conditions are not as bad as I make them sound. The housing project is working speedily and new residence halls are under way in all three divisons of the university.

As my plans now stand I intend to declare my major and minor upon entering school this fall. I have finally decided on Speech Correction as my major and Spanish and Psychology as a split minor. This is quite a load for four years in college but if I spend one year abroad, I can make up the foreign language in little time. Speaking of school abroad, my interest lies in Latin America only, and would like a year in one of its universities, preferably in Mexico. This is all pending my luck on a fellowship which I intend to start working on in the near future. So again, I hope you have your fingers crossed for me! Thanks, I knew you would: you did on my other scholarship.

Now back to the resort again—The waitresses here are from various colleges in the East. One of them is also a U of Illinois girl but I didn't know' her until she came here. We were both quite surprised to meet in Michigan.

This place by the way, has had a long column written about it in the Chicago Tribune about two years ago. This probably accounts for the fact that many prominent Chicagoans spend their vacations here. One guest, a Chicago radio announcer, had quite an interesting account of his vacation here over his radio program when he returned about a week ago.

Well, I hope this letter finds you in the best of health. I don't know when or if I'll be up that way this year, but will try to steal a week's rest before I return to school. And what can you suggest for a vacation that is better than a trip back to see relatives and friends in Independence.

Sincerely
Adeline

Tribute from Mr. Kirkpatrick and letter re senior scholarship, 1949.

Miss Adeline Kulig Wins Scholarship 1949

Miss Adeline Kulig, daughter of Wm. Kulig of Maule coulee, has been awarded the P. P. Reutinger cash endowment scholarship for her senior year at the University of Illinois at Champaign-Urbana.

The News-Wave editor is quite proud of this accomplishment. Adeline made her home with us during her senior year in Independence high school and endeared herself to members of the family.

Bereft of her mother when a babe, she was cared for by relatives here and there through her grade school days, and when high school days began she found a way to finish the four years without material help from home. Finishing high school, she secured employment in Chicago, then entered the University of Illinois under a scholarship, and now reaches the climax of her senior year. Maybe there isn't anything so wonderful about all this, but the average girl without funds would have sought a job and been satisfied at that. Not so, Adeline. She has what it takes to get up in the world, and she'll do it, too.

The following letter from her is published without her consent because we know home town folks are deeply interested in such worthy characters as Adeline:

Chicago, Ill., July 2
Dear Mr. Kirkpatrick: 1949

It has been a long time since I wrote to you. Another eventful year at the U. of Illinois has passed and this fall I shall embark on my senior year. Who thought I would ever make it?

I am now working for the Houghton-Mifflin Publishing Company in Chicago and I'm back in the money again. I haven't had such a good paying and resourceful job since the year before I went to college. No more resort work for me.

I am enclosing $2.00 for a year's subscription to the News-Wave and request to have the mailing address changed to 603 Addison, Apt. 3, Chicago, Illinois. I look forward to reading it every week.

I have just been awarded the "P. P. Reutinger" cash endowment scholarship for my senior year. Yes, I'm on-the-ball again and all set to take my senior year without working if possible. Next summer I would like to take a trip to the West Coast to visit some people I met in Chicago who are putting in a word for me at the Spencer Tracy Clinic. One of these women (friends I met here in Chgo.) knows the board members at this clinic. Looks like a grand opportunity and I may try it, now that my traveling abroad is not likely to take place.

I can't tell you more about the scholarship, except that it pays me $200.00 in cash, $100 for each semester. I wasn't expecting to win it so I destroyed all information when I was packing my clothes to leave school. How can one person be so lucky? Me, I mean.

It's about time for me to get back to work so will sign off here. My job as a correspondent at this office is keeping my hands full. But, I enjoy it.

Good bye for now. Hope this letter finds you happy and in the best of health. I also hope Wisconsin is much cooler than Illinois at this point.

Sincerely
Adeline